ECONOMICS, CULTURE AND SOCIETY— ALTERNATIVE APPROACHES:

Dissenting Views from Economic Orthodoxy

Contributors to This Volume

Lapo Berti, University of Milano, Italy

Willis W. Harman, Institute of Noetic Sciences, Sausalito, California, United States

Björn Hettne, Peace and Development Research Institute, Gothemburg University, Sweden

Mark A. Lutz, University of Maine, Department of Economics, Orono, Maine, United States

Oscar Nudler, The Bariloche Foundation, Bariloche, Argentina

Economics, Culture and Society— Alternative Approaches:
Dissenting Views from Economic Orthodoxy

Edited by Oscar Nudler
and Mark A. Lutz

The Apex Press
NEW YORK

United Nations
University Press
TOKYO • NEW YORK • PARIS

This volume integrates the series of books produced as an output of the Economic Aspects of Human Development Project of the United Nations University. The Project has been carried out by a network of scholars from various institutes and universities in Europe, Latin America, and the United States, coordinated by Dr. Oscar Nudler from the Bariloche Foundation in Argentina.

© The United Nations University, 1996
All rights reserved

Published by The Apex Press, an imprint of the Council on International and Public Affairs, Suite 3C, 777 United Nations Plaza, New York, NY 10017, USA, with the United Nations University Press, The United Nations University, 53-70, Jingumae 5-chome, Shibuya-ku, Tokyo 150, Japan (with exclusive distribution within Asia).

Library of Congress Cataloging-in-Publication Data

Economics, culture and society—alternative approaches: dissenting views from economic orthodoxy / Oscar Nudler and Mark A. Lutz, editors.

p. cm.

Includes bibliographical references and index.

ISBN 0-945257-73-2 (hard). — ISBN 0-945257-72-4 (paper). — ISBN 92-808-0864-8 (hard). — ISBN 92-808-0749-8 (paper).

1. Economics—Sociological aspects. 2. Development economics—Sociological aspects. I. Nudler, Oscar. II. Lutz, Mark A.

HM35.E26 1996 96-38310

306.3—dc20 CIP

The Apex Press
ISBN: 0-945257-72-4 pbk
ISBN: 0-945257-73-2 hard

United Nations University Press
ISBN: 92-808-0749-8 pbk
ISBN: 92-808-0864-8 hard

Cover design by Warren Hurley
Printed in the United States of America

Contents

matter, a belief shared by all traditional cultures and religions. The expansion of this materialist system has brought with it all sorts of negative consequences at a planetary scale ranging from the destruction of earth ecosystems up to the erasing of cultural differences. But Harman is optimistic since, according to him, a "new heresy" is rapidly growing, particularly in the developed North. Such heresy, which takes consciousness as a causal factor, implies a fundamental change of mind which is already impacting all social spheres of activity, including science, work, business, and so on. It is producing a "respiritualization of society." A new science, incorporating such changed metaphysical belief and thus leaving aside the metaphysical assumptions of Western science —objectivism, positivism, and reductionism—is emerging. At the same time, social rationality is displacing pure economic rationality and a redefinition of the goals of development is taking place. As we mentioned above, Harman does not elaborate in detail the consequences of his vision for economics and development economics, but it seems clear that it implies a sweeping critique of these disciplines in their present form. His position in this respect is the most radical since the other authors do not postulate a new science in general, but a new economics that is more attuned to modern science in particular and rational thinking in general.

On the Nature of the Normative Approach

In most of the cases, the chapters of this book include an explicit, detailed normative critique. The contribution by Berti is in this respect somewhat different. Its focus is more descriptive and historical than normative. However, a strong normative element is implicit. As he reminds us, it is clear that classical economics, with its one-sided emphasis on the market, served the interest of the bourgeoisie. In its turn, Marxism was intended in the first place as an expression of the interest of the working class. Berti's implied view is that economic science should express the richness and complexity of the entire economic process and, so doing, be at the service not of any particular

Contents

INTRODUCTION

On the Contents of This Book: An Overview

The group of scholars who, within the framework of the Economic Aspects of Human Development project of the United Nations University, have contributed to this volume are related to different traditions of thought, namely, the European cultural-historical approach to the economic process linked to the names of Karl Polanyi and Fernand Braudel, the "Human Economy" school in the United States, the "green" view of economic development with roots in the north of Europe, and the so-called "new paradigm" vision. There are, of course, some areas of consensus among these trends, but also important differences, as is shown below. However, one common stance providing unity to this series of articles is clearly discernible: all of them express deep dissatisfaction with the conventional type of economics, more particularly with the neoclassical revival that took place in the 1980s. The dissatisfaction is "deep" because it refers to the very foundations and the relevance of building economics. Let us review briefly the reason each author has for feeling dissatisfied and, by the same token, refer to the constructive suggestions for new directions in economics made in the chapters that follow.

The essay by Lapo Berti, constituting the first chapter of this volume, is a remarkable effort to shed light on the foundations of economics by integrating and building upon the works of Polanyi and Braudel. According to Polanyi, the attentions of classical and neoclassical economics have been exceedingly absorbed by one of the forms of integration of economic activity within society—the market—while remaining blind to much of the substantive economic activity based on other social practices such as reciprocity and redistribution. It is true that the rise of capitalism implied the dominance of the market but the other forms of integration never disappeared and even reached new important roles, such as redistribution in the welfare state or reciprocity through the informal sector. Lack of consideration of them inevitably means blocking our understanding of the economy, which is not an isolated compartment but an inseparable part of the social fabric. The impressive work of Braudel on the economic history of capitalism points in exactly the same direction. He described the economy as a hierarchical system or, in metaphorical terms, as a multi-story building having at the bottom material life or self-consumption economy, then the market economy, and at the top capitalism. The three structures change at different historical rhythms but the "determining factor is the whole movement." Thus a new economic paradigm recognizing such complexity and ongoing evolutionary dynamics will have to make room for coexisting, interacting organizational principles and be able to conceptualize the tradeoffs between them. Some work has already been done along these lines by Coase, Arrow, Williamson, Simon, and others. They provide valuable analytical fragments of the new vision but need to be framed within a comprehensive theoretical picture which would integrate economics into the realm of a new social science. The essay by Berti may be seen to set the stage for such a paradigmatic reorientation and enrichment of a substantive economic science.

The essay that follows by Mark Lutz focuses on the historical roots and development of the Human Economy school. It is highly critical of the core of conventional theory centering around the formal abstraction of Rational Economic Man. This core is especially ill-suited for meaningful normative guidance in the apprehension and amelioration of social problems. It leads to an overemphasis of material consumption as a goal of economic activity and neglects work quality and the higher needs of economic agents. Lutz criticizes instrumental rationality and would like to see a rational evolution not only of the means but also of the ends. Lutz stresses an end of intrinsic human worth, or dignity, which is negatively impacted by the wage system and excessive economic insecurity. The key demand is for a broadening of economics, especially when concerned with normative issues in general and development economics in particular. However, much of the descriptive, explanatory component of economics is not rejected—it is merely relegated to a limited "special case" status.

Hettne's chapter focuses on development economics, which he considers to be in an unsettled condition, if not in a state of crisis. Yet, this crisis he attributes primarily to the economic bias that has so far marked development studies. More specifically, since modern economics deals with individual maximization and choice in situations of scarcity, it has nothing of substance to offer in promoting meaningful development. He is also critical of both Marx and Keynes who stressed the state overly much to the neglect of reciprocity, cooperation, and specific local conditions and resources. In his perceptive essay he gropes toward outlining the framework of such a new development economics. The end product is a development approach that is more in tune with the cultural needs of particular regions rather than universal and centered around the nation state.

Willis Harman's chapter, which closes the book, does not focus directly, as in the case of the other chapters, on the foundations of economics or development economics. His views on the subject are to a large extent implicit in his picture of Western science and modern industrial society. According to Harman, this "production-focused" society, based on what was three or four centuries ago an ascending "scientific heresy," is no longer workable or sustainable. In particular, "present economic, corporate and social policies are, by and large, inconsistent with viable long term global development." At the core of the modern system, we find the doctrine of scientific materialism, with its implied rejection of the pre-eminence of consciousness over matter, a belief shared by all traditional cultures and religions. The expansion of this materialist system has brought with it all sorts of negative consequences at a planetary scale ranging from the destruction of earth ecosystems up to the erasing of cultural differences. But Harman is optimistic since, according to him, a "new heresy" is rapidly growing, particularly in the developed North. Such heresy, which takes consciousness as a causal factor, implies a fundamental change of mind which is already impacting all social spheres of activity, including science, work, business, and so on. It is producing a "respiritualization of society." A new science, incorporating such changed metaphysical belief and thus leaving aside the metaphysical assumptions of Western science—objectivism, positivism, and reductionism—is emerging. At the same time, social rationality is displacing pure economic rationality and a redefinition of the goals of development is taking place. As we mentioned above, Harman does not elaborate in detail the consequences of his vision for economics and development economics, but it seems clear that it implies a sweeping critique of these disciplines in their present form. His position in this respect is the most radical since the other authors do not postulate a new science in general, but a new economics that is more attuned to modern science in particular and rational thinking in general.

On the Nature of the Normative Approach

In most of the cases, the chapters of this book include an explicit, detailed normative critique. The contribution by Berti is in this respect somewhat different. Its focus is more descriptive and historical than normative. However, a strong normative element is implicit. As he reminds us, it is clear that classical economics, with its one-sided emphasis on the market, served the interest of the bourgeoisie. In its turn, Marxism was intended in the first place as an expression of the interest of the working class. Berti's implied view is that economic science should express the richness and complexity of the entire economic process and, so doing, be at the service not of any particular group or class but of society as a whole. Obviously, this is not only an epistemological recommendation but also an ethical imperative.

Referring now to the rest of the chapters, we can distinguish between two different ways of grounding a normative critique. Either it is grounded in terms of a particular image of what constitutes the whole person and *authentic human personality,* or else in the norm of *sustainability,* of "social reproduction" necessitating an "environmentally sustainable economics." Closely related to this second norm is also the goal of preserving cultural autonomy and diversity.

The first approach, centering around the human person, is particularly emphasized in the contribution by Lutz from the American "Human Economy" school. In this type of "moral humanism," human beings are pictured as having material and social needs, the fulfillment of which provide a standard for economic policies and socio-economic institutions. These needs are characteristic of our common humanity and are in that sense both transnational and transcultural. Accordingly, much space is devoted in Lutz's chapter to carefully discuss human nature, particularly its dual nature. Such a view of human duality or a "dual self" implies that we have deep down a choice whether to follow the inclinations of our lower selfish self or to respond to the needs of our higher self by acting "selflessly" or "disinterestedly." Lutz stresses this capacity of free will, which he sees as the very essence of being human and which gives an individual person uniqueness and also dignity.

This stress on personal uniqueness, community, and dignity leads Lutz to be critical of unbridled capitalist market forces compelling increasing uniformity as well as being reluctant to embrace the political principle of a strong and centralized bureaucratic state. His new economics is highly critical of consumerism and economic growth fueled by unlimited greed. It instead puts helping the poor as a top priority item on the socio-economic agenda. Other fundamental goals derived from his humanistic norm are meaningful work and economic democracy, or worker self-management.

Progress in this model would be characterized by an increase of genuine human welfare: the growing satisfaction of "reasonable" material needs without sacrificing the essential dignity of the person and without unnecessarily disrupting community and culture in the process. A good development policy would bring about progress in *this* sense. A necessary but not sufficient ingredient of this perspective is a democratic social control of the economy or, to use a more fashionable word, the "embedding" of the economy in society. But, to repeat, some cultures, including the contemporary western culture, lack development in this sense. Wherever we find exploitative and degrading institutions, whether due to configurations of power or otherwise, it is the task of a meaningful development economics to suggest ameliorative action.

The feasibility and persuasiveness of this type of normative critique hinges, of course, on the acceptability of the underlying image of human personality, particularly its non-material "higher" dimensions. Lutz is reluctant to rely heavily on modern psychology because it is by its very nature not well suited for coming to grips with the distinctive human capacity of free will choice. Instead, he finds a philosophical anthropology grounded not only in reason but also in common sense and casual introspection more to the point.

The real challenge of the "human-centered" perspective rests in convincing others that this point of view is more than merely subjective or ethnocentric, as illustrated, for example, by its heavy reliance on Gandhian thought.

The second way of criticizing modern economics is asserting that its general approach is marred by non-sustainability, particularly with respect to the natural environment. It underlies much of Hettne's chapter and parts of Harman's approach. Hettne, for example, recognizes sustainability as a "normative concept that has appeared in development theory as a consequence of the environmental concerns of the early 1970s and onwards." Its message is that any international economic order would not be viable "unless the natural biological systems that underpin the global economy are preserved." The value premise here is more naturalistic: whatever cannot be universalized and sustained is bad, whatever is sustainable in time and across the globe is in principle good. Societies and cultures have to reproduce themselves, and it is the task of a good development economics to heed this basic fact.

It is probably fair to say that this underlying value premise is hard to challenge and as a result rather compelling. Yet, it too has controversial implications and potential weak points. The reproduction of life, of culture and society, does by no means imply life fulfillment, a "civilized" culture and a "good society." Many proponents of the sustainability approach also tend to identify with an ethics known as "cultural relativism." Such a view precludes any values that would be valid transculturally, that would allow us to evaluate the goodness of cultures. The vacuum gets filled with a more pragmatic criteria of "workability."

Hettne's chapter, as we have seen, centers on the principle of sustainability, but it also grants that there are universal human needs pertaining to all cultures. Connected with this realization is his value premise of equality also pertaining to all cultures. Although he would leave satisfaction of higher, qualitative, and non-material needs to local philosophy and religion rather than to social science, the cultural autonomy pertaining to the "ways of life" is confined within certain boundaries that would presumably be inconsistent with cultural practices violating the postulate that all men and women are essentially equal. In other words, Hettne's position can be seen to aim at a modified sustainability norm by injecting, among other things, a dose of (universal) moral humanism. So, for example, when advocating the need for a territorial (rather than national) development strategy, he writes: "A development strategy informed by a territorial perspective must make efficient use of those resources which happen to exist in that particular area, and in a way that both sustains the ecological system and provides the people living there with their basic human needs." No doubt, this is a rather fertile blend of normative principles informed not only by ecological sustainability and cultural sustainability, but also by human need satisfaction. He sees them all as "complementary and mutually supportive." Hettne's chapter is most valuable in pointing to some solid common ground on which a viable alternative normative economic theory may have to be constructed.

We may want to add here that the human-centered alternative economists have reached an equivalent position by means of stressing the needs and dignity of future generations. The views of E. F. Schumacher—one of the greatest heroes of both the ecologically oriented Green movement and the human-centered alternative—are a good specimen for the integration of both normative principles.

The Harman chapter also operates with a combination of the two normative principles. On the one hand, his primary norm appears to be cultural sustainability, the norm of "workability" that we already alluded to above. Not surprisingly, he extolls the absoluteness of culture, the relativity of contemporary empirical and reductionist Western science, and sees the existing cultural diversity as a most precious resource and end. Like others arguing from a sustainability norm principle, he attacks the production/consumption orientation of modern economics as globally unsustainable, moribund, and to be replaced by an economics generating "meaning."

So far, he moves in the tracks of pure cultural relativism and anti-development, yet there is a twist: in all of this a human image that reigns with a certain unquestionable absoluteness and informs much of his normative thought. Through deep intuition and spiritual disciplines all human beings in all cultures can aspire to another kind of knowledge which is not only implanted within us, but is seen as absolutely universal. It lends itself to a critique of Western culture—and with it of economics—in absolute terms. The Western industrial paradigm has to yield; Western economists together with their peers in the other social sciences will have to awaken from their cultural hypnosis. The guiding paradigm for genuine development is to be built on the foundation of ancient spiritual traditions, inner circles, and doctrines and teachings allowing us to reach enlightenment.

In conclusion, the menu of choice in alternative economic thought is no doubt deeply influenced by the relative importance given to the underlying normative principles, one stressing ecological sustainability, the other proceeding from a conception of universal human needs and human dignity. In all three essays espousing an explicitly normative point of view, both principles are present but usually one is given greater priority over the other. To some extent this may indeed reflect Kenneth Boulding's observation quoted by Hettne, that the human-centered approach assuming Man to be the measure of all things is more in harmony with a Judeo-Christian world view, while the ecological approach is more consistent with an Eastern perspective rooted in Hinduism and Buddhism.

Whatever the motive for preferring one normative principle over the other, it appears that both have to be seen as essential foundational elements for a new alternative economics. Moreover, both fundamentally challenge the methodological individualism characterizing conventional economic thought. What counts are not existing desires, or preferences of individual economic agents, but considerations such as the needs of future generations, the requirements of a sustainable biosphere, or considerations of maintaining cultural diversity. This fundamental aspect alone indicates that there is much common ground among the several "alternative economic perspectives" in spite of the seeming diversity.

Alternative Economics and Capitalism

To begin with, there is the humanistic perspective, as portrayed by Lutz. The new economy is still basically production-oriented with an emphasis on full employment and job security. At the same time, there appears to be a certain acceptance of the principle of a market economy regulated by the state. The means of production, that is, land and capital, remain in private or corporate ownership of one kind or another but also much more accessible to the masses. However, Lutz, following here in the footsteps of the British socialist Tawney, claims that private property is "the instrument," and economic security "the object." When private ownership patterns no longer generate sufficient security for the workers, it becomes functionless property to be transferred to those who perform the constructive work: employees and laborers. Similarly, workers cooperative self-management is portrayed as superior to the degrading wage system. Such worker cooperatives cannot have a meaningful existence in a socialist command economy: workers and employees decide in one, central planners in the other. Conversely, capitalism has not been a hospitable environment either, but there is the example of the Spanish Mondragón cooperative movement organized in a manner that seems to promote operational efficiency as well as human dignity.

Although we look in vain for a systematic picturing of an entire economy running and interacting on such a new footing, Lutz is careful to make clear that we cannot realistically expect humanistic enterprises to be a promising proposition in a disembedded economy lacking effective social control. In particular, it requires a trade policy that is also mindful of long-run *social* consequences. Moreover, Lutz advocates what he calls a "correspondence principle" where the boundaries of the economic and social-political domains need to coincide. The key to this goal is not "free" trade but "managed" trade. It can be argued that, ultimately, an insistence on the correspondence principle can be seen to be transcending the very essence of capitalism. Immanuel Wallerstein, for example, has observed that "capitalism as an economic mode is based on the fact that the economic factors operate with an arena *larger* than that which any political entity can totally control."[1]

All said, we may summarize the Human Economy position as one affirming markets, albeit socially regulated, while strongly rejecting capitalism, especially the type of corporate capitalism dominating the world today.

The New Paradigm representative Harman paints a different picture both more radical and more capitalist. It is more radical in its vision of a post-industrial society that focuses more on the "production" of meaning and less on the production of goods. In his vision, there is a futuristic outline of a society that works more at home or not at all, where leisure is more important allowing people to engage in meaningful work and research while supported by public and private grants. The traditional link between production and income distribution would be severed. At the same time, Harman's new economic system remains essentially a capitalist one, although it is meant to be a more humane capitalism where management of private corporations would "invest in lives" and no longer for profits. All this is made possible by the imminent birth of a new spiritual consciousness changing the life goals of economic agents.

Since Harman trusts that this new evolutionary quantum leap is indeed about to occur on a global scale, he does not show much concern about the correspondence problem troubling Lutz. To the extent that capitalist market forces are seen to be self-regulated and self-restrained, there is less need for social control of corporate decision making. In a sense, one could say that with Harman, Adam

Smith's "invisible hand" doctrine is about to be replaced by a new coordinating principle grounded in an "invisible inner Self." From this we may infer that Harman's new humanity is affirmative of both the market and capitalism, providing the latter takes on a more spiritual and human face. Both principles are held to be compatible with the realization of the goals Harman envisions: social and political decentralization, deep ecology, feminism, inner peace, creative entrepreneurship and, above all, empowerment for the people to take responsibility for their own lives and for the necessary social change.

Economic thought emanating from the Green movement, at least in Hettne's vision, ought to reflect and manifest the "counterpoint" society. This is in part due to his conviction that a normative view of a new social reality is a necessary and integral part in helping to bring it about. In whatever the Swedish scholar has to say about the new social economy, his thoughts have most certainly been strongly influenced by Karl Polanyi's historical and social thought, which paves the way to recognize besides capitalism a principle of coordination: *reciprocity* described as "socially embedded forms of exchange in small symmetric communities." The concept manifests in what we call the "informal sector," the "household economy," local community-oriented cooperatives, and resource allocation. The state is important and necessary, but primarily to protect cultural integrity and encourage local and community economic initiatives. State centrism, together with what we may call "market centrism," is rejected, but there is a very definite and important role reserved for the market place.

In many ways, it appears that the new "green" blueprint of society resembles most what we may call "non-Marxian socialism" with a populist, anarchist, and utopian bent. Not surprisingly, it shares a certain affinity with the basic ideology of the Human Economy school, although it is perhaps more critical in orientation, pretending to be less clairvoyant about the vision of the future, and more pronounced in its emphasis on ecology and culture. It is also related to the more positive model of capitalist development discussed by Berti who in turn relies on the work of Polanyi and particularly Braudel.

The essay by Berti traces the evolution of Western society during the last few centuries. One of the highlights of this essay is a rather penetrating description of capitalism's essential nature. Specifically, Berti, following Braudel, demonstrates rather convincingly that there is a big conceptual difference between what we call "capitalism" and the "market." In fact, capitalism emerges as "counter-market," a force that seeks to circumvent, control, even abolish the market. It is probably no great secret that Berti's sympathies lie with the traditional and socially embedded market place rather than with the disembedded capitalist market system, but his analysis of the internal arrangements of the economic system and the ways in which it complies with the society's general dynamics "for the better or the worse" is primarily, if not exclusively, historical and *descriptive*. At the same time, it is also quite deterministic. According to Berti, individuals "entertain interests and modes of action that are the result of historical processes of functional differentiation within the economy." Elsewhere, he describes Braudel's historical dynamics as a gigantic "historical fresco" with "layers of movement and relations that gradually shape the ground on which capitalism settles and grows, while determining the historical configurations (i.e., the world economies)." We cannot know for sure where all this will lead us, but Berti does seem to have a basic faith that the historical process may be slowly working away from the market system toward a revival of the market place.

Concluding Remarks

We would like to conclude this overview by singling out four features of economic thought as they seem to recur throughout this book. Explication of, and a short comment to, each of those features may be helpful.

- **Completeness.** As emphasized by Berti and Hettne, economics, and *a fortiori* development economics, should transcend the narrow focus of conventional economics on the market and take as a research target the whole gamut of economic organizational forms. In this, they follow the methodology of the German

Historical School in political economy. It is true that the image of the economic system and its evolutionary dynamics associated with such a search for completeness is more resistant to the application of theoretically neat and mathematically simple models. The work of Braudel, who certainly had in mind the completeness goal when drawing his grandiose picture of material civilization, the development of "world economies," and the unfolding of capitalism, is often an example of the lack of precise, either/or boundaries that some find so exasperating. However, this type of work is also one of the best sources of learning about the evolution of the modern economic system. But it should not be seen as the only one: a certain amount of abstraction and precision is clearly legitimate. Still, there are very real costs to the denial of complexity and reality—especially in the area of socio-economic development. As pointed out by Nicholas Georgescu-Roegen, "standard economics, by opposing any suggestion that the economic process may consist of something more than a jigsaw puzzle with all its elements given, has identified with dogmatism. And this is a privilegium odiosum that has dwarfed the understanding of the economic process wherever it has been exercised."[2]

- **Interdisciplinarity**. Conventional economics has to a great extent remained isolated from the rest of the social sciences. In a way, this was a consequence of the just-mentioned narrow appreciation of its subject matter. For example, according to Lionel Robbins in his *Essay on the Nature and Significance of Economic Science,*[3] economics is the science which studies human behavior as a relationship between ends and scarce means which have alternative uses. Economics should start with given ends, given means, and given "orders of preference" and should not care about "why the human animal attaches particular values... to particular things." All the psychological, social, cultural, historical, and, needless to say, ecological factors intertwined with economic behavior were treated as "externalities" and, as such, outside the relevant domain of professional investigation by the economist qua economist. Such disciplinary isolation offers an explanation of such constructs as *homo oeconomicus*, regardless of its inadequate psychology of motivation. At the same time, conventional economics has not let go of the kind of mechanistic epistemology that no longer seems accepted in the natural sciences, as Harman claims. All these problems can be attributed to the lack of sufficient contact—not to say cross-fertilization—with other relevant fields of knowledge ranging from all other social sciences to social philosophy. Interdisciplinarity appears more as an essential means for enriching economics than a threat to its identity, as commonly perceived.

- **An Extended Value Basis.** Any part of nature or culture which has no market value is considered by conventional economics as value-less. This consequence of the commodification principle is strongly rejected by alternative economists. For example, Immler points out that this principle allows one to consider "the wild exploitation and destruction of the wealth of nature as 'productive labour' and as a 'positive contribution to the economic welfare of society'. . . . The same rationality which ensures the economic welfare of society concurrently constitutes a dreadful menace to the very existence of Man."[4] Dropping off the communication principle would obviously imply a redefinition of "productive labour" as pointed out by Freidrich List some one-hundred-fifty years ago, with special application to the assessment of gains and losses due to engaging in international trade. Moreover, it would open the door to a more comprehensive, holistic view of the economic system by placing into focus not only the so-called formal, monetarized sector but also the informal, non-monetary one. Once non-monetary economic activities are brought into the picture, particularly those in which household and local community-based relations are involved, the full range of implications of the economic system for human and social welfare and development will most likely be revealed more clearly.

- **Sensitivity to Cultural Diversity and Historical Roots.** This is a crucial feature of the image of economics emerging from this book, as stressed by Harman and Hettne with regard to devel-

> opment economics. It is increasingly recognized that economic development cannot be but the result of a socially managed interaction between economy and culture. The influence of socio-cultural factors on economic behavior and performance is, of course, not a new discovery. Once again, it goes back to the German Historical School on economic thought. Among its gems is Max Weber's classical study on the outcome of protestant reformation. Since then we have also the vast collection of studies in modernization theory done in the spirit of the American culturalist school and empiricist research methodology. However, cross-fertilization between this tradition and development economics has been minimal, if any at all.

The Japanese economist Michiro Morishima has aptly expressed all this concern with culture and history in connection to development economics:

> No country can progress while it disregards its own past which constrains its subsequent course of development. Historical considerations are equally important for the social sciences. Any social scientific thought which has paid no attention to history, although it may be effective as a first approximation to reality, can at times even be dangerous. Economic policies which lack any historical perspective are similarly extremely hazardous. A policy which has been proved to be successful for Japan may turn out to be unworkable in Britain and vice versa because of the difference in their ethos, in the ways of behaviour of their peoples and in all the other cultural characteristics which they have inherited from their respective parts.[5]

Of course, one may dispute Morishima's claim, as many other writers have done, especially—and quite convincingly—Robert Osaki. But sensitivity to cultural factors does not imply reducibility to the same. It is necessary is to keep an open mind on this delicate issue.

Similarly, sensitivity to cultural and historical diversity should be distinguished from the philosophical doctrine of cultural relativism which, as mentioned earlier, is not at all accepted by several of the contributors to this book.

The preceding discussion of the emerging economic vision should be regarded as no more than a rough indication of the general thrust of the essays that follow. We hope that the reader will find these integrative comments helpful toward a better understanding of the otherwise quite diverse essays in this book.

NOTES

1. I. Wallerstein, 1976, *The Making of the Modern World System*, New York: Academic Press, p. 348, emphasis added.
2. Nicholas Georgescu-Roegen, 1971, *The Entropy Law and the Economic Process*, Cambridge, Massachusetts: Harvard University Press, p. 318.
3. Lionel Robbins, [1932] 1984, *An Essay on the Nature and Significance of Economic Science*, London: Macmillan.
4. Hans Immler, 1986, "How Adam Smith Valued Nature," *Development* 3, p. 49.
5. Michero Morishima, 1982, *Why Has Japan Succeeded?*, Cambridge: Cambridge University Press.

I

SOCIETY AND THE MARKET: REMOTE AND LESS REMOTE SOURCES OF A CURRENT ISSUE

Lapo Berti

A Swinging Market

For some time the relationship of the market to society has re-emerged as a critical issue. It is not the first time, however. More than two hundred years after the Industrial Revolution laid the foundations of a "market society," the relationship between these two entities, society and the market, remains troublesome and conflicting. Since our societies have been dominated by market mechanisms, they have been unable to make this way of regulating economic activities, which has become firmly established and widely spread hand in hand with the expansion of industry, fully integrated into their system structure. Society has appeared unable to learn how to live peacefully with the market, and the latter still appears unable to comply with the rules of social cohesion. If two centuries of "market society" have made this interlock almost unbreakable, such a long period of time has not been enough to dissolve that contraposition between society and the market, or even between the state and the market, that almost appears to be part of its very makeup. Occasionally, the relationship between society and the market has become a critical issue. Whenever a crisis seems to challenge the functioning of markets by cutting into a society's cohesion, it calls the very nature of that relationship into question.

By subjecting production and distribution activities to a regime of interdependent markets based on information condensed into prices, prices which are mutually communicating and self-regulating, the autonomy that the economic system has acquired retains a twofold ambiguous character. At times, this autonomy exhibits a potentially dangerous tendency to upset the institutions, norms, and behaviors upon which society over time has built its own cohesion. At other times, the market appears as a powerful growth factor that enhances underlying opportunities, and which is a necessary condition for the regulation and integration of the resulting complexity.

Such a duality in the social role and rank of the market economy is finely matched by the ways in which the relationship between the market and society has been perceived and understood since the economic system began to exhibit an autonomy, by isolating and multiplying monetary exchanges. Cultural attitudes to the market have not been consistent or steady over time. In fact, they have undergone wide oscillations which, in turn, have caused various configurations of the economic system and its place in, and integration with, the social system. The history of these oscillations is part of the history of market society. The hub on which the pendulum is swinging is the role that the market is playing in the social order. How does the market organization impact on the structuring on social relationships? Has it a favorable or destructive effect? There is no doubt that we have witnessed a "market revival" for some years, i.e., a renewed attempt to uphold the market as the only and sweeping criterion for restructuring society. Yet, it is also true that the market has recorded other victories and downfalls heretofore.

In a highly stimulating, although by no means exhaustive, article, Albert O. Hirschman has identified four basic cultural attitudes toward the market and its role in society in the industrial history of the West: two favorable and two adverse ones.[1] The argument of doux-commerce was the first to appear, emerging during the seventeenth and eighteenth centuries, when trade began to expand and markets began to grow. The classical formulation of this view can be found in Montesquieu's *L'esprit des lois,* at the beginning of Book XX, in a passage that opens the discussions of the relationship between the laws and the economy.

> It is almost a general rule that wherever mild mores (moeurs douces) prevail, there is commerce, and wherever there is commerce, mild mores prevail. . . . Commerce . . . refines and softens (adoucit) barbarous ways, as we can see every day.[2]

According to Montesquieu, therefore, the market was an institution beneficial to society, because it brought about behaviors that rested on feelings of equity and a longing for peace. This was the prevailing view throughout the eighteenth century. It should be noted, however, that this view of the market was more or less explicitly built into a project of social and political construction. It was designed to pave the road for a "market society" as a method of overcoming the social and political order established under the Ancien Régime.

Next came the self-destruction argument. It was a favored view during the nineteenth century, finally established by the Marxian formulation, although it had a hardly surprising, yet intriguing, precedent. This was seen in the conservative reaction to the advancement of market society during the first half of the eighteenth century.[3] According to this argument, which—it should be stressed—identified market society with capitalism, the socio-economic system that set in as the market began to grow, already carried "the seed of its own destruction." Far from being a permanent acquisition in society's evolution, capitalism was then viewed as a transitional stage which was inevitably made such by self-destructive elements which were thought to be connate with the functioning of capitalism and the process of its establishment. As Hirschman has aptly noted, the self-destruction argument exhibited substantial differences as well as contrasting political implications. Marx viewed the transitory nature of capitalism as logically and historically founded on the internal contradictions that characterized the bourgeoise social formation. On the other hand, many conservatives in the eighteenth century, like many critics in our own century, thought that the self-destructive drive of capitalism originated in its ability to eat away the social, cultural, ethical, and traditional relations that could alone guarantee its functioning and survival.

To Marx and Engels:

> . . . the modern bourgeois society, which has, as if by magic, elicited such powerful means of production and exchange, resembles a magician who is no longer able to dominate the underground powers he himself evoked. . . . The weapons by which the bourgeois overthrew feudalism are now turned against the bourgeois itself. Yet, the bourgeois has not only fabricated the weapons that are causing its death. It has also created the men who will wield those weapons—the modern workers, the proletarians.[4]

The self-destructive power evoked by capitalism was the power behind the same productive forces it had brought to life. The growth of the market economy and the proliferation of trade had powerfully enhanced industrial expansion and maturity, thus making a strong productive apparatus available to society. Marx and Engels argued that the operation of this apparatus, along with the social wealth it could bring about, were incompatible with the structure of ownership relations on which the bourgeoisie's power was founded.

To the constructive critics of market society, however, the understanding of the self-destructive mechanism intrinsic to the capitalistic system was slightly different. It had an indirect, mediated effect, as opposed to the direct effect envisaged by the Marxian contradiction. The crucial distinction here was that the establishment of a market (capitalistic) structure was thought to imply the destruction of a fabric of social relations and rules of behavior that were necessary to secure the cohesion of the social body.[5] As could be expected of a conservative view, the emphasis was placed on "the world we have lost,"[6] the good old times regarded as a repository of those values on which civilized societies had been founded. The prejudice built into this argument was that capitalism was unable to create a society "of its own."

Obviously, Marx and Engels were fully aware of the destructive effects that the rise of the market and capitalism had on the previous social and cultural fabric. But they saw this as part of the capital's revolutionary force, so to speak, with the beneficial ability to advance society's productive forces by exceeding previous modes of production and destroying their related social formations. In itself, it was not the unavoidable precondition of its decline. More precisely, such a precondition was found within the capitalistic formation itself, rather than in the relationship between the capitalistic market and feudal forms, however unsolved or contradictory that relationship might be.

The two opposing arguments—doux-commerce and self-destruction—have not over time remained discrete as homogeneous or uniform blocks. As Hirschman has shown with scholarly elegance, a number of variations can be identified, but these can be conveniently merged into a basic pattern.[7] The picture may acquire different colors or shades but it hardly changes. The relationship between the disruptive power of the new arrangement of economic activities, and its impact on the existing social structure and traditional relational formations, still provides the hub around which any view of the social roles of the market and capitalism revolves. On the one hand, there will be a less triumphant view of the market economy's progress against which strong forces, associated with the traditional social universe, may seem to oppose effectively. On the other hand, there could be a positive view of the pre-capitalistic constraints that oppose the successful spread of a market society. This, in turn, would help to govern the integration of the capitalistic market into an existing social structure.

As a result, the third argument that Hirschman has identified is merely the reverse of the first assumption (doux-commerce). Here, the glass appears to be half-empty rather than half-full as it was formerly. The emphasis is on the obstacles or the constraints; traditional, pre-capitalistic, social formations are sometimes set up to prevent the market from unfolding all of its beneficial effects for social living. Finally, the fourth argument, that of a feudal blessing, is simply the negative version of the second assumption. According to this, "a feudal background is a favorable factor for subsequent democratic-capitalist development."[8]

As Hirschman has further emphasized, "however incompatible the various theories may be, each might still have its 'hour of truth' and/or its 'country of truth.'"[9] Moreover, at least some of these arguments can supplement one another usefully in order to account for any given situation. With this, the integration of the market into society then exhibits its fully complex and contradictory character. It is a consistently open issue never to be finally settled in the same way as the deployment of the economic system within the social system. Historically, the solutions that have been tried at one time or another, including those that appeared more stable than others, have actually all been temporary. This is due to the simple reason that they have always run along the shaky edge of a systemic equilibrium. Consequently, they have been exposed to the stresses to which the evolutionary dynamics of a social system are constantly subjected, as a result of the interaction of all of the system's building blocks.

Today, in the face of yet another "market revival," there may be an opportunity as well as a need to emerge finally from such crude polarity, and to escape the cultural, social, and political swings that such a revival involves. In short, this is a chance to rethink completely the issues posed by the "integration of the market into society." This step generally requires a new way of looking at the integration of the economy into society.[10] It then becomes necessary to shift our focus directly toward the crucial historical turning point: when the formation of a "market society" began to challenge the traditional link of the material activity of society's reproduction—the economy—with the social structure as a whole. This is the turning point wherein we must seek the native roots of an economic approach that still directs and distorts our vision and conception of the entire range of activities by which society reproduces itself.

Thus, an attempt will be made to put that crucial turning point into perspective in light of a critical approach emerging from two very different authors. Both Karl Polanyi and Fernand Braudel are rich with analytical and theoretical insights. Also shown will be how twentieth-century economic theory, generally confined to the splendid seclusion created by the "neoclassical revolution," has nonetheless been able to grasp on occasion the "anomalies" that the functioning of the model exhibits in respect of sometimes significant classes of phenomena, although it has not been pushed to promote a paradigmatic transformation. In fact, efforts worthy of a better cause have been devoted to reinforcing the validity and general applicability of the economic paradigm based on the metaphor of the *homo oeconomicus* and the market. Today, the incommunicability of economic science with the other social sciences appears as the main obstacle to the formulation of a less formal, more comprehensive, economic theory. In the closing section of this chapter, an attempt will be made to show how certain boundaries between social sciences can be crossed profitably.

On the Origins of a Market Society

The Discovery of the Market

Markets have always existed. Their origins are lost in time immemorial. Traces of this institution can be found in all social formations, however primitive they may be. But a "market society" is a comparatively recent occurrence, one, at least in its beginnings, that is geographically circumscribed. What differentiates it from other social formations is the fact that markets, far from playing an ancillary role, can organize society's reproductive activity extensively, thereby dictating its overall structure. In pre-capitalistic societies, as Polanyi has forcefully emphasized, even when markets and trade were a substantial presence, they were located at the margins of the social space and often even at the margins of the physical geographical space. Sometimes, they were accompanied by measures that tended to restrict their impact on the social structure. In any event, they sustained the circulation and distribution of a minor share of the goods and services needed for society's material reproduction. Most of these were distributed through such institutions as the family, the state, and the court or the monastery, which acted in such a way as to make the economy in its whole apparently "embedded" (as Polanyi puts it) in the social structure. In "market societies," however, society itself appears to be subordinated to the market's activity. Basic resources are almost entirely allocated and distributed through a system of interdependent markets that give rise to the formation of a price for each of them and determine their allocation while fixing the returns to their owners. A society's entire self-reproducing mechanism depends considerably on the functioning of the markets. The economy becomes disconnected from traditional social institutions, and tends to meld with the market system.

What caused a market society to emerge? It is a known fact that economic science, at its inception, was faced with this historical transformation; the manifestations and consequences of a market society began to attract the attention of a growing number of observers in the course of the eighteenth century, although markets and trade had been the objects of considerable thought since before then. Adam Smith focused on the "certain propensity in human nature . . . to truck, barter, and exchange one thing for another,"[11] as the natural foundation of a social order based on the market. He seemed to ascribe the character of an unbroken evolution in the history of mankind, to the formation of a "market society." The spread of trade and the resulting increase in the division of labor which accompanies it, should then be seen as simply the natural outcome of a gradual expansion of man's propensity to trade. Hence, in Smith's view, a sort of virtuous circle was established which involved society's entire development. Trade activities gave rise to a drive to increase gradually the division of labor, multiply goods, introduce and generalize the use of money, and expand the market. An enlarged market, in turn, stimulated an increased division of labor, enhanced trade and monetary flows, and so on. The wealth and welfare of nations grew as a result.

This was by no means a novel idea. Adam Smith's celebrated formulation had a centuries-long gestation behind it. In 1601, John Wheeler, the secretary of the Company of Merchant Adventurers and a resolute advocate of the social dignity of mercantile activities, wrote that "there is nothing in the world so ordinary and natural unto men, as to contract, truck, merchandise and traffic one with another."[12] That society's well-being was closely related to this most "natural" of man's inclinations was an idea that could be traced back to the end of the fourteenth century. A 1363 Venetian act of law stated: "As there is nothing that could better multiply and increase the wealth of our city than fostering and enhancing the practice of mercantile trade, let it be conducted here rather than elsewhere in the best interests of the commonwealth and private individuals alike."[13] Such a broad horizon is ample evidence of the long and laborious development of a culture that had to face the new role that an ancient economic institution—the market—was beginning to play in Western societies. The idea of a "market society" did not issue from Adam Smith's mind as a fully developed concept. Rather, it took shape over several centuries, during which the presence of markets increased along with the perception of their influence on society. The vision that Smith brought to full awareness was not so much the perception of the market as it was a conception of the market as a self-consistent economic system able to organize the social order and dictate its rules of behavior.

The market was then thought to be endowed with a sort of spontaneity which provided opposition to the state's more or less arbitrary intervention. In eighteenth-century England, and even more in Scotland, this view acquired an almost commonplace status. Hume wrote in 1752: "According to the most natural course of things, industry and arts and trade increase the power of Sovereign as well as happiness of the subjects and that policy is violent which aggrandizes the public by the poverty of individuals."[14] This style of reasoning was the very root of the antithesis between the state and the market or, if we are to choose Smith's language, between the Sovereign and the trader.[15] These are the very terms in which the market's social role has been largely concerned up to this day. The most clear-cut formulation of this thought can be traced back earlier, to an explicit criticism of mercantilism. In the words of Sir Dudley North, a British gentleman who had participated in commerce as a member of the Levant Company and had later become Lord Mayor: "No people has ever become rich because of the interventions of the State. It is instead peace, industry, freedom and nothing else that make commerce and wealth grow."[16]

In this respect, Adam Smith's reflections, usually regarded as the origin of economic science, instead appears as the point of arrival of a cultural evolution primarily devoted to winning social dignity for the trader's activity and role and, secondarily, including the market mechanism within an organic view of social operations. In England, where this process was particularly prominent, this shift has been aptly shown by Joyce Oldham Appleby to have slowly but unambiguously taken place during the seventeenth century.[17] In thousands of writings, booklets, pamphlets, treatises, and leaflets, the new advocates of free trade tried to legitimate the merchant's function and activity in social terms through a varying degree of analytical skills. The powerful spread of market transactions had posed the question of how to understand this newly evolving social reality in its specificity, in the same way that the emergence and rise of a mercantile class had posed the question of its own place in society. The vast multifarious economic literature of seventeenth-century Britain was the result of both issues. This, at least in part, can explain the peculiar traits of the economic theory that emerged from the new market pattern and its gravitation toward the principle of free trade.

The first task was to rescue the merchant's social figure and activity from the protracted dispute that had surrounded it throughout the Middle Ages. The merchant was unduly likened to the figure of the moneylender, thus associating his status with the general condemnation of interest and profit as expressed in the Bible.[18] A response that facilitated the fulfillment of this task came with the notion of the "invisible hand" that slowly emerged between the seventeenth and eighteenth centuries, culminating in Adam Smith's classical formulation.[19] Far from being a danger for social cohesion the merchant's self-interest, which focused entirely on the attainment of maximum personal gain, was shown to be the main source of society's welfare and harmonious development. This was the cultural riverbed into which the argument of doux-commerce began to flow like a flood.

A more general task was to find the moral legitimation and analytical justification for market relations. This was handled through the notion of *homo oeconomicus*. A specific view of human nature as the foundation of market society emerged in the wake of a newly dominant rationalism: man was driven by self-interest to pursue gain as an instrument to improve his condition. As would often occur later on, particularly in the area of economic theorizing, a micro-societal behavior was assumed to explain a macro-societal structure.

In such an interlocked environment, the biggest consequence was that the whole of economic life was seen as regulated by natural processes, so that it appeared sufficient to let Nature work through its own will for free trade activities between men, in order to produce the highest degree of common welfare through a sort of unintentional cooperation (the "invisible hand"). No other notion as powerful as this one, that of a natural order in economic relations unaffected by social devices or political interference, was brought to life during the seventeenth century.[20]

This core vision also originated a language that would become prevalent in economic theory with innumerable, yet elusive, consequences, through such terms as natural price, natural rate of profit, natural rate of exchange, and the very notion of equilibrium. We take a passage by Pierre de Boisguilbert as evidence of the introduction of such a link:

> Nature (or Providence) alone can enforce this kind of justice, provided that, however, once again, nobody else should interfere with it. Here is how it succeeds in doing so. First, it establishes an equal need to buy and sell in all and any branches of commerce, so that the desire of profit alone becomes the reason for any trade or exchange for both the buyer and the seller. In fact, it is precisely because of this equilibrium, of this sort of balance, that both are forced to comply with, and yield to, the rules. . . . Any departure from this law, which should be held sacred and yet it is even too often disregarded, is the first cause of public misery. The equilibrium among all commodities, which is the only means to preserve general opulence, is seriously endangered in many ways as a result.[21]

This remarkable passage already contained, *in nuce*, all the features of the analytical approach around which both the classical and neoclassical economic theories were to revolve. The market was seen as a huge self-regulating machine which operated under the power supplied by the individual's drive to profit and could coordinate the various individual drives in order to achieve the state of equilibrium in which maximum common welfare could be attained. In light of this conception, the Sovereign should keep off and leave Nature or, as Boisguilbert went so far as to say, Providence free to unfold all of its beneficial effects. Although the creed of economic liberalism was to undergo cultural and analytical refinements in the following centuries, its message had been clearly announced. The argument for a "market society" had received its first accomplished formulation. The idea was *laisser faire* ("to let them act"), implying that society's survival and well-being should be left to the free action of those natural forces from which the inclination to trade and the motive of gain originated.

The perception of this new social machine, the market (understood as a generalized system of economic transactions covering all available goods and services even to include land, labor, and money, on which society's welfare ultimately depended), made its way through the seventeenth century in successive approximations, but always under the compelling pressure of the interests that commerce itself set in motion. The conceptualization of a differentiated self-contained economic system within a social system took place under the sign of the disrupting flood of market dynamics, the scars of which it would bear for a long time to come. The identification of the economic system with the market system, on which Polanyi focused his cultural and ideological criticism, had its origin and justification precisely in this approach.

Beginning in the seventeenth century, the way of thinking that gradually established economics as a specific separate subject matter, resulted in a particular area of the scientific discourse; "political economy," later known as "economics," developed as a response, in relation to questions posed by the market's new reality. Such a close definition of economic thought, which singled the market out as a unique comprehensive object, provided a powerful constraint, then a historic "necessity" which could hardly be challenged. An emerging class, the mercantile bourgeoisie, had gradually built a vision of society's working which perfectly matched its interests, and was now putting it forward as a way of governing. In this sense, economics was politics, and so it remained even with the neoclassical economists, when the clarity of "political" as a modifier of "economy" was nearly lost. The nature and limitations of "economic discourse" find their justification and explanation in this sort of "original fault," which betrays its secret. A more difficult undertaking would be to understand and justify the persistence of that view of economic reality into which that need and that "original fault" have been dissolved for so long, thus leaving the field open to far more complex analytical and political demands. Indeed, if the market still is the propellor or, if you will, the dominant factor of our economies, it has been also obvious for at least a century that it has only covered a portion (even a variable one) of their scope, and not the entire economic expanse. Other subjects have occupied the economic space, and other organizing principles have emerged alongside, and in competition with, the market.

The industrial revolution in the second half of the eighteenth century did not modify the background of the picture. The economy was still identified with the market. Beginning around that time, however, the logic of trade fully penetrated the scope of production, thus making the market's dominance even more general—or seemingly so, at least. Theoretical speculation went on to follow the tracks of the *homo oeconomicus*[22] as the only paradigm upon which a scientific analysis of economic activities could be founded. Producers had long remained at the margins of the trade flow, but they now became part of it in their own right. The perfect type of entrepreneur emerged as an economic subject who strictly applied the logic of market transactions, based on the search for profit and maximization of utility, to the entire scope of production activities.[23] Manufacture, as a specific form of production organization, was the most apparent outcome of the market's resulting pressure on the productive sphere, and triggered a process of generalization of market-oriented production. Although the forms of production that had preceded the capitalistic system still survived, they were relegated to a dark area at the boundaries of the bright "transparent" area of the market; they entirely escaped scientific attention only to be rediscovered and revitalized in more recent times under the pressure of the innovating drives that have strained and brought out every fibre of the social and economic fabric.

All these processes contributed to reinforcing the all-embracing image of the market economy and promoting it as the ideological pattern for a society whose functioning and cohesion were expected to be almost exclusively regulated by market transactions. Not even Marx's corrosive criticism succeeded in chipping the seemingly impervious coating of this image. Marx did succeed in assigning a historically limited, transient dimension to it, but he could not challenge its pretension to ascendancy in a given phase of social evolution. As such, the market's cultural hegemony became so pervasive that nobody could venture that the economy could be something more than, and different from, a well-framed system of price-controlled transactions. Only the comparative view of anthropology would later inject doubts about the truth of the whole picture.[24]

THE MARKET AS AN IMPOSITION

Within the scope of this research, Polanyi's contribution appears to be crucially relevant in at least two respects: (1) as a criticism of the "economistic fallacy" that identifies the market system as the economic system *tout court*, thus viewing market society as the climax of an unbroken historical evolution, and (2) as the foundation of a view of the economic system that reckons with the many ways in which economic activities can be regulated by, and integrated into, a social system.

The core of Polanyi's thought, which also led him to his more mature insights, was already fully outlined in his most celebrated work, *The Great Transformation*, conceived in the late 1930s and written during World War II.[25] The source of this insight, which has the self-regulating market as its focus, was the experience of the Great Depression and the political and social crisis of the 1930s. That sequence of dramatic events was seen by Polanyi as the ultimately necessary outcome of an economic and social system, the market-dominated system, that had reversed the millenarian relationship of the economy with society by making the latter subservient to the former. The Great Transformation, which according to Polanyi affected liberal institutions during the 1930s, underlaid a "turning of the tide towards socialism"[26] which placed the economy-to-society relationship back into man's hands. As a result, the polemic objective that is at the heart of Polanyi's research began to take shape as a utopian society entirely governed by the principle of a market that becomes self-regulating based on flexible prices, and, simultaneously, by the classical and neoclassical economic theories which had been the necessary ideological and cultural pillars of the market economy's rule. From this, Polanyi's more general anthropological research design drew its original mark and motive, i.e., from the need of theoretically founding a radical criticism of liberal ideology by showing the fallacy of a pretended generality of the market system.

First of all, Polanyi denies any legitimacy to the typical assumption of the liberal creed according to which the market system simply was the outcome of a natural evolution deeply rooted in man's very makeup or, according to Adam Smith's celebrated formulation previously quoted, in that "certain propensity in human nature" that is the "propensity to truck, to barter, and to exchange one thing for another."[27] Polanyi tries to show that heretofore markets have never been anything more than accessories to economic life.[28] Whether markets were related to long-range external trade or to local trade, they have—in the long history of civilization—always provided a separate institution outside society, something placed at society's margins that society has always tried to ward off by a number of limitations and defences. Only when an internal market was created in the form of a system of interdependent markets based on price variations as a self-regulating device, was this relationship reversed. At that point, the market then penetrated society, gradually subdued all of its relations, and transformed things that had never been commodities in the first place—labor, land, and money—into merchandise. Society itself now changed into a "market society," governed by the opposing and interdependent motives of hunger and gain.

All that is not, says Polanyi, the result of a "natural" evolution of society. Contrary to what historians have been often led to maintain, it was not the intensification of trade or the spread of money that "naturally" brought about the rise of an economy or, more generally, a society which was either hinged on the market or structured around the relations that were established through trade within the market. The market economy was the result of a political action, a violence brought against the social body to adjust it to the needs of a form of production which was organized around complex machines and processes.[29] It was the factory system that, through the more and more complex coordination problems it posed, required the flows of production inputs, intermediate goods, and final goods to be provided by a system of interdependent markets.[30] It was the state that saw to it that these conditions should prevail. Again, it was the state's intervention that, as British history from 1795 to 1934 tells us, forcibly created a labor market by turning impoverished mobs into new industrial troops or a reserve army. It was the state that subjected land to the rule of merchandise. Finally, it was the state that made even money a commodity in self-regulated supply through the establishment of a central bank and a gold-based monetary system.

Evolution is then out of the question. It was a break artificially injected in order to further the factory system. As Polanyi has emphasized, a final evidence of the artifical and violent nature inherent in the establishment of the market economy is provided by the many forms of self-defence society has meted out to protect itself from the intrusiveness of the mercantile logic. Since the time when the market economy started its triumphal progress through society until its downfall in the late 1920s, the pattern of modern society can be viewed as the result of a dual process: the market was continuously expanding but its movement was met by a contrary movement that controlled its expansion in certain directions.[31] Although Polanyi has only briefly outlined this development, filling in the picture is not difficult. Think, on the one hand, of the disrupting effects resulting from the fact that the destinies of man, land (i.e., the environment), and money are still largely dependent on market logic. Apart from the labor market, upon which society has always tried to weave a web of constraints and protections, it is unnecessary to dwell on the devastating effects of the mercantile use of land resources in terms of depletion, waste, or pollution. Likewise, it is almost superfluous to mention the shattering economic and social consequences of the recent monetaristic attempt to bring the operations of the money system back to a narrow view of the market as a "self-regulating" entity. On the other hand, it is true that some the most significant socio-economic innovations in the half-century since the years of the Great Transformation have concerned precisely the refinement of cultural and economic tools, designed to control the use of land and the supply of money. What remains to be said is that, while Polanyi believed that the intrinsic contradiction of the "dual process" had resulted in the downfall of market society, the experience that has built up since the late 1930s seems to suggest that it is connate with its evolutionary pattern. If it is true that the vigorous expansion of the market system during the nineteenth century was only a partially successful process of adjustment to the needs posed by a form of production organized around complex machine systems, it is also true that such a strain has been a constant condition (although variable over time) of modern economies.

This early core of thought about the nature of our market societies and their crisis initiated the strategic objective of Polanyi's theoretical design, which was to redefine "the place of economies within societies" in an anthropological perspective. In addition, it was necessary to relocate the nature and function of a self-regulating market as a specific unique institution of capitalistic economy in a specific historical phase, rather than a general form of "the economic."

Following *The Great Transformation,* a work permeated with a keen polemic spirit and driven by a resolute social commitment, Polanyi devoted his efforts to consolidating the analytical structure of his own insight, that the self-regulating market system was a historical anomaly. *The Livelihood of Man* was based on an extensive comparative survey into primitive, ancient, and modern economic systems. Polanyi planned, as evidenced by this posthumous and most highly systematic work, to continue his battle against "our obsolete market mentality" by stressing the uniqueness and the artifice of the "market economy" as opposed to the presumed character of generality and naturality that the traditional economic theory ascribed to it. In order to achieve his goal, he was led to rethink radically/profoundly the theoretical status of the economy and the market, and to reconceptualize the distinction between them. We will now be concerned with this aspect of his argument.

As the foundation of his entire approach, Polanyi introduced a basic analytical distinction between the two meanings combined in the current usage of the term "economic": a substantive meaning and a formal meaning.[32] He related the former to the institutionalized interaction of man with his natural and social environment, a relationship designed to provide man with the means to satisfy his wants. As such, the "economic" dimension was inherent in any social system, regardless of both the institutional forms it would take over time and ways in which it was integrated into society. The latter meaning of "economic" was taken to refer to a behavior that resulted from a need to choose an allocation from among the many uses for means that are insufficiently available. This behavior corresponds to an approach to rational action oriented in the means-to-ends relationship, which only prevails in situations where man's livelihood is dominated by scarcity.[33] Contrary to the dominant economic belief, the character of scarcity is not in itself intrinsic to the category of the economic in its "substantive" meaning. It is not enough merely for certain goods to be available to an insufficient extent in order for them to become scarce and require a choice.

> . . . For a scarcity situation to arise, not only an insufficiency of means but also choice induced by that insufficiency must exist. Now, insufficiency of means does not induce choice unless at least two further conditions are given: more than one use for the means, otherwise there would be nothing to choose *from;* and more than one end, with an indication of which of them is preferred, otherwise there would be nothing which to choose *by*.[34]

These conditions only apply in a market-dominated society, where the general introduction of purchasing power as a means of appropriation changes the process by which wants are satisfied, into the allocation of insufficient means having alternative uses, particularly money.[35] Here, individuals' choices result in interdependent flows through a system of markets, which regulate the prices of all the goods and services that are required by the economic process—thus originating all forms of income. According to Polanyi, only an economy of this type can lend itself to the classical and neoclassical analytical approach, with its hypostatization of a *homo oeconomicus* who acts upon the motive of gain and who thinks according to the logic of a rational choice, i.e., by allocating insufficient means to alternative ends. The traditional economic analysis, as a victim of the "economistic fallacy" that "equate[s] the human economy with its market form,"[36] lives and dies with the self-regulating market system. As soon as, and to the extent that, such a system no longer governs the whole sphere of society's reproductive relations, classical and neoclassical theories lose most of their relevance.

This is a major result that has gone unnoticed by economists for too long. The whole debate about the economic theory that has rather fruitlessly occupied these last fifteen years can be reapproached and made more fecund. Polanyi may be charged with having been, at least in part, the victim of his own anti-economistic bias, and with having let himself be subjugated by his own discovery to some extent. The self-regulating market system has never covered the entire span of "substantive economy," even during the "one-hundred years's peace" as Polanyi defines the period of what has been thought to be associated with its full establishment. This image certainly is more the result of Polanyi's passionate self-deception than a careful reconstruction of the twentieth-century economy. Yet, it shows what no other economic theory has been able to show. Above all, it reminds us that, in any event, the utopia of a self-regulating market was the dominant, hegemonic political ideology during and beyond the period studied by Polanyi.

The market's all-embracing presence forcefully established itself in the heart of European society in the first half of the nineteenth century, with the pretension of occupying it in full. According to Polanyi, this was the historically determined factor that explained the assertion of an economistic culture[37] erasing the far wider social territory that is occupied by "substantive economy" from social imagery, and removing it from the economic analysis. If one wishes to understand the economy in a given period or territory in any depth, one should refer to this "substantive" meaning of economy, and adopt a view which allows for an overall review of the many ways in which the interaction between man and his environment is realized and institutionalized so that material wants can be satisfied and society's reproduction can take place.

Polanyi's answer to this analytical question is based on the notion of the "forms of integration," which he developed by reviewing anthropological evidence. "Forms of integration . . . designate the institutionalized movements through which the elements of the economic process—from material resources and labor to the transportation, storage, and distribution of goods—are connected.[38] In *The Livelihood of Man,* Polanyi thought he could identify three major forms of integration in the human economy through the history of cultures: reciprocity, redistribution, and exchange.[39] In *Dahomey and the Slave Trade,* however, he also mentioned a fourth form, household economy, which does not seem to be identifiable with reciprocity.[40] Obviously, it was still a crude and elementary analytical approach, of a somewhat temporary character. Polanyi was fully aware of the fact that this was just the beginning.[41] Yet, it is a convenient starting point to analyze the place of the economy in society and the different institutional forms that provide social integration to economic activities, and to outline a tentative formal model of an economic system outside of the analytical pre-assumption of the market model.

The "forms of integration" can be thought of "as diagrams representing the patterns made by the movements of goods and persons in the economy, whether these movements consist of changes in their location, in their appropriation, or in both."[42] Reciprocity describes a social situation in which goods and services are allocated and distributed through flows between points (people or groups) in a symmetrical arrangement. It is a situation similar to that of trade, except that the latter requires the presence of the motive of gain, and a price mechanism, i.e., the presence of a market. Finally, redistribution describes a social situation in which goods are made available through flows and reflows from a center that governs their allocation. In this view, the household or family economy could be seen as a form of integration in which goods and services are produced and distributed based on cooperation within a household.

For the "forms of integration" to be able to operate, they must rest on "supporting structures"[43] or institutions which organize the underlying individual behaviors by providing them with continuity, consistency, and effectiveness. Two major features of the model of the forms of integration must be highlighted. First, as Polanyi himself emphasized, these forms should not be viewed as stages of development that come after one another in a forced sequence.[44] Quite to the contrary, they can exist one besides another at different levels and in different sectors of an economy. Obviously, one of them will play a dominant role and affix its mark onto the whole of the economic system, but it can also undergo a temporary eclipse during which subordinated forms are restored to relevance.

In the second place, one should consider whether they are "embedded" in society. This criteria is crucially relevant to Polanyi's argument, and allows us to single out the self-regulating market as an institution separated from other forms of integration. For the first time in the history of economies and societies, the self-regulating market is identified as an economic structure entirely separated from society: "Livelihood is secured primarily by economic institutions that are activated through economic motives and governed by economic laws. Institutions, motives, and laws are specifically economic."[45] In Polanyi's view, such an economic system can function irrespective of such non-economic institutions of society as the family, the state, or religion. This may very well be an extreme caricature of the market system, in which Polanyi is somehow a victim of his hypostatization of the self-regulating market principle; in some respects, it is similar to its polar opposite, to the vice which he assigned to neoclassical economists. Yet, it allows us to single out what characterizes the economic system as it begins to change within Western societies with a special institution as its starting point—the competitive market. What makes up the economy as a system[46] is precisely its separation and self-containment within the social system, or the fact that such motives and behaviors as gain and self-interest can be singled out and institutionalized, which guarantees the execution of economic activities irrespective of the influence and cooperation of non-economic variables.

Such an analytical approach is the source of a view of the economic process which is not only hinged on the form of the market, according to the image that has been imposed by the liberal ideology and sanctioned by the refined constructs of neoclassical theories, but also appears as a process of distinct, variously interlocked institutional forms. Certainly, there is still one form that prevails over the others—this is the status of market exchange in our societies—but this dominance appears less as an inflexible, immovable pattern than as a fluctuating arrangement, or the result of a continuous interplay caused by the way in which, and the extent to which, each institutional form contributes in realizing the overall satisfaction of wants from time to time, i.e., in securing the performance of the economic system. In its substantive meaning, the "economy" should still be seen as a complex, hierarchical system, constantly traversed by "hierarchizing" processes that move and reshape the relative positions of the different forms of integration, depending upon the demands arising from the wants that the social system expresses and recognizes from time to time. The "double motion," which according to Polanyi defines the basic pattern of market society, must be understood more aptly, as a complex, multi-pole movement in which society and the economy interact in a much more bending and winding way than has been believed heretofore.

Obviously, we are just at the beginning of a criticism of the dominant economic theory and ideology. We are still far from the construction of a model of the economic system that could overcome the narrow boundaries enforced by traditional economic theory. Similarly, we are still far from beginning to reckon with the insights to be derived from other areas of social research while interacting with disciplines that deal with the same domain of phenomena. But the road has been paved.

Some temporary acquisitions are emerging upon which the foundation for a criticism of economics can be laid. In the first place, we know that the market is not the only institution designed to regulate economic activities, in the same way that gain is not the only motive. Further on, we will refer to recent studies showing that, even in the case of the market, gain is not the only standard against which trade is regulated. As a result, when the economy is viewed under a substantive light, it appears as a composite system which fulfills its functional task of allocating resources and producing and distributing goods and services through a number of motives and institutions variously merging with one another during historical evolution. Finally, we know that different institutions exist which, at different levels and in different areas of an economy, provide for the integration of economic activities in the social structure.

We can then rule out, once and for all, the idea that there is, or must necessarily exist, a linear, univocal process called "modernization," the sense of which is given by the principle of formal rationality as expressed by the market economy, in which the birth and growth of our societies appear to occur. The process leading to the establishment of a market society that is characterized by the integrating function of trade is neither univocal nor irreversible nor even linear. As the market economy creates and wins spaces within society, it elicits many conflicting forces which oppose it, adjust to it, intersect it, and ceaselessly combine in designing and redesigning the overall configuration of the economic system and the market's role within it. In this view, economic crises can be seen as a crucial stage within which the dominant form of integration is no longer able to meet the demand from the societal structure of wants. A sweeping readjustment process sets in, which also includes the requalification and refunctionalization of secondary or marginal forms of integration. For example, it is along these lines that one can see the boom of the "hidden economy" in the 1970s, which occurred in all the capitalistic countries affected by a crisis, i.e., a growing inability of the given market-relation configuration to face the economy's "substantive" problems. Also, it might be along these lines that one should read the so-called "market revival," i.e., the re-emergence of economic needs that are better served by the market principle.

The Dynamics of Capitalism: F. Braudel

In view of the issue we are concerned with here, which is the issue of the origins of the "market economy," and the structure of an economy in which the market as an institution plays a dominant role, Fernand Braudel's historical work offers some findings that can be usefully integrated with those offered by Polanyi within a new synthesis, the main lines of which we will now attempt to sketch. In his monumental work, designed to trace the development of capitalism from the fifteenth through the eighteenth century,[47] Braudel has outlined a model which—although it is mainly addressed to a description of the historical evolution of capitalism—exhibits an analytical structure that can be usefully combined with Polanyi's schematic in an attempt to outline the basic traits of a more general model of the functioning of the capitalistic economy and its development.

Any attempt to trace back and articulate Braudel's analytical approach may prove a hard task, since it has not the degree of formalization that is typical of an economist's model, as it is fully embedded in the historical record. Moreover, Braudel rightly conceives models as experimental constructs that must be continuously subjected to the test of facts, and modifed accordingly. His models are not, therefore, stable and fixed, but flexible and subjected to gradual adjustments. Yet, their main lines can be easily identified.

Underlying Braudel's approach to history, there is his careful attention to, and distinction between, different paces of historical development. There is the slow pace of change marked by centennial drifts, in which the economic process and society's life seem to reproduce themselves in almost constant, unchanged forms. It is the long-term perspective of "an almost immovable history," as Braudel says, or, if you will, the development of civilization's deep structures. Then, there is the faster, recognizable pace of economic cycles. Finally, there is the fast pace of events. While these paces diachronically mark historical becoming, they synchronically define a structural configuration or a hierarchy of movements, in which social life is reproduced.

Besides this differentiation of temporal paces, Braudel's moving historical picture shows another dimension that plays a major explanatory role in his analysis, although it has been traditionally overlooked by economists. This dimension is geographical space with its characteristic and distinct features. Geography is also at work in the stratifying processes that it, in turn, helps to create by giving rise to differences and differentials in economic potentials. Different paces of economic and social life are distributed over, or condensed in, geographical space in different patterns.

Such a complex analytical framework, which tends to become "a general interpretation of human history,"[48] enriches the background of the great historical fresco painted by Braudel with layers of movements and relations that gradually shape the social ground on which capitalism settles and grows. Simultaneously, this framework determines the geographical distribution of centres and peripheries within large geographical and historical configurations—"world-economies" in Braudel's terminology. This basic approach prepares and compacts his research ground in ways that appear surprisingly similar to those just identified in Polanyi's work. To be clear, I am not going to strain either author's purport by misrepresenting their statements or even ascribing intentions to them that they did not have. I am only trying to collate hints coming from their own works, and to work through the challenging puzzle that they appear to suggest, beginning with the questions being articulated here: What is the capitalistic economy? How does it relate to the market economy? How do both shape the societies in which we live?

Like Polanyi, Braudel begins by considering that "there is not one but several economies, and their evolution patterns may either clash, mutually support or even contradict one another."[49] Braudel, like Polanyi, is aware that "what is mainly described is the so-called market economy, i.e., the mechanisms of production and trade that are related to the activities of farms, stores, workshops, exchanges, banks, trade fairs, and obviously the marketplace." And he is also aware, again like Polanyi, that the discourse represented by economic science has taken shape "around these clear, 'transparent' realities," and economics has, as a result, retired into seclusion since its very beginning, in a privileged show to the exclusion of anything else.[50]

The historian's task is to try to shed some light on those areas of the economy that have been dimmed by the somewhat intrusive brightness of markets, thus escaping the attention of economic scientists entirely absorbed by "trade games." Braudel discovered that one dim area, "often hardly discernible for lack of adequate historical evidence," is the one lying, so to speak, below the market, which he has broadly termed "material civilization" to emphasize the fact that it almost indistinctly includes a wide range of activities intended for the daily reproduction of material life occurring on a long-term basis. This is the "inert mass of day-to-day living" barely touched by the reality of markets, which long remain outside this self-reproducing dimension of society. This lower primordial layer of economic life (the habits and flows of which change very gradually during the course of human history) appears to become integrated with society through the workings of a number of institutions—the family above all. Traditions and cultures have sedimented in this layer over hundreds, or even thousands, of years. It is the compressible but not suppressible, let alone suppressed, support on which every other form of economic activity has come to rest.

This definition is by no means a rigorous one, and may displease economists obsessed with formalism, but it allows us to throw some light on a reality which, until recently, included the great majority of the activities intended for reproduction, and has not disappeared even to this day, if it is true, as Braudel also believes, that "a slightly disguised trade, services directly exchanged, and the so-called 'moonlighting,' as well as the many forms of homework and do-it-yourself jobs" represent its modern version.[51]

Here we are not very far from the reality Polanyi included under the heading of "reciprocity," although the definitions involved can be hardly matched as they originate from different research agendas and meet different analytical needs. Yet, both authors seem to move in a converging manner in their search for forms of organization of economic activity that precede and accompany market activities.

Above this almost immoveable sea of material life, Braudel saw a more or less thickly woven network of market exchanges, a reality that almost keeps to itself for a long time, and does not contain in its substance, the reasons for its own evolution. Markets at the margins of collective settlement, at the boundaries of societies, are known to have always existed everywhere. The exchange system organized into market forms, with its many well-defined variations, can supplement but cannot modify, and even less replace, the reproduction of society based on self-consumption. It provides a thin, yet steady communication channel "between the vast world of the producer, on the one hand, and the equally enormous world of the consumer, on the other"[52] without ever being able to touch or attract the much larger part of production that flows directly to consumption without taking the market's circuitous route. Both economic realities can live together in an almost steady equilibrium for a long time. ". . . [T]he fundamental characteristic of the pre-industrial economy," says Braudel, "is the coexistence of the inflexibility, inertia, and slow motion characteristic of an economy that was still primitive, alongside trends—limited and in the minority, yet active and powerful—that were characteristic of modern growth."[53]

One should not be led to think, however, that Braudel conceived of the world of trade as a homogeneous whole immovable within itself. In fact, the purpose of the second volume of this monumental work was precisely to show the great variety of forms and solutions that are apparent within this only seemingly immovable reality. The problem will be, indeed, to develop a model to explain its evolution.

Braudel lingers at length over the multiform ever-changing reality of markets through the three centuries which are the object of his narrative, in order to see and cause others to see, as he often describes the historian's task to be. The result is a number of facts, uses, and circumstances which seem to make the modeling of these developments a hopeless exercise. The overlapping and intermixing of times and places in which each instance of the boundless reality of exchange can appear, make it almost impossible to fit them within the comfortable patterns of a time sequence able to show neatly the individual steps of an evolution. It then appears appropriate and reasonable to take a different route.

It may be true that over a reasonable time frame for exploring the issue of the market economy, i.e., from the late Middle Ages onward, all the "tools of exchange" had already been present. Indeed, some of them—elementary markets, hawkers, shops, trade fairs, and bourses—had been present since time immemorial. As a result, any genetic study is almost invariably doomed to be lost deep in the shadows of time. A more profitable approach appears to be one under which consideration is given to the various clusters, in which different tools of exchange are combined in a predetermined structure. Such a model will be largely dynamic enough to account for the accelerations, delays, and frictions that staggered paces necessarily involve. Elsewhere, I have gone so far as to suggest that it will be a systemic model. Even the market economy, like the economy in its whole, will then have to be viewed as a complex system, wherein operations are determined by the interaction of many elemental time-dependent mechanisms (and subjects).

This is the route Braudel himself indicated in his wisely allusive style, intrinsically rigorous yet, hardly prone to put forward any final statements or clearcut definitions. In a few densely written pages at the end of his first review of the "tools of exchange," under the conservative heading "Assumptions for a Conclusion," Braudel outlines what he cannot help calling "a model,"[54] which is an attempt to read the evolution of the European economy in the fifteenth to the eighteenth century as a sequence of different combinations of "mechanisms of trade," or a "differentiated history," in which their roles were continuously changing, such that "each century had its own special countenance."[55]

In the fifteenth century, especially with the economic recovery of the second half-century, "artisanal shops or, even better, urban markets were the driving force. These markets imposed their wishes upon others."[56] In other words, economic flows were dominated by the establishment and consolidation of the towns. When and why did the spread of the market assign a dominant role to this institution in society's economic organization? Certainly, trade must be intensified and compacted in order for the market reality to come to life and to begin to flow through the social fabric; it thus triggers a process of gradual subordination of economic life to the rules of monetary exchange. Yet, although this is the answer provided by conventional wisdom, it only shifts the problem sideways.

Braudel's answer is more complex and yet careful at the same time. The spreading of the economic area occupied by market activities is a lengthy process taking centuries to develop in full. Yet, "the market economy served as the link, the driving force, the restricted but vital area from which flowed encouragement, energy, innovation, enterprise, new awarenesses, growth, and even progress."[57] Possibly because of such a dynamic pattern, the market economy gradually began to differentiate two levels within itself that were to have different outcomes and developments: a lower level of marketplaces, shops, and hawkers, and an upper level of trade fairs and bourses.[58]

Although Braudel is not clear about that phenomenon, the duplicity of the exchange economy in his terminology, later to give rise to the differentiation between the market economy proper and capitalism, laid the foundations of that very transformation which was to install the market in the very heart of society's economic life. Only when the market entered the whirlpool created by the huge power of attraction of capitalism, did it shed its traditional features as a marginal place and tool of exchange to become the driving belt of capitalistic development. Only then did the need emerge to subject the entire process of society's reproduction to the logics of exchange. Without capitalism, there could be no market society.

What characterized the economic evolution of the West was less the fact that, as one is often led to believe, markets began to appear at a certain point in its history, than that the transformation to which they were subjected was a result of a set of circumstances. Elemental markets, as Braudel terms them, or traditional forms of exchange, were introduced into a new dynamic pattern which gradually redefined their nature and function to make them a "system." It swallowed them, made them grow up to its own size and, in turn, became subjected to their rule. Undoubtedly, the most significant fact was the introduction of the town, "a heavy unit,"[59] into the economic loop. The combination of towns and markets brought about a set of synergetic flows apt to modify the market's role and operations and to define a self-contained space for the economy.[60] Here, the foundations of capitalism were laid.

The first possibly fundamental synergy, one necessary premise for a "capitalistic process" to set in,[61] was the one actuated by the scale at which the town inevitably posed the economic problem of its very livelihood. This implied that the market was assigned increasingly complex tasks, and it was pushed to expand the range of its action, thus reaching and interconnecting more and more remote areas. Urban organization reduced the scope of economic life covered by self-consumption, while encouraging the division of labor and social differentiation. Both were loaded springs that acted for the expansion and consolidation of markets. Exchange activities acquired strength and continuity as a result, and began to branch out and differentiate from within. Hence, in the upper exchange bracket, foreign trade or long-range trade developed and enormously expanded the market's area of influence and dynamics. Economic life now became susceptible to a new genetic mutation, such as to give rise to a new form of organization of economic activity—the capitalistic form. Although the new form grew in a close symbiotic association with the market economy upon which it depended, it did not merge with it. In fact, it has constantly tended to bypass the rules and go beyond the boundaries of the market economy. Braudel is very keen on this distinction. Although capitalism thrives on the market economy, tends to subjugate it to capitalism's own interests and underlies this economy, it is not the market economy itself. It is a "second area of opacity above the clarity of the market economy and it is, somehow, its upper limit."[62] The market proper is the economic area where exchanges take place in a regular, predictable, or, so to speak, "transparent" fashion, based on rules and uses dictated by tradition and routine. Capitalism, however, tends to eliminate or bypass such rules and creates an economic space in which exchanges are all but transparent and symmetric. It tends to extend the trade chains between production and consumption to multiply opportunities of gain, exploit and continuously reproduce economic gaps, and impose unequal exchanges. In short, it aims at extending profit margins to the largest possible extent. It is not by chance that the forge of capitalism is widespread long-distance trade, the friend of rulers and states.

To emphasize this peculiarity of capitalism, Braudel has gone as far as to suggest that it should be called "a counter-market":[63] "A strong and progressing market economy . . . is the necessary—though not sufficient—condition for the formation of a capitalistic process."[64] For what we post-festum call a "capitalistic process" to develop, and take shape and substance, society must have developed from within the organizational and institutional conditions for its reproduction and substance.

This is the second basic prerequisite indicated by Braudel: "Society must act as an accomplice."[65] In particular, according to Braudel, society should be sufficiently differentiated within itself to bring about a hierarchy of dominating and dominated groups and to allow for some measure of mobility between them. And, in the second place, continuity of accumulation must be provided in some institutionalized form. Braudel does not explicitly say so, at least in this passage, but a specific determining link appears to exist between society's hierarchization and capitalistic accumulation. A strong, stable hierarchization of society even appears to be the necessary background for one or more groups firmly established in a dominant position to accumulate, and concentrate in their hands, a substantial and increasing share of the wealth that society itself has at its disposal. Family relations, and various forms of inheritance and ownership, are major institutions which, in their concrete historical configurations, help make the accumulation of wealth possible (or inviable). The ways and times of accumulation will then depend on the forms wealth will take from time to time—land, money, industries, or securities. Historical phenomenology is particularly rich, and the forms of wealth that can be identified in it are rather complex. But what must be stressed in this connection is that, for the process of formation and growth of large assets to develop in private hands, the social structure must be shaped to allow for and facilitate it. "The entire process implies a long, very long, preliminary gestation. In fact, thousands of factors of a political or "historical," more than specifically economic and social, nature must have come into play. A multi-century overall movement is at work in society."[66]

Not even this would be sufficient, however necessary it may be, without a third basic prerequisite: the formation of that global trade system that we call "the world market." Clearly, this heading will historically include very different realities from time to time. Despite its array of institutions, and the capillarity of its relations, the world market that we see today has very little to do with, for example, the sixteenth-century world market, intersected as it was by just a few, however decisive, trade flows. Yet, without the operation of long-distance trade, one could hardly understand the formation of the activities, figures, and organizations that are at work at the upper limit of the exchanges, and from which capitalism strictly originated. In short, with a summary statement that I believe Braudel would share, one could say that no long-range trade means no capitalism, as long-range trade is already capitalism. As Braudel must also be well aware, such a statement sounds quite disgraceful, even provocative. It is susceptible to the most infamous indictment for a historian—anachronism. Is it correct to talk of capitalism before the Industrial Revolution? Is a broader usage of the word legitimate?

Answering these questions in an exhaustive, analytically grounded manner would mean to possess an already accomplished model of the historical evolution of the capitalistic system. However, one could reason by assumptions, by putting together the pieces of an argument found only in the form of reflections sparsely scattered throughout Braudel's narrative. One could think of long-range trade, which draws its *raison d'être,* but not necessarily its origin, from the existence of full-fledged town markets, i.e., adequately wide and diversified ones (with viable money flows). Such trade has provided the innovating economic device resulting in a whole set of movements and synergies within the system, which acted in an accelerated fashion on the process of wealth production and distribution. In this view, Fernhandel could be construed as a sort of accelerator of the economic dynamics of which urban markets were the main organizational support. A sufficiently wide and diversified solvable demand probably provided an adequate impetus for the threshold of long-range trading ventures to be stepped over in view of the potential for huge profits. Originally, the market was driven by luxury consumer items, particularly spices and fabrics, but these could have hardly supported anything but a primitive stage of wealth accumulation. Only the full development of urban consumption in all of its breadth and variety could have provided that firm base of certainty and continuity that is a prerequisite for the stabilization of capitalistic assets. This is already an advanced phase of capitalistic development, though.

The decisive aspect of long-range trade is, in any event, that it brings about the rise of the level of profit that, in turn, accelerates or is even a condition of, the accumulation process. As long as economic activity, including trade, retains a fundamentally reproductive dimension, accumulation remains slow, or at least is not such as to become an economically and socially determining factor. Here again, the paces and their variations and accelerations are the keys to qualitative changes, although it is still difficult to establish levels or indicate dates for them. As soon as the accumulation pace accelerates because of the profits that are made possible by the consolidation of long-range trade, however, accumulation itself qualifies as a social function, thus triggering society's restratification.

In Braudel's model of the historical dynamics of capitalism, the decisive hint is the distinction of capitalism from the "market economy" and the area of "self-consumption": ". . . [C]apitalism does not overlay the entire economy and all of working society: it never encompasses both of them within one perfect system all its own. . . . *Capitalism* is the perfect term for designating economic activities that are carried on at the summit, or that are striving for the summit."[67] Capitalism, therefore, far from being identical to the market economy as suggested by the established economic theory and free-trade tenets, is something basically different, often conflicting with it, so that, as we have seen, Braudel has been even compelled to talk of a "counter-market." "The area of the counter-market is the domain of shifting for oneself and overpowering. Here the ground of capitalism is ideally located—yesterday as well as today, before as well as after the industrial revolution."[68] The activities in this area are regulated by other mechanisms. Braudel uses the terminology of the French economists, particularly François Perroux, in speaking of "organization." Certainly, this is the domain of monopoly, of the ability to assert hierarchies. These terms will come up again later on.

To sum up, the image of the economic system emerging from Braudel's investigation is that of a multi-story building.[69] At the bottom, there is "material life," in the sense of a very basic, self-sufficient economy based on self-consumption; above it, the sequence of the upper levels of economic life with the many exchange mechanisms, the "market economy;" and, finally, the topmost economic activity, "capitalism." It is a hierarchical structure, endogenously generated by the interaction of its various components, without any of them actually being dominant. Braudel is convinced that "the determining factor was the movement as a whole and that the extensiveness of any capitalism is in direct proportion to the underlying economy."[70] It is evident that the area of the economy as defined by Braudel's work exhibits somewhat ephemeral, or at least partly mobile, boundaries. Since he is fundamentally an empiricist in his methodological approach, Braudel is only slightly inclined to clear-cut definitions, and would not be prepared to do what he blames on the economists, regarding: "the economy as a homogeneous reality, apt to be taken out at our own will from its historical context and measured as it is, because nothing could then be intelligible except numbers."[71] An economist would very likely repay him with the same mistrust and Braudel himself is not free of doubts. In particular, this applies to the lowest level of the economic hierarchy, the material civilization, which he is unwilling to include under "economy."[72] The very distinction between the "market economy" and "capitalism" appears to be intentionally deprived of normal rigor. At times, the market economy seems to be fully separated from capitalism; at other times, it branches out to two levels, the upper level being occupied by capitalism. These are fluid concepts, and broad fluctuating definitions likely to be flexibly adjusted to complex and varying descriptions without any thought being given to reclassifying reality in a rigid final manner. It is a refreshing exercise for an economist willing to expose himself to the resulting suggestions even if only for the purpose of an analytical work.

The Market's Eclipse: From the Invisible Hand to the Visible Hand

"Fictitious Commodities" Removed from the Market

Polanyi believed that the 1929 crisis marked the irreversible end of society founded on the utopia of the market's self-regulating ability. As we know today, that was, in fact, just the beginning of a deep change in our social systems. Its outcome has been a new combination of the different forms for regulating economic activity that historical and cultural evolution has made available. Under the inspiration of Keynes's doctrine, that change resulted in the emergence of so-called "mixed economies," or economies characterized by a certain division of roles between the state and the market, and their more or less harmonious coexistence. We are now beginning to realize that not even that portrait was adequate to picture the complexity of the ways in which economic activity has become integrated into mature capitalistic societies.

However passionate and fascinating Polanyi's argument about the end of the self-regulating market might be, it was affected by the old state/market polarity to which it was captive. He only worked it into a direction contrary to the current one, and advocated the state's remedial action to restore society to full control over its own economic system. What escaped Polanyi in even his most ingenious and provocative work was the far more complex and diversified, even ambiguous, relationship between the various forms by which economic activity is regulated and integrated. In fact, the state that Polanyi's "planistic" frame of mind viewed as the vindicator of the supremacy of social claims, was "more intimately adjusting society to the economy,"[73] thus giving rise to a new economic constitution of capitalistic societies, not to mention the other new and traditional forms of organizing and regulating the economy that found a place in this area. True, Polanyi, as we have seen, developed an anthropological model in his later works to account for these multipolar dynamics. But the bill of the "economistic fallacy" had been settled, and his criticism of the market society was to remain in its original form.

In his most famous work, however, Polanyi found a way to stress that the market's victory had never been final, not even at the time when the "market society" was at its best: For a century, modern society's dynamics was governed by a double movement: the market was continuously expanding but this movement was met with a contrary one that controlled this expansion in certain directions.[74] In Polanyi's view, one of the most radical and devastating consequences of the establishment of a market economy was the transformation of man and nature into the species of labor and land. This shift was absolutely necessary, if production was to be organized on the basis of market exchanges. But the effects of this transformation on the social structure have been disruptive. The enslavement of man and nature to the logic of profit resulted in the dangers intrinsic in the exploitation of the worker's physical power, the destruction of family life, the devastation of local environment, the spoilage of forests, the pollution of streams, the deterioration of craftsmanship, and the general degradation of living.[75] As these dangers began to be felt, antibodies developed in the social body, which tried to preserve its traditional constitution, at least by regulating the assimilation of change. In Polanyi's view, this process began in the 1880s, and this conflict between society and the market went on until the final crisis in 1929. As society was led to comply with the needs of the market mechanism, malfunctions in that mechanism created cumulative stresses in the social body.[76]

Money was the first of the "fictitious commodities"[77] to be rescued from the market's rule and placed under the state's protection. In a few wonderful pages in which Polanyi confidently and originally handles the deep significance of money circulation in a capitalistic economy, he shows how a monetary system founded on money as a commodity, which the market mechanism tends to produce and the free-trade ideology would like to have, is incompatible with the expansion of production and trade that is made possible by a mature industrial system.[78] This insurmountable barrier, an intrinsic contradiction of the market system, compelled the state to replace money as a commodity, with money as a sign able to meet the needs of production and trade on a path of sustainable growth. To Polanyi, it also was a major cause of its decline.[79]

It was then the turn of land and labor to be gradually taken out of the market's domain. Thus, paradoxically, "while, on the one hand, markets were spreading over the entire surface of the globe, and the amount of commodities circulating in them developed to incredible proportions, on the other hand a network of political steps and measures became integrated into powerful institutions designed to control the market's action in respect of labor, land, and money."[80] This was the source of the monopoly over the issuance of money by central banks and of their power to control the conditions of monetary circulation. From this moment on, monetary authorities, instead of the market, were to determine the price of money. Trade unions and labor legislation were born; they would replace the market in fixing the price of labor until it became a price almost entirely administered in a triangular bargain—in which the state and the organizations of employees and employers were involved to varying degrees. The number of constraints would increase on the free purchase and sale of land or nature in the interests of a sort of collective ownership. The recent growing environmental concerns are just the latest chapter of a conflicting story with often unsatisfactory outcomes, which, however, shows how the market has always seen its full control of "land" fiercely challenged.

According to Polanyi himself, a society in which the economy was entirely governed by a system of self-regulating interdependent markets has never existed or, if it has, it has only lived a very short life—some twenty years or so. Society, which has seen the market economy progress and conquer one area of its reproduction after another, has long opposed it with pre-modern social, productive, and institutional forces, while, as Braudel has thought, the market economy itself has never lacked the forces to outflank and beat it and to substitute hierarchical for exchange relationships. Moreover, Polanyi's own analysis has shown that, in about the middle of what was expected to be the market economy's century, powerful actions were implemented to restrict and control the market's dynamics. Polanyi's "double movement" certainly is a useful metaphor, except that it does not, contrary to his allegation, describe the crisis of the self-regulating market. His metaphor only accounts for the dynamics of a society in which the market has acquired a central position. In a sense, it has identified its "laws of motion." The clash between the market's "imperialistic" drive and the resistance of customs, organizational structures, and ideologies in conforming with its rules—and in challenging it in the achievement of the goals that society sets for itself from time to time—are innate to market society. The actual configuration this society takes and the role the market plays in it as the regulator of economic activity are the outcomes—always temporary and precarious—of this clash.

The idea of a society in which survival is internally regulated by the market has never been fully substantiated by historical evidence. Rather, it belongs to the utopian projection of an ideology—free trade—that has tried to approach society as an entirely economic machine. To be able to refute that ideology, and in his concern for the devastating consequences it appeared to have on social balance, Polanyi thought it his duty to demonstrate the historical downfall of its alleged material foundation—the self-regulating market system. As a result, he overshot, so to speak, his own target, resulting in a conflict with what his own research strategy suggested to him, i.e., identifying the place of the economies or different economic forms (including the self-regulating market) within society.

The Keynesian Compromise

The maximum protection explicitly accorded to society against the disruptive operation of the market's mechanism was certainly reached by what has been described as the "Keynesian compromise" in a mixed economy.

By recognizing that the capitalistic market system was not in itself able to guarantee the goal of full employment through which society's economic well-being could be identified, John Maynard Keynes paved the way to a structural involvement of the state in the management of the economy. Involuntary unemployment was viewed as a signal warning of the deficiencies of the market mechanism in achieving an optimum allocation of resources. Keynes's analysis went to the roots of the elemental certainties on which the dominant economic theory had erected its building since Adam Smith's days. Keynes was perhaps the most acute and final critic of this individualistic approach precisely because he did not come from an adverse ideological background, and based his arguments on an extensive review of the capitalistic system and the opportunities to change it, while preserving its essence.

In this respect, the crucial point was Keynes's recognition that the entrepreneur's instinct, "animal spirits," and individual drive to the pursuit of profit did not necessarily give rise to the attainment of a state of full optimum use of the available resources, contrary to the confident expectations of Adam Smith and all of his successors. In social terms, the rationality of the market mechanism received a final blow as a result. The market principle could no longer be uncritically assumed to be the founder and guarantor of the social order. Keynes acknowledged that the community's superior interest must be served through a deliberate action by the state, with the support of sound intermediate organizations which reflected social interests. Keynes even thought that this was the new frontier of free trade:

> The transition from economic anarchy to a régime which deliberately aims at controlling and directing economic forces in the interests of social justice and social stability, will present enormous difficulties both technical and political. I suggest, nevertheless, that the true destiny of New Liberalism is to seek their solution.[81]

Indeed, back in 1924, in a clear and insightful pamphlet against the current thinking of the times, Keynes bid farewell to the traditional free-trade ideology:

> The world is *not* so governed from above that private and social interests always coincide. It is *not* so managed here below that in practice they coincide. It is *not* a correct deduction from the Principles of Economics that enlightened self-interest always operates in the public interest.[82]

In the well-known Chapter XXIV of his *General Theory*, Keynes was even more explicit: "The outstanding faults of the economic society in which we live are its failure to provide for full employment and its arbitrary and inequitable distribution of wealth and incomes."[83] The free-market model that the classical theory had worked up was powerless in the face of these problems because "its tacit assumptions are seldom or never satisfied," and it cannot, as a consequence, "solve the economic problems of the actual world."[84] If "the destruction of existing economic forms in their entirety" is to be avoided, and, at the same time, a "successful functioning of individual initiative" is to be ensured,[85] which to Keynes, were the prerequisites of an economic order compatible with the criteria of freedom and efficiency, a kind of compromise needed to be found whereby society's material reproduction was not left to the market's forces alone. Room must be left for collective action in organizing economic activity and, above all, some socialization of economic decisions needed to be established, particularly of those concerning investment: ". . . the duty of ordering the current volume of investment cannot safely be left in private hands."[86] Society needs to reassert, through its collective and representative bodies, the laws of its own cohesion on the market.

THE MARKET'S FAILURE

If, in the real world, an economy entirely organized as a system of interdependent self-regulating markets has never existed, one must still recognize that even the orthodox economic theory (or at least its most capable advocates) soon realized the limitations of a picture that portrayed the economy as a function of the mechanism of perfect competition. A careful reading of Walras's work, free of any ideological preconceptions, will show that even he as one of the founding fathers of the neoclassical approach was fully aware of the lack of self-consistency in the market model, of the fallacy of assuming that its pure essence was either a relevant description of reality, or a prescriptive model.[87] Walras's complex position has not been recognized in the subsequent development of economic theory; however, along the lines Walras indicated, there have been (at least from Marshall onward) references to the failure of the market as a mechanism for the allocation of resources. It would be interesting, along with the "wonderful and progressive wanderings" of the market theory, to write the history of the many, often painful, reflections about the market's limitations, deficiencies, and inequities that have paved the road of economic theory in the twentieth century. The result would certainly be a far less homogeneous or solid theoretical picture than the dominant academic wisdom may wish to offer—perhaps even a more attractive and stimulating one. Yet, the resulting portrait would not have been very different, however challenging it might appear. Like the good intentions upon which the road to hell is paved, no such reflections or re-thinking have ever led to a reversal of course, allowing us to go beyond the market ideology and put reality back in perspective. We remain within a domain where the market's centrality is thought of as an allocation mechanism, propelled by the ideology of its superiority in terms of efficiency and equity. Even the most penetrating considerations concerning the market's "failures" have, at most, enhanced rather than challenged the great social record of the market idea. In this way, *ad hoc* assumptions are generated which reinforce the substance of the paradigm rather than lay the foundations of an alternative paradigm.

Based on the anthropological view outlined by Polanyi and the historical model developed by Braudel, it might be possible to provide consistency, within the boundaries of a different economic paradigm, to a number of analytical hints that, in the evolution of recent and less recent economic theories, have tried to reaffirm the elements that escape or oppose the market logics. Particularly in these last few years, a rather heterogeneous school of thought has gained strength, which has been responsible for some vigorous attempts to show how principles other than the market logics are at work beyond the rationale governing the market's behavior. Although the scholars who are prospecting in this vast field of investigation have not started from homogeneous methodological approaches, often being driven by far different scientific motives, they have either voluntarily or involuntarily given rise to an image of the economy's "other face" (in Braudel's words). This has occurred by evidencing the substantial phenomena that can hardly be accounted for on the basis of the market's maximizing logic, and then by eliciting, more or less directly, the formulation of a more complex and diversified economic paradigm than the one that has sedimented around the core of the neoclassical theory.

The history of the market's failure began, strictly speaking, with *The Economics of Welfare* (1920) by Arthur Cecil Pigou. It is here, for the first time, that we find an attempt to provide an explicit and systematic account of the market's "failures" in the form of so-called "externalities." These are the unexpected, positive or negative, effects of individual economic subjects' activity which are not recorded by the price mechanism, thus determining a bias in resource allocation and a reduction in overall economic well-being. According to Pigou's well-known conceptualization, a difference can be introduced between the private and social cost of the use of factors. In other words, the market "fails" precisely in its crucial function—optimum resource allocation. In the face of this unequivocal inability of the market to regulate the whole of transactions in an optimum fashion, the legitimacy of the state's intervention in the economy has found a place for the first time, within a theoretical view that basically retains its free-trade character in an analytically unquestionable way.

The road Pigou first opened was later to follow a long and winding path taking it to the barren beaches of the "new economics of welfare."

In any event, it remained a somewhat secluded path, one along which one could easily encounter certain thorny questions concerning market efficiency, indignantly repudiated by the dominant doctrine which went undeterred on the polished road of perfect competition and the perfect transparence of the market's price mechanism. The function of this alternative route essentially was to keep the highway of economic theory clear by preventing useless, and inelegant, complications from building up on it. In both its original and revisited versions, welfare theory found itself involved in the task of disposing of any analytical difficulties likely to clog the gears of the main model, rather than paving the road for the construction of new conceptual structures.

At a later stage, Ronald H. Coase's seminal work on the nature of the firm (1937) was to prove decisive in this history. Coase questioned the assumption that the market should be regarded as the only organizing form of economic activity. In analyzing the nature and meaning of the firm in economy, Coase proposed that the firm could exist as an alternative solution to the market approach for a number of transactions: "It can, I think, be assumed that the distinguishing mark of the firm is the supersession of the price mechanism."[88]

Coase's argument is not entirely rigorous, and his basic definitions are not fully satisfactory. For example, it is clear that the argument could have acquired greater significance and general relevance if Coase had referred, as his argument only implied, to "organization" or "hierarchy" instead of to the "firm," as Oliver Williamson was to do later on. Nor is the application of his theory to both the explanation of the advent of the enterprise and to its actual dimension fully satisfactory. It would have been more correctly applied only to the latter. Yet, the road Coase paved with his contribution has proved highly productive in that it has led to an enhanced image of organizational processes that take place in the economy and, at the same time, has led to a revitalization of the market's role.

Coase's key idea was that the use of the price mechanism in organizing the productive process involved a cost. In Coase's view, this cost emerged from two circumstances, the mere mention of which is already disruptive in comparison to the received theoretical model of the market, such as the one built upon the marginalist theory that assumes the absence of attrition and perfect predictability. Quite to the contrary, Coase denied that every economic subject was fully aware of all the relevant prices; in the second place, he stressed the existence of uncertainty as a factor that dictated entrepreneurial decisions. The "firm" was then viewed as an organizational form that became mandatory when the combination of the factors of production gave rise, through markets, to costs that could be avoided or abated by organizing the flow of inputs through hierarchical relations.

Since he only produced a few examples, Coase did not systematically develop these lines of analysis. However, it is not difficult to harvest the crop that his reasoning brought to fruition. Once some of the most restrictive assumptions on which the pure market model is based, such as perfect knowledge and perfect predictability, are discarded as unrealistic, it becomes clear at a minimum that exchanges based on the price mechanism are not the only way to organize that part of economic activity which deals with production. Above all, it is not always the most effective means. Besides, and instead of, this kind of exchange, there appeared the function of a hierarchical organization. Organization rules out the market mechanism and replaces it with the mechanism of control and guidance.

Kenneth J. Arrow is probably the author who, more than anyone else, tried to develop an actual theory of the market's failures by depicting them within a stringent analytical framework. Such a systematic presentation of the market failure was used by Arrow to ground his detailed justification of the state intervention, or "rules of social behavior," to guide market mechanisms for efficiency and equity.[89] However, the scientific project within which this operation was conducted came from one of the most powerful and successful attempts to reinforce and perfect the model of general economic equilibrium. This was constructed by extending the rules of the market approach to behavior constituted outside of, or even opposed to, it. In other words, it seems that the schema of general economic equilibrium reveals imperfections and inconsistencies at the analytical level that must be reckoned with when developing a clear definition of the market's potentials and limitations in resource allocation.[90] At the same time, it could on a prescriptive level maintain its role unchanged and even dictate the rules of those behaviors that are part of collective action. The analysis of the market's deficiencies and failures led Arrow to a logical generalization of the form of market exchange and of all activities which take place within the economic domain.

To bring the analysis of the market's failures within a unified interpretational outline, Arrow employed the transaction-cost argument originally advanced by Coase. This is the assumption that, generally speaking, exchanges can only take place at a cost, and "the operating costs of the economic system" must be considered. The existence of transaction costs implies that situations may occur which prevent markets from being formed and alternative organizational approaches from being worked out. As mentioned earlier, Arrow recognized that these alternative approaches might include the use of "rules of social behavior" making transactions possible, or re-establishing efficiency where the market was either deficient or absent altogether.[91]

Arrow's rigorous analysis of the market's theoretical functioning, and his accurate appraisal of its failures, inevitably led him to make an explicit criticism that questioned the legitimacy of the market economy in social terms:

> The price system does not provide within itself any defensible income distribution, and this is a key drawback. In fact, the price system tends to obscure the fact that low income is a restriction of freedom. . . . The market in no way prescribes a just distribution of income and the idealization of freedom through the market fully disregards that for many relatively poor people this freedom is circumscribed indeed.[92]

Arrow seemed unaware of the radical nature of such an objection. In fact, it undermined the liberal construct that had since its origins identified market freedom as freedom altogether, and founded the legitimacy of a "market society" upon this identification. Certainly, the theoretical market model could be retained and accompanied, as Arrow's scientific plan envisaged, by criteria of justice resulting from the very rationality that generated economic behavior, which would then allow the "closure" of that model in terms of distribution outcomes. While this may be enough for an economist, in fact, the entire free-trade project collapses as a result. This is a paradoxical result. A more rigorous assertion of the market model and its underlying rationality becomes associated with the implied demonstration of the market's illegitimacy in playing the role of the originator of the social order, which the free-trade ideology assigned to it in the first place.

THE INVISIBLE HAND

As far back as the second half of the nineteenth century, firms in various industries began to exhibit a tendency to achieve a size, and pursue behaviors (trusts, monopolies, etc.) that challenged the very functioning of a pure market system based on competition. Braudel would have not found it difficult to identify a tendency to "bypass" the market, which he viewed as a basic trait of the deep nature of capitalism. But it took almost one hundred years for economic theory to accept the idea that this was something that could not be reduced to the ideal laws of a market economy. Even in the late 1960s, when John Kenneth Galbraith revived the idea that the "new industrial state" or a system dominated by large corporations represented a substitute structure for the market, it had not yet lost its scandalous charge. Only the extensive studies of Alfred D. Chandler, Jr., devoted to the origins of the large corporation in the American economy, finally attracted the economist's attention to the fact that besides the invisible hand, there was a "visible hand," just as strong and efficient, governing wide areas of economic activity.

Once again, the source of this school of thought was Coase's often-quoted essay (1937), but more recent developments have gone well beyond his original insight. Indeed, a theoretical argument has emerged whereby the market is deprived of its leadership in organizing the economic system, and is delivered into the hands of the modern large corporation that covers most of the economy's territory and only leaves almost interstitial areas to the market proper. The reasons for this evolution, which has gradually reduced the scope and significance of market mechanism, can be traced back to two basic features of economic development over the last one hundred years. These are the growing role of technology, and the growing interdependence of economic decisions within an increasingly complex environment that has resulted from the market's expansion. Both processes have combined to increase the margin of uncertainty in which production decisions are made. Technological evolution has implied—and in part still implies—that decisions must be made to invest in fixed assets of increasingly larger size over increasingly longer periods of time. Growing interdependence involves a greater turbulence of, and reduced controls over, the contents and consequences of decisions. Both circumstances are such that organizational approaches must be sought to reduce uncertainty and abate the associated costs. This is the justification for business understandings, trusts, joint ventures, and various other forms of collusion between economic subjects that are intended to reduce the impact of market relations within the whole of the transactions on which an economic entity must rely for its own survival.

Oliver E. Williamson has developed this approach with the highest degree of analytical rigor and depth. Although within a very careful research strategy that does not depart from orthodox microeconomics,[93] Williamson at the same time overtly supports J. Commons's institutionalistic approach—hardly welcomed by the profession's establishment. Williamson has built a strong analytical structure providing a valuable contribution to the critique of the all-embracing market ideology. The economic universe has been described on the basis of a set of factors that makes its image far different from the picture presented by the neoclassical theory. On the one hand, Williamson emphasizes two "environmental" factors—uncertainty and/or complexity, and presence of a limited number of exchanging subjects—which involve the removal of some characteristic, essential assumptions of the neoclassical approach. On the other hand, he stresses that both factors become decisive in reducing the market's ability to coordinate and make transactions possible, since each of them combines into one "human" aspect: bounded rationality and opportunism, respectively.[94] As far as the former is concerned, Williamson shares Herbert Simon's criticism of the behavioristic fundamentals of the neoclassical theory. The assumed perfect rationality of *homo oeconomicus*, compatible only with a highly simplified environment, has been contrasted by both Simon and Williamson, with the bounded rationality of those who act in a highly complex world in which the number of opportunities being offered systematically exceed the individual's knowledge and processing abilities. The result would be an economic subject who, instead of pursuing optimum outcomes based on an exhaustive bargaining where all the elements are known, will be content with achieving "satisfactory" results based on adaptive sequential decisions, and willing to use an organization rather than incomplete or costly markets to achieve his goals.

The notion of "opportunism" is also useful in expanding the range of behaviors to be considered in analyzing economic subjects and the relationships resulting from their interaction. Opportunistic behavior combines with a "small numbers" situation to generate the pursuit of collusive strategies that tend to replace market transactions since they afford more favorable results to individual economic subjects. Once again, the microeconomic review of behaviors shows that the use of the market is not necessarily the only possible outcome of a rational behavior, particularly since rationality is assumed to be "bounded."

FROM THE MARKET'S FAILURES TO THE MARKET'S LIMITATIONS

The literature on market failure can be viewed within a theoretical context that makes the market the central mechanism of the economy, and grants it a dominant rank in theoretical investigation. As we know, a prescriptive value has often been associated with this representation—the market as the optimum organizing model. Any phenomena or behaviors not complying with such a model are perceived as "failures."

The market failure argument can be, so to speak, decontextualized, i.e., removed with a positive sign to a different analytical context. As a result, the market's assumed "failures" become as many limbs of the general economic model, thus evidencing a number of ways in which economic activity can find its most economically and socially suitable organization. In particular, two forms emerge as important substitutes for the market: state organization and hierarchy.

Here, it is easy to recognize two issues already discussed by Polanyi and Braudel in their analyses of the economic system. Polanyi saw the state's redistributing activity as a fundamental form of the economy's organization. Braudel viewed hierarchy as the specific dimension in which capitalism has developed. These are, therefore, two forms that the historian and the anthropologist can easily recognize in their material, but that the economist has a hard time trying to include in his theoretical model as fully legitimate components constrained as the model is by the market metaphor.

A theoretical issue arises as to how to understand the ways in which those different forms of organizing the economy flow through the economic system, and which laws regulate their interaction and substitution relationships. We are not concerned with a taxonomy of economic forces. We are rather interested in identifying the meaningful relations that regulate the system's linkage and, thereby, its evolutive dynamics.

Conclusions

In a celebrated essay of 1947, Polanyi subjected what he described as "our obsolete market mentality" to a fierce criticism, and showed that it was at best the heritage of an age which has now finally come to an end. In his view, the future was open to the prospect of a process whereby the economy could be again integrated into society, and subjected to the latter's rule, by finally giving up the utopia of a self-regulating economy founded on market mechanisms. In this way, certainly at a difficult time, he tried to re-legitimate a contrary utopia—socialism.

In the following years, under the pressures of the problems arising from the need to reorganize the postwar economy, the "Keynesian compromise" won widespread acceptance as a mixed system resulting from a particular combination of state actions and market forces. Although the outcome of this "reform" of capitalism, far from being what Polanyi might have expected from the state's intervention (i.e., bringing the market economy back under society's control) was its precise opposite (i.e., the adjustment of society to the market's operations), there is no doubt that the first twenty-five years after the war saw the rise and consolidation of a thick network of controls designed to harness the market's dynamics and secure its compliance with social equilibria. Moreover, the forms of the interaction between different mechanisms designed to regulate economic activity have so proliferated that market relationships have almost merged into a relation system characterized by widely diversified organizing principles that have profoundly altered its distinctive traits.

It is known that for some years now we have witnessed an ideological counteroffensive tending to restore the market to its place as the highest, if not the only, mechanism to regulate the economy, and as the primary foundation of social order. We have already said that in our view it is high time to come out of this static contraposition and its resultant swinging behaviors, but we must also understand the features and reasons of this seeming "market revival" in its invocation as the deep, uncheckable power society's "marketization" process is supposed to have. The argument we have tried to advance here is that the reasons behind such a revival of the "market mentality" are not only ideological, but also derive from structural changes that favor the restoration of market relations and the market's organizing role. These are deeply rooted in the changes that have taken place in the social system and in the economic subsystem in the last ten years, along with a faster growth of the processes of differentiation, diversification, and segmentation of the relevant issues and operating approaches. The revival of the market mentality is designed to meet an increasing need to decentralize decisions as a response to the increased complexity of social and economic systems. This underlying trend has then combined with a flood of technological innovations that tend to assert and enhance the growth of societies' global interdependence and complexity. The arguments that have been discussed so far allow us to state that even this "market revival" can only be of a partial and transient nature. It does not imply society's full marketization, nor does it mean the final suppression of any other economic form. It merely implies a change in their relative ranks, and a restructuring of their ways of interacting. Here is, in a sense, the dynamic substance and systemic cohesion of a "market society." This is a statement of fact, rather than the declaration of an ideology. Free trade thought should be relegated to where it belongs—to the museum of ideologies.

The preceding pages are just a tentative summary prospection. They are, in a sense, a sort of feasibility study for a research strategy designed to shape a new paradigm of political economy. Herbert Simon once said, on the occasion of the Nobel Award for Economic Sciences (1978), that the same principle applies to scientific and economic theory as applies to politics: "You can't beat something with nothing, or defeat a candidate by merely pointing to his faults or deficiencies."[95] I fully share this view, in the same way that I am convinced that an alternative does exist or, at least that, again in Simon's words, "there exists an embarassing demand for alternatives."[96] More than that, there exist, as I have tried to show, individual, often well-developed, analytical fragments which appear apt to be framed within a new theoretical picture. What is lacking is a logical thread upon which to weave the canvas of this recomposition. Polanyi's powerful dismissal of the "economistic fallacy" allows us to proceed toward the construction of an economic theory which, far from being haughtily secluded from the other social sciences—sociology, anthropology, history, and psychology—must be committed to the search for contact lines and overlapping surfaces, in order to achieve the general aim of explaining the ways in which the social fabric develops and changes.

The discussion of Polanyi's contribution has shown how one could hardly understand the workings of the economic system unless it is related to the modes upon which its integration into society depends, from time to time, in ever-changing combinations. Also, in a complex social system, the economy appears to be institutionalized to varying degrees and in different forms, which is a result of both historical evolution and of the diversification and adaptation processes that have occurred at different stages, and are still interacting with one another.

Braudel's historical analysis has, in turn, helped us to see how at least three forms of organizing economic activity can be identified in the multi-century evolution that led to the establishment of a capitalistic economic world. One was the traditional form, basically oriented toward self-consumption, which had its regulatory level in the elemental institutions of social organization (the household, the court, the monastery). Then came the form of the market economy, the result of the gradual differentiation and atomization of the economic system that first evolved in the late Middle Ages through the widespread use of money in trade and price as an information channel. This market economy, as Braudel has aptly illustrated, emerged alongside the self-consumption economy, and then enveloped, overpowered, and compressed it—depending on time and opportunities—but never succeeded in suppressing it. The market economy, in turn, has been overpowered, conditioned, and exploited by the capitalistic economy proper, ruled first by the big international merchants and bankers, and then the large firms in which the state has been present ever since. Here, the factor that regulates economic relations is not the transparent exchange at market prices, but the power, hierarchy, and organization that have generated and established monopoly positions.

The consequences of this research approach are substantial. One result is that the economy can no longer be seen as the social space in which the absolute rationality of *homo oeconomicus* works in an exclusive capacity. It rather defines a cluster of relationships—those upon which society's reproduction ultimately depends—that has accomodated and legitimated motives and behaviors less oriented to maximum gain than to different value systems and strategies reckoning with the constraints with which human rationality is customarily met. One should recognize once and for all that the economic system is not acted upon by a homogeneous, undivided motivational horizon (the one of *homo oeconomicus*), but that it thrives on a plurality of motives and concerns pressing to shape it in their own image and likeness. The economic universe is inhabited by individuals who are not, in the first place, closely related in standard behaviors based on absolute rationality. Rather, they entertain different interests and modes of action, which are the result of historical processes of functional differentiation within the economy, and therefore are, in the second place, agents of conflict.

If there is anything to be recovered from the idea of "scarcity," which in orthodox economic discourse is supposed to preside over the very constitution of the economic issue, then it is the implicit consequence that the use of any resource can only result in conflict. For, if there is no absolute synoptic rationality likely to lead to the optimum use of resources, i.e., the *only one* rationally admissible use as the source of *certain choices*, then the allocation of "scarce" resources will always take place based on choices being made under conditions of *uncertainty* under basically *equivalent* conditions. One use is preferred over another, not because of a rational ranking whereby *only one* optimum solution is identified, but on the basis of power relationships arising from resource distribution and, more generally, from society's material constitution.

Different economic forms orginate from the need to integrate behaviors motivated by different logics which, at least in part, conflict with one another. The logics of behavior encountered in the market and finding their integration according to the forms and modes of exchange can only satisfy some of the wants and interests society exhibits. In turn, these logics elicit others that again demand to be integrated, hence, the need for a reallocation by the state or the hierarchy ranking or replacing long exchange chains. Thus the viability of the "household" economy, self-consumption, and reciprocity, in turn, replaces the market in order to avoid its costs and complexity, and finds its integration standard in elemental and/or traditional forms of relationship.

A second consequence is the refutation of the venerable unequivocal image of economic evolution. The most widely accepted version of this, and one still fairly widespread, was that of "the stages of growth"; once any economy has taken the pathway of development, it is bound to follow a sort of compulsory route from the condition of a traditional society to the final stage of mass consumption.[97]

This is no trivial result. The stage theory is as old as economic thought itself and in that sense shows its original sin. Its profoundly ideological character becomes even more apparent if we look at its older versions, which candidly exhibit their apologetic intentionality. Adam Smith, embodying the stage of qualification and articulation in the long evolution of this subject as well as others, said: "There are four distinct stages mankind has gone through: I, the age of hunters; II, the age of shepherds; III, the age of farming; and, IV, the age of commerce."[98] This is what Ronald Meek in a fascinating essay described as "the four-stage theory," where mankind is viewed as progressing from the state of the ignoble savage to that of doux-commerce, according to a philosophy of history that viewed historical evolution as a progress toward the best form of organization, in which the current state always is, by definition, the most advanced and the best one. A century later, the early German historical school, especially Bruno Hildebrand,[99] again proposed a stage theory of economic evolution based on three steps, those of the natural economy, followed by the monetary economy, and then the credit economy. The central element of this was obviously an admiration for the wonderful development of credit institutions, in the same way as the admiration for the remarkable effects of the mercantile economy was the locus of economic theory a hundred years before.

The last consequence to be mentioned here concerns the domain of economic policy. We now know that a refutation of the "economistic fallacy" does not, contrary to what Polanyi expected, allow us to envisage a new age in which society could re-acquire with the state's help its control over the economy. This would mean relieving the economy from the dominant character that market dynamics had given to it as an autonomous internally consistent system. The age of the self-regulating market, as I have ventured, has probably never existed—at least not in the all-embracing form, as Polanyi had suggested. In any event, it was not an intermission. The gradual accelerating extension of market relations to wider and wider areas of the economic space until it occupied, although never entirely so, the domain of production (as occurred during the nineteenth century) cannot be regarded as an isolated phenomenon in historical evolution which brought about a particular configuration of the economic system that entered a crisis and finally disappeared. Quite to the contrary, the "marketization" of social life triggered a sequence of adjustments and reactions which, in turn, modified the market's nature and role. Besides these changes—albeit very slowly and in cycles that become only occasionally visible—the internal arrangement of the economic system also changes along with the ways in which it is aligned with society's general dynamics.

The market economy proper, one exclusively regulated by price-based exchange relations, now appears to be what it has always been, a political myth, or the conceptual projection of a societal ideal grounded on the free activity of individuals isolated in themselves. It is the myth of the invisible hand that establishes the social order, undetected by the individuals who participate in it with their isolated actions and yet unwittingly determine it through that elemental vehicle of communication and organization: exchange. The market, however, remains what it has been since the very beginning, a powerful tool instrumental in the organization and enhancement of economic activity, or a mechanism remarkably lending itself to stir and rally energies that may result in the satisfaction of human and social wants. Yet, there is nothing in the nature of such a mechanism that compels it to work necessarily in this direction.

As a result, the free-trade pretension to have the entire economic space occupied by the market can be dismissed. Also dismissed is its promise that the achievement of maximum well-being for individuals and society alike would be thereby secured. In fact, one has to recognize the legitimacy and relevance of other forms of organizing economic activity for *both* the production and the distribution and enjoyment of commodities and services. The result is a host of issues, entirely new to the economist, which his science is poorly equipped to handle. The task is to determine which combination of the various forms of organization and integration of economic activity should apply from time to time. Adequate criteria must be found to establish the conditions for an appropriate trade-off between alternative forms. The final and most important point is that decision-making modes and processes must be identified so that society is enabled to select the mix of economic forms best suited to the structure of its wants, its culture, and its social constitution.

A corollary to this analytical finding is that the development of an economy can no longer be related to the extension and intensification of market exchanges. The improvement in the economic condition of any given society can be the joint product of different organizational forms. Hence, policymaking for development could become a more complex and difficult, yet perhaps less inhuman and a more effective task. The question is no longer how to proceed without departures or hesitations on the road of modernization that is guided by a market mechanism, but to grasp and develop the opportunities, resources, and potentials that are concealed even in older forms of organization and regulation of economic activity, which a linear development of the market logic may tend to compress and cancel, and which could, instead, derive strengths and efficiencies from a new economic and social context. Contrary to what Marx thought, there is a future for the small firm even in the age of market globalization, in the same way as there is a future for homework even in the age of computer-aided telecommunications. Economic activity has not finally left other areas of social life in order to establish a separated system of its own, as the oversimplifying view of orthodox economic theory would have it; instead, it constantly tends to generate, "invent," or recover links with the most diverse social institutions. It may very well be that in highly complex social systems, society is no longer able to restore a simple, transparent control relationship with the economy, and with the market in particular. However, means can certainly be found to prevent society from yielding—unarmed and unaware as it may be—to the market's separate logic.

NOTES

1. A.O. Hirshman, 1982, "Rival Interpretations of Market Society: Civilizing, Destructive, or Feeble?," *Journal of Economic Literature* XX, pp. 1463-84.

2. Ch. L. Montesquieu, [1748] 1961, *De L'esprit des lois*, vol. 2, Paris: Garnier, pp. 80-81.

3. See A. O. Hirschman, 1977, *The Passions and the Interests: Political Arguments for Capitalism Before Its Triumph*, Princeton: Princeton University Press.

4. Karl Marx and Frederick Engels, 1987, "Manifest der Kommunistischen Partei," *Marx and Engels Works*, vol. 4, Geneva: International Publications, pp. 467-68.

5. Hirschman, 1982, "Rival Interpretations," *op cit.*, pp. 1466 ff.

6. See Peter Laslett, 1970, *The World We Have Lost*, 2nd ed., Cambridge: Cambridge University Press.

7. Hirschman, 1982, "Rival Interpretations," *op. cit.*, p. 1481.

8. *Ibid.*

9. *Ibid.*

10. K. Polanyi, 1977, *The Livelihood of Man,* Harry W. Pearson, ed., pt. II, New York: Academic Press.

11. A. Smith, [1776] 1976, *An Inquiry into the Nature and Causes of the Wealth of Nations,* Oxford: Clarendon Press, p. 25.

12. J. Wheeler, [1601] 1931, *A Treatise of Commerce,* New York: Columbia University Press, p. 2.

13. J. Wheeler, 1916, in R. Cessi, "L'Officium de Navigantibus e i sistemi della politica commerciale veneziana nel secolo XIV," *Nuovo archivio veneto,* serie II, t. XXXII, p. 130.

14. D. Hume, [1752] 1953, "Of Commerce," *Political Essays,* New York: The Liberal Arts Press, p. 134.

15. Smith, 1976, *An Inquiry, op. cit.,* p. 819: "No two characters seem more inconsistent than those of trader and Sovereign."

16. D. North, [1691], rev. 1954, "Discourses upon Trade" in *A Select Collection of the Early English Tracts on Commerce,* R. McCulloch, ed., London: Cambridge University Press, p. 540.

17. J. O. Appleby, 1978, *Economic Thought and Ideology in Seventeenth-Century England,* Princeton: Princeton University Press.

18. See B. Nelson, 1949, *The Idea of Usury,* Princeton: Princeton University Press; and J. Le Goff, 1986, *La bourse et la vie: Economie et religion au Moyen Age,* Paris: Hachette.

19. Hirschman, 1977, *Passions and the Interests, op cit.,* pp. 10, 16-17.

20. See Appleby, 1978, *Economic Thought, op. cit.*

21. Pierre de Boisguilbert, [1712] 1843, "Dissertation sur la nature des richesses, de l'argent et des tributs" in *Economistes Financiers du XVIIIè Siècle,* E. Daire, ed., Paris: Guillaumin, pp. 409, 411.

22. J. Viner, 1937, *Studies in the Theory of International Trade,* New York-London: Harper & Brothers.

23. See W. Sombart, 1902, *Der Modernen Kapitalismus,* 2 vols., Leipzig: Duncker & Humblot.

24. See, for example, the works of M. Mauss on gift (1923-24, "Essai sur le don," *Année Sociologique*, II, p. 1); and B. Malinowski on the economics of the Trobriand Islands (1922, *Agronauts of the Western Pacific*, London: Routledge & Kegan Paul).

25. K. Polanyi, 1944, *The Great Transformation: The Political and Economic Origins of Our Time*, New York: Holt, Rinehart & Winston.

26. Polanyi, 1977, *Livelihood of Man, op. cit.*, p. xviii.

27. Smith, 1976, *An Inquiry, op. cit.*, p. 25.

28. Polanyi, 1944, *Great Transformation, op. cit.*, ch. vi.

29. *Ibid.*, ch. xxi.

30. Polanyi, 1977, *Livelihood of Man, op. cit.*, pp. xlviii-1.

31. Polanyi, 1944, *Great Transformation, op. cit.*, ch. xi.

32. K. Polanyi, C. Arensberg, and H.W. Pearson, 1957, *Trade and Market in the Early Empires: Economies in History and Theory*, New York: Free Press, ch. xiii; Polanyi, 1977, *The Livelihood of Man, op cit.*, ch. ii; and Polanyi, 1971, "Karl Menger's Two Meanings of 'Economic'" in *Studies in Economic Anthropology*, G. Dalton, ed., Washington, DC: American Anthropological Association.

33. M. Sahlins, 1972, *Stone Age Economics*, Chicago: Aldine-Atherton.

34. Polanyi, 1977, *Livelihood of Man, op. cit.*, p. 26.

35. Polanyi et al, 1971, *Trade and Market in the Early Empires, op. cit.*, ch. xiii.

36. Polanyi, 1977, *Livelihood of Man, op. cit.*, p. 20.

37. See L. Dumont, 1977, *Homo aequalis: Genèse et épanouissement de l'idéologie économique*, Paris: Gallimard.

38. Polanyi, 1977, *Livelihood of Man, op. cit.*, p. 35.

39. *Ibid.*

40. K. Polanyi, 1966, *Dahomey and the Slave Trade: An Analysis of an Archaic*

Economy, Seattle: University of Washington Press.

41. See Polanyi, 1977, *Livelihood of Man, op. cit.,* p. xliii: "No more than a beginning can be made in this book."

42. *Ibid.,* p. 36.

43. *Ibid.,* p. 37.

44. *Ibid.,* pp. 42-43.

45. *Ibid.,* p. 47.

46. See my "L'economia come sistema," n.d.

47. F. Braudel, 1979, *Civilisation matérielle, économie et capitalisme (XV-XVIII siècle),* 3 vols., Paris: A. Colin; and 1977, *Afterthoughts on Material Civilization and Capitalism,* Baltimore: Johns Hopkins University Press.

48. F. Braudel, 1979, 1982, *The Wheels of Commerce: Civilization and Capitalism, (Les jeux de l'échange*, vol. 2 of *Civilisation matérielle),* New York: Harper & Row.

49. Braudel, 1979, 1988, *Les structures du quotidien: le possible et l'impossible..* (vol. 1 of *Civilisation matérielle*), Paris: A. Colin.

50. *Ibid.*

51. *Ibid.*

52. Braudel, 1977, *Afterthoughts, op. cit.,* p. 16.

53. *Ibid.,* p. 5.

54. Braudel, 1979, 1988, *Les jeux de l'échange* (vol. 2 of *Civilisation matérielle),* Paris: A. Colin.

55. *Ibid.*

56. Braudel, 1977, *Afterthoughts, op cit.,* p. 24.

57. *Ibid.,* p. 12.

58. *Ibid.,* p. 23.

59. See Pirenne, 1927, *Les villes du Moyen Age,* Bruxelles: M. Lamertin.

60. *Ibid.*

61. Braudel, 1979, 1988, *Les jeux de l'échange, op. cit.*

62. Braudel, 1979, 1988, *Les structures du quotidien, op. cit.*

63. Braudel, 1977, *Afterthoughts, op. cit.,* p. 52.

64. Braudel, 1979, 1988, *Les jeux de l'échange, op. cit.*

65. *Ibid.*

66. *Ibid.*

67. Braudel, 1977, *Afterthoughts, op. cit.,* p. 112.

68. Braudel, 1979, 1988, *Les jeux de l'échange, op. cit.*

69. *Ibid.*

70. Braudel, 1977, *Afterthoughts, op. cit.,* p. 63.

71. Braudel, 1979, 1988, *Les structures du quotidien, op. cit.*

72. *Ibid.*

73. A. Salsano, 1966, "Polanyi, Braudel e il re del Dahomey," Introduzione to K. Polanyi, *Dahomey and the Slave Trade, op. cit.,* p. XXVIII.

74. Polanyi, 1944, *Great Transformation, op. cit.*

75. *Ibid.*

76. *Ibid.*

77. *Ibid.,* ch. vi.

78. *Ibid.,* ch. xiii.

79. *Ibid.,* ch. vi.

80. P. Rosanvallon, 1981, *La crise de l'Etat-providence,* Paris: Seuil, p. 32.

81. J. M. Keynes, 1931, *Essays in Persuasion*, London: Macmillan, p. 335.

82. J. M. Keynes, 1926, *The End of Laissez-Faire*, London: Hogarth Press, p. 39.

83. J. M. Keynes, 1973, *The General Theory of Employment, Interest, and Money* (Collected Writings, vol. vii), London: Macmillan Press Ltd./St. Martin's Press for Royal Economic Society, p. 372.

84. *Ibid.*, p. 378.

85. *Ibid.*, p. 380.

86. *Ibid.*, p. 320.

87. See G. de Caro, 1985, "Léon Walras dalla teoria monetaria alla teoria generale della produzione di merci," Introduzione in L. Walras, *L'economia monetaria*, Rome: 1st. Encicl. Italiana.

88. R. H. Coase, 1937, "The Nature of the Firm," *Economica*, p. 389.

89. K. J. Arrow, 1969, "The Organization of Economic Activity: Issues Pertinent to the Choice of Market Versus Nonmarket Allocation" in Joint Economic Committee, U.S. Congress, *The Analysis and Evaluation of Public Expenditures: The PPB System*, vol. I, Washington, D.C.: Government Printing Office, pp. 47-64, 76.

90. K. J. Arrow, 1985, "The Potentials and the Limits of the Market in Resource Allocation" in G. R. Feiwel, ed., *Issues in Contemporary Microeconomics and Welfare*, New York-London: Macmillan.

91. Arrow, 1969, "The Organization," *op. cit.*

92. K. J. Arrow, 1985, "Distributive Justice and Desirable Ends of Economic Activity" in G. R. Feiwel, ed., *Issues in Contemporary Microeconomics and Welfare*, New York-London: Macmillan, pp. 137-38.

93. See O. E. Williamson, 1975, *Market and Hierarchies: Analysis and Antitrust Implications*, New York: Free Press, p. xi.

94. *Ibid.*, pp. 9, 21.

95. H. Simon, 1981, "Economic Rationality: Adaptive Artifice" in *The*

Science and the Artificial, Cambridge, Massachusetts: MIT Press, pp. 31-61.

96. *Ibid.*

97. See W. Rostow, 1960, *The Stages of Economic Growth,* Cambridge: Cambridge University Press.

98. A. Smith, *1762-63 Notes,* vol. I., pp. 26-27, cited in R. Meek, 1976, *Social Science and the Ignoble Savage,* London: Cambridge University Press.

99. B. Hildebrand, 1864, "Naturalwirtschaft, Geldwirtschaft und Kreditwirtschaft," *Jahrbücher für Nationalökonomie und Statistik* 2.

BIBLIOGRAPHY

Appleby, J. O., 1978, *Economic Thought and Ideology in Seventeenth-Century England,* Princeton: Princeton University Press.

Arrow, K. J., 1969, "The Organization of Economic Activity: Issues Pertinent to the Choice of Market Versus Nonmarket Allocation" in Joint Economic Committee, U.S. Congress, *The Analysis and Evaluation of Public Expenditures: The PPB System,* vol. I, Washington, D.C.: Government Printing Office, pp. 47-64.

________, 1985, "Distributive Justice and Desirable Ends of Economic Activity" in G. R. Feiwel, ed., *Issues in Contemporary Microeconomics and Welfare,* New York-London: Macmillan.

________, 1985, "The Potentials and the Limits of the Market in Resource Allocation" in G. R. Feiwel, ed., *Issues in Contemporary Microeconomics and Welfare,* New York-London: Macmillan.

Bagnoli, V. Barbagli, ed., 1981, *La moneta nell'economia europea, secoli XIII-XVIII,* Firenze: Le Monnier.

Becattini, G., 1981, "L'interpretazione sraffiana di Marshall" in R. Bellofiori, ed., *Tra teoria economica e grande cultura europea: Piero Sraffa,* Milan: F. Angeli.

Bell, D., and I. Kristol, eds., 1981, *The Crisis in Economic Theory,* New York: Basic Books.

Bloch, M., 1954, *Esquisse d'une histoire monétaire de l'Europe,* Paris: A. Colin.

Boisguilbert, Pierre de, [1712] 1843, "Dissertation sur la nature des richesses, de l'argent et des tributs" in E. Daire, *Economistes Financiers du XVIIIème siècle,* Paris: Guillaumin.

________, 1966, *Pierre de Boisguilbert ou la naissance de l'économie politique,* Paris: Institut National d'Etudes Démographiques.

Bosanquet, N., 1983, *After the New Right,* London: Heinemann.

Braudel, F., 1977, *Afterthoughts on Material Civilization and Capitalism,* Baltimore: Johns Hopkins University Press.

_________, 1979, *Civilisation matérielle, économie et capitalisme (XV-XVIII siècle),* 3 vols., Paris: A. Colin.

Brentano, L., 1916, *Die Anfänge des Modernen Kapitalismus,* Munich: Akademie der Wissenschaften.

Bücher, K, 1913, *Die Entstehung der Volkswirtschaft,* Tubingen: Verlag der H. Lauppschen Buchhandlung.

Cessi, R., 1916, "Officium de Navigantibus e i sistemi della politica commerciale veneziana nel secolo XIV," *Nuovo archivio veneto,* serie II, t. XXXII.

Chandler, A. D., 1977, *The Visible Hand,* Cambridge, Massachusetts: Harvard University Press.

Coase, R. H., 1937, "The Nature of the Firm," *Economica* 4, pp. 386-405.

Commons, J. R., 1934, *Institutional Economics,* Madison: University of Wisconsin Press.

Cox., O. G., 1959, *The Foundations of Capitalism,* New York: Philosophical Library.

Dockès, P., 1969, *L'espace dans la pensée économique du XVIème au XVIIIème siècle,* Paris: Flammarion.

Dopsch, A., 1930, *Naturalwirtschaft und Geldwirtschaft in der Weltgeschichte,* Wien: L. W. Seidel & Sohn.

Dumont, L., 1977, *Homo aequalis: Genèse et épanouissement de l'idéologie économique,* Paris: Gallimard.

Fahrquhar, J. D., and K. Heidensohn, 1975, *The Market Economy,* London: Philip Allan Publishers.

Ferguson, A. [1767] 1966, *An Essay on the History of Civil Society,* Edinburgh: Edinburgh University Press.

Galbraith, J. K., 1967, *The New Industrial State,* Boston: Houghton Mifflin.

Gras, N. S. B., 1939, *Business and Capitalism: An Introduction to Business History,* New York: Augustus M. Kelley.

Hahn, F., 1982, "Reflections on the Invisible Hand," *Lloyd Bank Review* (April), pp. 1-21.

Heilbroner, R. L., 1975, *The Making of Economic Society,* Englewood Cliffs, New Jersey: Prentice-Hall.

Heimann, [1929] 1982, *Soziale Theorie des Kapitalismus,* Frankfurt: Suhrkamp.

Hicks, J., 1969, *A Theory of Economic History,* Oxford: Oxford University Press.

Hildebrand, 1864, "Naturalwirtschaft, Geldwirtschaft und Kreditwirtschaft," *Jahrbücher für Nationalökonomie und Statistik* 2.

Hirschman, A. O., 1977, *The Passions and the Interests: Political Arguments for Capitalism Before Its Triumph,* Princeton: Princeton University Press.

________, 1982, "Rival Interpretations of Market Society: Civilizing, Destructive, or Feeble?," *Journal of Economic Literature* XX, pp. 1463-84.

Hume, D., 1752, *Of Commerce in Political Discourses,* Edinburgh: R. Fleming.

Kahn, A. E., "The Tyranny of Small Decisions: Market Failures, Imperfections and the Limits of Economics," *Kyklos,* pp. 23-46.

Kaldor, N., 1972, "The Irrelevance of Equilibrium Economics," *Economic Journal,* pp. 1237-55.

Keynes, J. M., 1926, *The End of Laissez-Faire,* London: Hogarth Press.

________, 1931, *Essays in Persuasion,* London: Macmillan.

________, 1973, *The General Theory of Employment, Interest, and Money,* (Collected Writings, vol. vii), London: Macmillan Press/St. Martin's Press for Royal Economic Society.

Knight, F. H., 1921, *Risk, Uncertainty and Profit,* Boston: Houghton Mifflin.

Kriedte, P., H. Medick, and J. Schlumbohm, 1977, *Industrialisierung vor der Industrialisierung: Gewerbliche Warenproduktion auf dem Land in der Formationsperiode des Kapitalismus*, Göttingen: Vandenhoeck & Ruprecht.

Landes, D. S., 1969, *The Unbound Prometheus: Technological Change, 1750 to the Present*, New York: Cambridge University Press.

Lane, F., 1982, *I mercanti di Venezia*, Torino: Einaudi.

Laslett, P., 1970, *The World We Have Lost*, 2nd ed, Cambridge: Cambridge University Press.

Le Goff, J., 1980, *Marchands et banquiers du Moyen Age*, 5th ed., Paris: PUF.

_________, 1986, *La bourse et la vie: Economie et religion au Moyen Age*, Paris: Hachette.

Leibenstein, H., 1976, *Beyond Economic Man*, Cambridge, Massachusetts: Harvard University Press.

Letwin, W., 1963, *The Origins of Scientific Economics: English Economic Thought 1660-1776*, London: Methuen.

Locke, J., [1690] 1988, *Two Treatises of Government*, Peter Laslett, ed., 3rd rev. ed., Cambridge: Cambridge University Press.

Malinowski, B., 1922, *Argonauts of the Western Pacific: An Account of Native Enterprise and Adventure in the Archipelagos of Melanesian New Guinea*, London: Routledge & Kegan Paul.

Marchi, A., 1981, *Il pensiero economico inglese prima di Adam Smith*, Torino: Loescher.

Marchionatti, R., 1985, *Gli economisti e i selvaggi*, Torino: Loescher.

Marshall, A., 1920, *Principles of Economics: An Introduction*, London: Macmillan.

Mauss, M., 1923-24, "Essai sur le don," *Année sociologique*, serie II, t. 1.

Meek, R. L., 1976, *Social Science and the Ignoble Savage*, London: Cambridge University Press.

Montesquieu, Ch. L., [1748] 1961, *De l'esprit des lois*, Paris: Garnier.

Nacamulli, R. C. D., and A. Rugiadini, eds., 1985, *Organizziazione & Mercato*, Bologna: Il Mulino.

Nelson, B., 1949, *The Idea of Usury*, Princeton: Princeton University Press.

North, D., [1691] 1856, 1954, "Discourses upon Trade" in J. R. McCulloch, ed., *A Select Collection of Early English Tracts on Commerce*, London: Political Economy Club, Cambridge University Press.

North, D. C., and R. P. Thomas, 1973, *The Rise of the Western World*, Cambridge: Cambridge University Press.

Pirenne, H., 1914, "The Stages in the Social History of Capitalism," *American Historical Review*, pp. 494-515.

_________, 1927, *Les villes du Moyen Age*, Bruxelles: M. Lamertin.

_________, 1935, *Histoire économique et sociale du Moyen Age*, Paris: PUF.

Polanyi, K., 1944, *The Great Transformation: The Political and Economic Origins of Our Time*, New York: Holt, Rinehart & Winston.

_________, 1947, "Our Obsolete Market Mentality," *Commentary* III (February), pp. 109-17.

_________, 1966, *Dahomey and the Slave Trade: An Analysis of an Archaic Economy*, Seattle: University of Washington Press.

_________, 1968, *Primitive, Archaic and Modern Economies*, New York: Doubleday & Co.

_________, 1971, "Karl Menger's Two Meanings of 'Economics'" in *Studies in Economic Anthropology*, G. Dalton, ed., Washington D.C.: American Anthropological Association.

_________, 1977, *The Livelihood of Man*, New York: Academic Press.

_________, C. Arensberg, and H. W. Pearson, 1957, *Trade and Market in the Early Empires: Economies in History and Theory*, New York: Free Press.

Postan, M. M., 1944, "The Rise of a Money Economy," *Economic History*

Review XIV, pp. 123-34.

Romano, R., and V. Tucci, eds., 1983, *Economia naturale, economia monetaria: Storia d'Italia* (Annali, VI), Torino: Einaudi.

Rosanvallon, P., 1979, *Le capitalisme utopique*, Paris: Seuil.

_________, 1981, *La crise de l'Etat-providence*, Paris: Seuil.

Rostow, W., 1960, *The Stages of Economic Growth*, Cambridge: Cambridge University Press.

Rothschild, K. W., 1947, "Price Theory and Oligopoly," *Economic Journal*, pp. 299-320.

Sahlins, M., 1972, *Stone Age Economics*, Chicago: Aldine-Atherton.

Sen, A., 1977, "Rational Fools: A Critique of the Behavioral Foundations of Economic Theory," *Philosophy and Public Affairs* 6.

Simon, H. A., 1981, "Economic Rationality: Adaptive Artifice" in *The Science and the Artificial*, Cambridge, Massachusetts: MIT Press, pp. 31-61.

Smith, A., [1776] 1976, *An Inquiry into the Nature and Causes of the Wealth of Nations*, Oxford: Clarendon Press.

Sombart, W., 1902, *Der Moderne Kapitalismus*, 2 vols., Leipzig: Duncker & Humblot.

_________, 1913, *Der Bourgeois zer Geistesgeschite der Moderne Wirtschaftsmenchen*, Munchen: Duncker & Humblot.

Sraffa, P., 1926, "The Laws of Returns under Competitive Conditions," *Economic Journal* 36, pp. 535-50.

Titmuss, R. M., 1971, *The Gift Relationship: From Human Blood to Social Policy*, London: Allen & Unwin.

Viner, J., 1937, *Studies in the Theory of International Trade*, New York-London: Harper & Brothers.

Walras, L., 1985, *L'economia monetaria*, Rome: 1st. Encicl. Italiana.

Wheeler, J., [1601] 1931, *A Treatise of Commerce,* New York: Columbia University Press.

Williamson, O. E., 1975, *Market and Hierarchies: Analysis and Antitrust Implications,* New York: Free Press.

_________, 1980, "Emergence of the Visible Hand: Implications for Industrial Organization" in A. D. Chandler and H. Daems, eds., *Managerial Hierarchies: Comparative Perspectives on the Rise of Modern Industrial Enterprise,* Cambridge, Massachusetts: Harvard University Press.

II

THE REFORMING OF ECONOMICS: RETROSPECT AND PROSPECT

Mark A. Lutz

The History of the Humanistic School

J. C. Simonde de Sismondi (1773-1842): The Father of a New Economics

The Swiss count J. C. Simonde de Sismondi was an early admirer of Adam Smith's ideas, and he popularized them in a book that was a French presentation of Smith in 1803, *De la Richesse Commerciale* (*On Commercial Wealth*). Like his teacher, he advocated free trade and came out strongly against monopolies, custom houses, colonial privileges, and the kind of government intervention prevailing at that time. The book was not an outstanding success, but it did generate enough professional reputation to induce a university to offer him the vacant chair of political economy. He refused and devoted himself to the study of history instead. And it was here that he learned to be more cautious in trusting the prevailing method of abstract theoretical deduction from first principles, especially when applied to the complex social reality. Instead, he was led to consider political economy from a more historical and institutional point of view.

In 1826 he published his second book on economics entitled *New Principles of Political Economy*. It was an attempt to rewrite the science anew and in the light of some of the newly recognized empirical facts: particularly the novel and so far unexplained economic "panics" or crises which he personally witnessed hurting so many workers in England and the European mainland. The timing of his book helped its promotion, since 1819 marked the worst commercial crisis yet. Another slump hit in 1826, and from then on there were recurring ups and downs in roughly four-year intervals. Sismondi visited England in 1818, 1824, and 1826, and observed:

> In this astonishing country [Great Britain], which seems to be submitted to a great experiment for the instruction of the rest of the world, I have seen production increasing whilst enjoyments were diminishing. The mass of the nation here, no less than philosophers, seems to forget that the increase of wealth is not the end in political economy, but its instrument in procuring the happiness of all. I sought for this happiness in *every* class, and I could nowhere find it.[1]

At the same time, he felt that events since 1819 had confirmed his new principles:

> Seven years have passed, and the facts appear to have fought victoriously for me. They have proved, much better than I could have done, that the wise men from whom I have separated myself were in pursuit of a false prosperity; that their theories, wherever they were put in practice, served well enough to increase material wealth, but that they diminished the mass of enjoyment laid up for each individual; that they tended to make the rich man more rich, they also made the poor man more poor, more dependent, and more destitute.[2]

All the suffering he encountered in England and so vividly described, he now attributed to a "false economical system" where the pursuit of wealth took precedence over people.

Self-interest under the operation of the invisible hand, rather than producing widespread prosperity and happiness in uplifting the laborers and the poor as had been one of Smith's original intentions, had instead produced a new and miserable social class, the industrial workers. They were increasingly victimized by the business cycle manifesting itself in periodic crises of overproduction and high unemployment.

Sismondi explained the problem as a recurring lack of consumption power among the masses of laborers. The newly manufactured goods could not be sold at a profit and so glutted the markets. The chief villain was an unfettered drive to expand output, in part fueled by new technologies, which boosted the profits of the entrepreneurs but which did not trickle down to raise the subsistence wages of the work force that lacked any bargaining power.

In his *New Principles*, as well as in much of his later writings, Sismondi focuses on the kind of issues which constitute the foundation of humanistic economics. The end of production is not "useful and elegant things [and] to cover the sea with vessels and the land with railways but to secure the development of Man, and of all men."[3]

Sismondi, in attempting to promote the ultimate end of human welfare, focused instead on basic human needs. The happiness of communities, he wrote, necessitates "abundance, variety, and wholesome lodging," as well as that "the future will not be inferior to the present, and that a poor man can by the same labour obtain at least the same enjoyment." To him, "no nation can be considered prosperous if the condition of the poor, who form part of it, is not secure under the four relations which just enumerated." And he adds, "subsistence in this degree is the common right of Man and should be secured to all those who do what they can to forward common labour; and the nation is so much more prosperous, the more every individual is assured of having a share in these comforts of the poor."[4]

The new system of factory-oriented manufacturing which had come to dominate the economy gave little consideration to human need; even worse, it tended to do more harm than good. Two of its characteristics were especially detrimental: unrestrained competition and the rapid mechanization of labor. Formerly independent masters of a trade were now being "forced to descend to the rank of a man who works by the day, of a proletary," all in the name of cheaper production and greater material wealth of a few. And all this to the applause of the orthodox school of political economy which had also "by its arguments, seconded the power of money, and the seduction of cheapness."[5]

Faced with this alarming situation and its even more dismal prospects for the future, Sismondi saw it a prime responsibility of state action to ameliorate the condition of mankind. Industrialization and urbanization had to be slowed down, the small farmer and independent artisan protected from extinction. The workers should be allowed to associate in trade unions, to enjoy shorter working hours, greater economic security by having employers finance the maintenance of their income during illness, periods of layoff, and old age. Finally, there was a need for public employment programs to employ the unemployed. These public jobs would also have to be meaningful so that in their execution the workers can regain their "complete being."

In conclusion, it should be noted that Sismondi, for all his critique of capitalism, was not a real socialist. He remained a strong believer in private property, a circumstance that did not keep him from deploring the increasing separation between property and work that industrialization brought about. At the very core of his reform proposals was the reuniting of property and labor. At the same time, his endorsement of private property was always contingent on the social welfare it produces. "The fundamental condition of society is, that no one shall die of hunger; it is *only* on this condition that property is acknowledged and guaranteed."[6]

For Sismondi, social progress was expected to occur not so much by violent revolution as climax of relentless class antagonism, but rather by means of gradual ameliorative and redistributive action of an enlightened legislature. Tragically, he was too much ahead of his time and so destined to die disillusioned. "I shall leave this world without having made any impression, and nothing will be done" were some of his last words.[7]

Sismondi's pessimism may have been somewhat premature, and certainly unwarranted in one aspect; he did make a very strong impression on the young Thomas Carlyle whose job it was to translate into English his first sketch of humanistic economics, an article on

"Political Economy" commissioned by Brewster's *Edinburgh Encyclopedia* (1815). Inspired by Sismondi's new perspective, he later became quite famous for his attacks on Mammon-worship, and a political economy portrayed as a "dismal science" that would reduce all human relations to the cash-nexus and considerations of profit and loss. But more importantly, Carlyle was to assume the role of a mentor for John Ruskin, another towering figure in the history of humanistic economics.

JOHN RUSKIN (1819-1900)

Ruskin was one of the most prolific English writers of the nineteenth century. Romantic idealist that he was, he wanted to bring the wonders of art to the ordinary working man. Unfortunately, he soon encountered a serious problem: workers were neither interested in art nor interested in attending the evening lectures specially designed to make them learn to appreciate it. After some years, Ruskin concluded that the real problem was not with the workers, but their degraded economic status having stunted their aesthetic needs and sensibilities.

After making this discouraging discovery, Ruskin turned his interests to economic affairs and political economy. The result was a book titled *Unto This Last*, published in 1864. It starts out with the following paragraph:

> Among the delusions which at different periods have possessed themselves of the minds of large masses of the human race, perhaps the most curious—certainly the least creditable—is the modern soi-disant science of political economy, based on the idea that an advantageous code of social action may be determined irrespective of the influence of social affection.

In a nutshell, Ruskin accuses economists of trying to prescribe social policy on the basis of self-interest only. He then continues:

> Of course, as in the instances of alchemy, astrology, witchcraft, and other such popular creeds, political economy has a plausible idea at the root of it. "The social affections," says the economist, "are accidental and disturbing elements in human nature; but avarice and the desire of progress are constant elements. Let us eliminate the inconstants, and by considering the human being merely as a covetous machine, examine by what laws of labor, purchase and

sale, the greatest accumulative result in wealth is attainable. Those laws once determined, it will be for each individual afterwards to introduce as much of the disturbing affectionate element as he chooses and to determine for himself the result on the new conditions supposed.[8]

In the above quote, Ruskin has been merely attempting to paraphrase this contemporary, J. S. Mill, representing the most respected learned opinion on the subject. To Mill, self-interest was not the only motive force; there were, of course, other "disturbing" forces, but those, according to this principle of the "Composition of forces," could be taken into account later and mechanically added or subtracted from the conclusion deduced from self-interest alone.

In other words, the would-be economist policy maker starts out with the principles based on abstract self-interest, and then tries to adjust the results here and there to approximate real-world behavior of real people. Ruskin strongly disagreed, saying that "the disturbing elements in the social problem are not of the same nature as the constant ones; they operate, not mathematically, but chemically, introducing conditions which render all previous knowledge unavailable." He then masterfully compares economics to an abstract science of gymnastics which assumed that men had no skeletons: "It might be shown, on that supposition, that it would be advantageous to roll the students up into pellets, flatten them into cakes, or stretch them into cables; and that when the results were effected, the re-insertion of the skeleton would be attended with various inconveniences to their constitution."[9]

Similarly, in considering men as actuated "by no other moral influences than those which affect rats or swine," political economy ends up denying the motive power of the Soul, and "the force of this very peculiar agent, as an unknown quality, enters into all the political economist's equations, without his knowledge, and falsifies every one of their results." Ruskin proceeds to illustrate the point by referring to the employer-employee relationship. There the "greatest average of work" cannot be attained on the basis of antagonistic self-interest, but instead derives from justice, mutual good will, and a cooperative spirit. True, he admits that it is not "so easy to imagine an enthusiastic affection among cotton spinners for the proprietor of the mill"; similarly, it may be asking too much to expect a general attitude of self-sacrifice toward the company. But to him all this lack of "moral animation" is to a considerable degree to be explained by the prevailing practice of engaging "a workman at a rate of wages variable according to the demand for labor, and with the risk of being any time thrown out of this situation by chance of trade." "Now," he warns, "under these contingencies, no action of the affections can take place, but only an explosive action of disaffections."[10] The remedy suggests itself in the regulation of wages and employment. Only if workers are assured a just and living wage as well as permanent employment will they see any reason to more fully exert themselves on behalf of their employer.

As much as Ruskin turned again and again to government to protect the poor by interfering into the wage determination process, he, like Sismondi, was more of a social reformer than a socialist. He was even, as the following quotation demonstrates, a true believer in genuine private enterprise.

> "Private enterprise" should never be interfered with, but, on the contrary, much encouraged, so long as it is indeed "enterprise" (the exercise of individual ingenuity and audacity in new fields of true labor), and so long as it is indeed "private," paying its way at its own cost, and in no wise harmfully affecting public comforts or interests. But "private enterprise" which poisons its neighborhood, or speculates for individual gain at common risk, is very sharply to be interfered with.[11]

Whatever Ruskin's ideology, he had few kind words for economists: "As no laws but those of the Devil are practicable in the world, so no impulses but those of the brute [says the modern political economist] are appealable to in the world. Faith, generosity, honesty, zeal, and self-sacrifice are poetical phrases; there is no truth in man which can be used as a moving and productive power."[12] To him and his numerous sympathizers, political economy as preached by its mercenaries was indeed "a lie," and responsible for *all* the evil of his times.

Needless to say, Ruskin's vituperative verbal onslaughts were largely ignored by his adversaries. Still, he may have been the first Englishman to cry out loudly against the dangerous tendency of assuming self-interested Economic Man in social description because of the inherent tendency to inspire its use for prescription as well.

Ruskin, thanks to his strongly developed moral sense, could see deeper in these matters than his contemporaries. What he saw made him angry and even drove him to sporadic bouts with insanity. On the other hand, his penetrating and outspoken critique also threatened the intellectual and commercial establishment of his day, as is evident by the following comment published in the *Manchester Examiner and Times*: "He [Ruskin] is not worth our powder and shot, yet, if we do not *crush* him, his wild words will touch the springs of action in some hearts, and ere we are aware, a moral floodgate may fly open and drown us all."[13] Of course, he was not crushed and he did touch some hearts, among them John A. Hobson, Arnold Toynbee, Frederick Soddy, Richard Tawney, Richard T. Ely, and, above all, Mohandas K. Gandhi. But he also had some effect on the British development of economics. So the famous Alfred Marshall, for example, credited Ruskin's "splendid teachings" with having clarified something that the earlier economists were not making sufficiently clear; namely, that "sordid selfishness" and the desire for material wealth are by no means the only human motives.

JOHN A. HOBSON (1858-1940)

Hobson had studied classics at Oxford during the 1870s where John Ruskin's influence had been extraordinarily strong and a general interest in reframing society was sweeping that university. Hobson recounts that he had read and admired *Unto This Last*, but first "regarded it rather as a passionate rebellion than as a critical and constructive work." But some years later he recognized that Ruskin's insistence upon interpreting the terms "wealth" and "vitality" was not a mere freak of the literary verbalist, but a genuine scientific demand. More than that, he admits that "from him [Ruskin] I drew the basic thought for my subsequent economic writings."[14]

In essence, we can interpret Hobson's human welfare economics as a serious lifelong attempt to put Ruskin's artistic thought into a vigorous and scientific framework. Furthermore, he attempted to integrate Ruskin's writings as far as possible within the at that time prevailing language of Marshallian economics.

In 1889 he had published, together with A. F. Mummery, his famous "over-saving" heresy which, upon insistence of economist H. S. Foxwell, brought about his being fired from his London University extension lectureship in political economy and literature. (A detailed account of these events can be found in Kadish [1990].)[15] Embittered, he was driven into a "mixed life of lecturing, controversial politics and journalism," which he recounts must have been "damaging to orderly thinking," but had the valuable compensation of enhancing his understanding of economic processes by "taking them out of the textbook mold and putting them into their proper human significance."[16]

John Hobson's work trying to explain business cycles by a lack of consumption demand continues one of the humanistic elements of Sismondi's "new" political economy. Although economic orthodoxy entrenched behind the so-called *Say's Law* declared for a long time such a research question as off limits to a respectable political economy, this attitude radically changed in the 1930s when it took the shocking lesson of the Great Depression together with the reputability of the leading economist, John Maynard Keynes, to recognize as entirely valid what up to then was mere heresy. Several years before he died, Hobson was rehabilitated and given due credit for his pioneering thought on this particular humanistic issue. But at that time nobody bothered to reexamine the rest of his economic thought which had suffered credibility after his unwarranted exclusion from university teaching. Yet it is precisely Hobson's contribution here that laid much of the foundation for a serious and coherent new human economy. Let us briefly survey this important work.

By the turn of the century, Hobson already realized that the great socio-economic problems facing society at that time could not fruitfully be discussed, not to mention solved, by the orthodox economics prevailing. "A science which still takes money as its standard of value, and regards man as a means of making money, is, in the nature of the case, incapable of facing the deep and complex problems which impose the Social Question."[17]

Yet, the human problems relating to poverty, private property, housing, wages, hours of labor, insurance, taxation, and state interference with private property were also *economic* in nature and cause. What was needed, therefore, was a *general* survey of the economic system and its problems from the standpoint of *human* values. He grants that "social students, of course, are justified by considerations of intellectual economy in isolating these several problems for certain purposes of detailed inquiry," but at the same time observed that these "special and separate studies of the various problems must then, in order to be socially serviceable, be subjected to the guidance and direction of some general conception, . . . assessing them by reference to some single standard of the humanly desirable."[18] Hobson's book, *Work and Wealth* (1914), was meant to provide the groundwork for such a comprehensive, "general conception fit to serve as a guiding theoretical framework for Human Economy."

Hobson's Human Standard of Value

Influenced strongly by the sociological and psychological theories of his day, he had a strong inclination to approach questions of human nature and society from a biological point of view. Man to him was a psycho-physical organism, and society he viewed as a collective organism with a mind and will of its own. A decade later he backed away from the latter assertion but held on to the former.

In his *Economics and Ethics* (1929), we read:

> Whether the sole end or purpose of the social activities and institutions that form community is the growth and enrichment of personality or whether community may be regarded as a collective conscious being with values of its own, is a question to which we are not here bound to give an answer.[19]

What was unquestionable, however, is that "individual welfare is dependent upon, and in chief part derived from the development of community"[19]

With social organism theory receding, Hobson was increasingly inclined to focus on the *development of individual personality* as the ultimate standard of value. Economic institutions that stifled personality growth, that "shattered" the wholeness of Man, would be targeted for criticism.

Although human personality appears of paramount importance in Hobson's system, it needs to be stressed that for him true enrichment and enlargement of personality could only take place through social interactions and relations. Higher individual consciousness implied a greater social consciousness. The social consciousness he had in mind was not more mechanical "like-mindedness" due to similar cultural upbringings, but an active awareness of and willingness to contribute to the common good and a common purpose. Individual personality differences and personal uniqueness would not only be brought out more in voluntary social intercourse and cooperation, but it would also be essential for enriching and developing genuine community.

Hobson approaches the concept of human welfare through *desirable* human values that well-ordered personalities will exhibit and manifest. But these values are not looked for in the "high abstractions of philosophy dealing with Beauty, Truth and Goodness," but instead "it will be better to begin our search for values . . . in the lower levels of human nature—the instincts, appetites and behavior of the animal man." And he observes that "this method recommends itself the more in that most economic 'goods,' which we shall seek to correlate with human good or value, are devoted to the satisfaction of the physical needs of man."[20]

And when we consider these lower values, we will most likely find Hobson's solid fact: "all men, in their constitution of body and mind, and in their natural and spiritual heritage and environment are much more alike than unlike."[21] These values are "natural" in the sense of being rooted in the organic structure or makeup of Man, and this "quite apart from his personal choice and direction."

Then there are the higher values; being more personal, more "conscious," more interesting, they derive from human purpose and operate primarily by reason and will.[22]

Hobson then sees a hierarchy of values as *objectively* valid for all sorts of men or of societies. His argument is as follows:

> If nature makes so much nisus [directive activity] towards the preservation and growth of a species, and if social cooperation plays the distinctive part it seems to do in human survival, then it may be argued that the higher values attaches to the conduct and the emotions which sustain society in the elaborate structure it has attained, and assist it to further useful needs of cooperation.[23]

Accordingly, he deduces a criterion of human welfare in its higher reaches by the need for "feelings, beliefs, interests, activities and institutions, which bring men into closer, conscious, willing cooperation for as many different sorts of work as possible, or to put it otherwise, which enrich the human personality through the largest measure of sociability."[24]

As overall result, there is not only the lower hierarchy of "sane economy": necessities, comforts, and luxuries but a rightly ordered functional society, "where service would be perfect freedom, the will of the members cooperant towards the well-working of the whole."[25]

And as a guide to such social justice, he relies on common sense, not merely that sense which exists the same in each person, but a genuine "sensus communus" which animates and forms a flow of thought and feeling where people put their minds in the common stock and "get together" in a spiritual way. Lower perspectives dominated by the narrow more selfish self now must yield to clearer appreciation of the general will, the common good.

In his book, *Work and Wealth* (1914), John Hobson proceeds to apply his human standard to analyze production, consumption, and distribution in turn. He faults conventional economics of assuming that costs occur only in production while consumption consists of utility only, a value that is measured by the buyer's willingness to pay. For him, assignments of costs and utilities are measured according to how they affect the development of personality. So, for example, artistic production when truly creative has little or no cost except "in instances where depraved public tastes, springing directly from luxury and idleness, debauch the natural talents of artists, and poison the very founts of the creative power of a nation." Under such circumstances, the production of "base forms of art, music, the drama, literature, the plastic arts, must necessarily entail the highest human costs . . . for such an artist poisons not only his own soul but the social soul, adulterating the food designed to nourish the highest faculties of man."[26]

Similarly, monotonous, routine, machine-tending labor is psychologically much more damaging than the more creative work of the independent craftsman. Additionally, monotony of narrow manual toil also "imposes on the victimized worker a corresponding narrowness of consumption and enjoyment." Other heavy human costs are involved in unemployment and uncertainty of regular work.

Competition, too, producing anxiety and stress, has a higher psychic cost than a more cooperative means of social coordination. The analysis of the categories proceeds in great detail, but there is not much sense repeating it here. He advocates a great measure of social control over private economic decision making. Workers, he argued, were entitled to an adequate "living wage," a system of free public education and public health, old age pensions, housing, insurance, and sufficient leisure for recreation, etc. In addition to this, he believed that it was not only necessary to supply more meaningful work, but also to envision a system where workers will have a "voice" in management. Such a demand would be "an essential condition for the growth of the sense of industry as a social service." And Hobson reminds us that "so long as the thoughts of a worker do not, and cannot, go beyond the near implications of his labour-bargain, and his sense of cooperation is confined to his trade-union, it is idle to suppose that the more general problems of our economic system can be rightly solved."[27]

In the demand for a voice in the control of business with workers sharing in decision making and profits, Hobson saw as a natural vehicle for bringing about "a wider and more conscious sense of the solidarity and social value of the economic system as a whole."[28]

Hobson's Road to Social Consciousness: Security, Fairness, and Meaningful Work

Let us in closing briefly articulate some of the essentials in Hobson's view of human economy and focus in particular on what may very well be his most profound insight: that economic security tends to act as a catalyst for a higher degree of social motivation and moral personality.

Hobson paints the human person as multidimensional, with a lower and a higher nature. Although economics was properly more concerned with the relatively uniform nature of the former, it could not afford to ignore the latter, and this essentially for two reasons. First, the realization of the higher self as the most important aspect of personality growth was to be encouraged, or at least not discouraged and thwarted by the industrial system. Second, the intellectual and spiritual energies released by greater use of our more deeply human faculties would do much to "raise the moral efficiency of the individual as a wealth producer and consumer."[29]

In both cases, it is important to ascertain a direct link between economic institutions and the higher aspects of human personality. If such a link cannot be established, there is no good reason why we should not leave economists to continue in their restrictive diet studying the interaction and collisions of narrow selves, and when it comes to factors making for more individual concerns regarding ethics, morality, and spirituality, listen instead to the sermons of the high-minded philosopher or the spiritual teacher. Without linking economics to the "higher"—or as some prefer to call it, the "inner"—the distinctly *human*, humanistic economics evaporates; there is simply no more need for it. In such a scenario, economics would be restricted to satisfying the material wants emanating from our "narrow self" to a maximum possible extent and nothing more—essentially the contribution we have today with orthodox economics. In contrast, a strong belief that there is such a linkage has always been assumed by the practitioners of the humanistic school, but nobody has demonstrated it more clearly than John Hobson. It provides the very bedrock of his attempted "human interpretation of industry" (elaborated in his last chapter of *The Industrial System*, [1909])[30] and the substance of his books on human welfare economics. Let us look in more detail at these three catalysts for a more moral economy.

Economic Security

Of all three, the theme that security will elevate the character, enrich personality, and facilitate the transition from a quantitative to a qualitative economy is the most insightful and perhaps operationally the most important. One encounters it already in his earlier writing, particularly in his *Industrial System*, but it is further elaborated in his *Work and Wealth* (1914).

Let us look at a handful of relevant quotations:

> A weekly wage of bare efficiency with regular employment is socially far superior to a higher average wage accompanied by greater irregularity of work. The former admits of modes of living and ready money payments: it conduces to steadiness of *character* and provision for the future without anxiety. Rapid and considerable fluctuations of wages, even with full employment, are damaging to character and stability of standards: but irregularity of employment is the most destructive agency to the *character*, the

> standard of comfort, the health and sanity of wage earners. The knowledge that he is liable at any time, from commercial or natural causes that lie entirely outside his control, to lose the opportunity to work and earn his livelihood, takes out of a man that confidence in the fundamental rationality of life which is essential to the soundness of character. Religion, ethics, education can have little hold upon workers exposed to such powerful illustrations of unreason and injustice of industry and society.[31]

> All proposals by organized public effort to abolish destitution give rise to fears lest by doing so we should sap the incentives to personal effort, and so impair the character of the poor. Among such critics there is entertained no corresponding hope or conviction that such a policy may be the better and securer conditions of life and employment it affords, sow the seeds of civic feeling and of social solidarity among large sections of our population where life had been little else than a sordid and unmeaning struggle.[32]

In his later writings, the point is made with even greater force:

> When moralists talk of altering human nature they are often misunderstood to mean that instincts and desires deeply implanted in our inherited animal outfit can be eradicated and others grafted on. Now no such miracles are possible or needed. But substantial changes in our environment or in our social institutions can apply different stimuli to human nature and evoke different physical responses. For example, by alterations in the organisation and government of businesses and industries, so as to give security of employment and of livelihood to workers, and some increased "voice" to them in the conditions of work, it seems reasonably possible to modify the conscious stress of personal gain-seeking and to educate a clearer sense of social solidarity and service. The insecurity of livelihood has been a growing factor in the discontent of modern workers, and it increases with an education that reveals the "social" cause of that insecurity in the absence of any reliable economic government. Security is, therefore, the first essential in any shift of the relative appeal to personal and social motives. The second essential is such alterations in the government of businesses as to give to the ordinary worker some real sense of participation in the conduct and efficiency of the business.[33]

The stress on security as gateway to a more elevated consciousness rests on the simple realization that selfishness is *not* an exclusive characteristic of human nature but a lack of realizing a common consciousness because of the selfish struggle for livelihood imposed by the existing competitive industrial system. Remove insecurity and workers will be less susceptible to considerations of immediate personal gain.

But it is not only the worker whose consciousness is affected by security; it is a general characteristic of our human psychological makeup, thereby including the masters of industry as well:

> In most manufactures, though the employer is not in business "for his health," but primarily to make profits, the skill and intricacy of the practical operations which he conducts absorbs much of his attention, and pride in the character of his business and the quality of its products dignifies his conduct. Just in proportion as he is not forced to concentrate his thought and feeling upon the art of getting business away from other firms and pushing his claims against theirs in the market does his work take conscious shape in his mind as the social function which it really is. Just in proportion as the competitive activities assume prominence is he compelled to sink this social feeling, to push his goods in conscious rivalry with those of other firms, and to cultivate those arts of sweating, adulteration and deceit which seem necessary to enable him to sell goods at a profit.[34]

The impact here of insecurity and morality is established through the struggle of existence intrinsic to competitive process.

The economic implications for Hobson's security postulate are obvious. By generating a maximum possible degree of security through appropriate social institutions, we, *as economists,* can recommend economic reform that helps generate a climate conducive to the improvement of individual and social character. Full employment and social security are primary means in this respect. In making this argument, he appeals to common sense and common experience for confirmation.

Economic Justice

The same is true for his second catalyst, the effect of a justly ordered economic system on the extent of self-seeking. Here Hobson's case is closely intertwined with his analysis of "measured surplus," which constitutes one of his primary attacks on the capitalist economic system and its distribution of income. "Only by resolving unearned into earned income, so that all property is duly earned either by individuals or by societies, can an ethical basis be laid for social industry. So long as property appears to come miraculously or capriciously, irrespective of efforts or requirements, and as long as it is withheld irrationally, it is idle to preach "the dignity of labor" or to inculcate sentiments of individual self-help."[35]

A new "rationality of the economic order will give to all that confidence in man and that faith in his future, which are the prime conditions of safe and rapid progress," and the effect of "setting on a human basis the industry of the country would, of course, react upon all departments of life, Religion, Family and civic morality." And he concludes:

> . . . [S]o far as the economic activities can be taken into separate consideration, it is evident that this justly ordered environment would do much to raise the physical, and more to raise the moral efficiency of the individual as a wealth producer and consumer. But its most important contribution to the value and the growth of human welfare would lie in other fields of personality than the distinctly economic, in the liberation, realisation and improved condition of other intellectual and spiritual energies at present thwarted by or subordinated to industrialism.[36]

The argument for justice and fairness as a means to self-realization is obviously closely intertwined with economic security, itself a vital component of a well-ordered social system. As such, it may share a similar degree of intuitive plausibility as does the security postulate, but in contrast to that, the practical policy implications are more remote and ambiguous. Nevertheless, Hobson's pointing to capitalist maldistribution is certainly a worthwhile starting point. And it cautions us to "inculcate sentiments of individual self-help" in a general context that lacks basic social justice; a warning that is well worth pondering for many contemporary writers and advocates of human economy.

Meaningful Work

Meaningful work, including a fair measure of participatory industrial democracy as a builder of personality and human economy, is perhaps the best known among the three linkings and also perhaps the least controversial. Here, more than anything else, he was strongly inspired by the work of John Ruskin.

While any human being has the innate capacity to wholeness, the actually prevailing "conditions of labor" are realized as an invasion and a degradation of their humanity, "offering neither stimulus or opportunity for a man to throw himself into his work. For the work only calls for a fragment of that 'self' and always that same fragment. So it is true that not only is labor divided but the laborer. And it is manifest, so far as his organic human nature is concerned, [that] its unused portions are destined to idleness, atrophy, and decay."[37]

Although Hobson refrained from using the word "alienation," it is, of course, precisely what he has in mind with his "divided labourer." The individual worker victim may not be consciously aware of his sorry state and even deny it. Yet, "a man who is not interested in his work and does not recognize in it either beauty or utility, is degraded by that work, whether he knows it or not."[38]

Good work, on the other hand, integrates human body, mind, and soul; it allows personal judgment and initiative and serves as expression of the worker's personality and its creative urge. Under a regime of participatory industrial democracy work, it educates "a clearer sense of social solidarity and service" and breeds a "sensus communus" so essential for the higher self. "The workshop is the natural unit of self-government where available, the area in which the individual workers are thrown into close and constant association for purposes related to their common conditions of employment and those conditions of neighbourhood and society dependent on the former."[39]

At the same time, Hobson was somewhat skeptical about the prospects of the "most radical of the new social-economic reforms: ousting the owners of capital from the government of industry and putting labour in their place."[40] He worried about questions of securing the necessary finance capital and maintaining necessary labor discipline. Instead, he preferred the more realistic capitalist alternative "qualified by a large participation of labour in the management through profit sharing and co-partnership."[41]

In conclusion, all three of Hobson's catalysts are believed to bring about a "change of heart," a qualitative progress in human morality and consciousness center one way or another on the social institutions related directly or indirectly to work. No wonder work assumes in his humanistic economics a paramount position akin to the focus on consumption in ordinary economics. In Hobson's moral economy, it is the means of integrating the human personality, elevating character and bringing about the organic social welfare he dedicated his life and activities to.

Much has already been said about Hobson's bold move to lay the groundwork for a comprehensive humanistic economic alternative. But we cannot leave him without mentioning yet another key contribution regarding the methodology of economics. It concerns his critique of economic man, the standard-bearer of orthodox economic science.

In the introduction of his *Economics and Ethics* (1929), he writes, "it is doubtful how far the term scientific can be claimed for the central purpose of this treatise. There may be a science of monetary values, and therefore of economic processes so far as reducible to monetary values. But in human valuation we have no such quantitative standard of reference."[42] He noted that a scientific analysis treats all differences as differences in degree while ignoring qualitative differences, which is precisely also the "scientific" method of neoclassical economics with its treatment of preferences, its common standard of desirability, and its profound mechanical maximization calculus in satisfying these preferences. He observed: "All desires, interests and values were treated as words of a single undifferentiated stuff, expressible in units of that stuff, pleasure, pain, utility, satisfaction, happiness or whatever name was assigned to it, and amenable as such to the measuring rod of money."[43] Even as early as 1914, in an insightful, pioneering discussion occupying much of his last chapter in *Work and Wealth*, he critically analyzes what economists mean "when they insist that qualitative differences, the desires and satisfactions which have such widely diverse origins and natures, can be weighted and measured against one another, and that the problems of industry are essentially and ultimately quantitative."[44] In the process, he anticipates much, if not most, of the problems relating to the difference between comparability and commensurability, which will be addressed more fully in the second part of this chapter. Suffice it to say that he clearly realized that "when organic matter attains the character of self-consciousness, the qualitative considerations reach a maximum and the interpretation and directive power of science a minimum."[45] It would seem to follow that, given a humanistic interpretation of the proper functioning of an economic system, and taking into account the distinctly human characteristic of self-awareness, a true economics is bound to be more qualitative than quantitative, more of an art and philosophy than a science.

In short, with Hobson, the choice among systems of normative economics is between bad economic science based on illegitimate calculation and good economic philosophy driven by an intuitive sense of the common: Hobson's enlightened common sense.

MOHANDAS GANDHI (1869-1948)

Gandhi was on his way to becoming an Oxford-graduated lawyer when his outlook changed radically, a development apparently triggered by reading John Ruskin. Gandhi, in his autobiography, tells us that *Unto This Last* was "the one book that brought about an instantaneous and practical transformation in my life."[46] The new Gandhi soon emerged as one of the best-known disciples and practitioners of humanistic thinking that the world has yet seen.

Gandhi, as a true humanist of the Ruskian tradition, was all in one: economist, sociologist, philosopher, political activist, and spiritual leader. But in all activities he was driven to the same end: the molding of India's institutional framework so as to allow a maximum quality of life.

In a sense, he paralleled John Hobson's attempts to infuse economic activity with the ideals of John Ruskin. Hobson wrote about welfare in an industrialized market economy. Gandhi, on the other hand, applied the humanistic ideals to the problems of undeveloped India. Like Ruskin and Hobson, he deplored the divorce of economic activity from human and ethical norms. Economic activity should be geared to the human welfare for all ("sarvodaya"). The goal of an economic system, he wrote, "is human happiness combined with full mental and moral growth."[47] Beyond the provision of the basic necessities of life (food, clothing, shelter), the economic system has to produce in accordance with the basic human needs and values of equality, nonviolence, and creative labor.

Since poverty and mass starvation were no doubt the most challenging problems for India at that time, any economic development had to be primarily oriented to raising the poorest to subsistence. Yet Gandhi advocated a development strategy that would not only do just that, *but at the same time* also provide for the higher (social) needs of rural Indians. Only in such a way could the development effort be sustainable. As Gunnar Myrdal put it: "Gandhi clearly perceived that development is basically a human problem concerning attitudes and institutions. It must imply that people everywhere begin to act more purposefully to improve their living conditions and then also to change their community in such a way as to make these strivings more possible and effective."[48]

The Gandhian idea of development can be briefly summarized as follows: He advocated a restructuring of the colonial economy that would emphasize self-reliant, egalitarian village economies in the rural areas. Work, both agricultural and industrial, had to be brought to the unemployed rural masses. It was the function of machines to serve, not replace, people.

> I am not fighting machinery as such but the madness of thinking that machinery saves labor. Men "save labor" unless thousands of them are without work and die of hunger on the streets. I want to secure employment and livelihood not only to part of the human race, but for all. I will not have the enrichment of a few at the expense of the community. At the present the machine is helping a small minority to live on the exploitation of the masses.[49]

In fitting with the decentralized village-based economy, industry had to be small-scale, traditional, employing nonviolent, nonalienating technology that would allow labor and laborers to acquire a maximum of human dignity and moral substance. Similarly, the nation's education system would have to be reoriented toward teaching the young the importance and dignity of all labor, in particular manual "bread labor," irrespective of class or caste.

As radical as Gandhian economics may sound, it is not conventionally socialist, even though he would allow for a sector of nationalized large-scale industry in the urban areas which would complement the more cooperative small-scale rural workshops.

Gandhian economics is the development branch of Ruskin's and Hobson's industrial economics. It still shines as a pioneering model offering poor countries real alternatives.[50]

RICHARD H. TAWNEY (1880-1962)

Tawney, like Hobson and Gandhi before him, had studied at Oxford and thus early in life was exposed to the thought of John Ruskin, the Slade professor at that university. Afterwards, he took a job as an assistant in economics at Glasgow University where he worked under William Smart, a boss who he complained was "bitten by the exchange idea." It was in Smart's department that Tawney learned that the "austere heights" of theoretical economics were not his "spiritual home." And in 1913 he confided to his diary: "There is no such thing as a science of economics, nor ever will be. It is just cant, and Marshall's talk as to the need for social problems to be studied by 'the same order of mind which tests the stability of a battleship in bad weather' is twaddle."[51]

Disenchanted with economics, Tawney decided to devote his career to history, which to him was "a study not of past events, but of the life of societies, and of the records of the past as a means to that end."

At the core of Tawney's thought, is his vision of a "functional society," a social ideal equivalent to Hobson's "well-ordered society"; and in his popular book, *The Acquisitive Society* (1920), he most eloquently contrasts his ideal vision with the actual social order of his day. In the acquisitive society, production and accumulation are the end, but in a functional society, they are merely the means to a more noble end: the provision of life to body and spirit.[52] And to the defenders of the status quo, he asks a "simple question":

> . . . [T]o those who clamor, as many now do, "Produce! Produce!" one simple question may be addressed: "Produce what?" Food, clothing, house room, art, knowledge? By all means! But if the nation is scantily furnished with these things had it not better stop producing a good many others which fill shop windows in Regent Street?[53]

In contrast to the acquisitive society which caters to wants and preferences, it is the very function of Tawney's "functional society" to satisfy human needs as best as possible. And just like the economy, so also economics has its function: wise economics will "consider the economic end for which economic activity is carried on and then to adopt economic organization to it."[54]

Equipped with the need-based criteria, Tawney spent much ink in reexamining the concepts of equality and property. He questioned the relevance of monetary inequality as an important issue, but instead never tired of arguing for an equality based on equal opportunity for life fulfillment. For this very reason, he also was repelled by the "material needs" equality preached in Marxian circles. What really mattered was "social needs" equality respecting man's "higher instincts" of social service, solidarity, and "self-fulfillment"; and he envisioned an order of perfect equality where "all its members may be equally enabled to make the best of such powers as they possess."[55]

The central theme of Tawney's *Acquisitive Society* revolved around the issue of ownership. He accepts the institution of property only as long as it has the function of satisfying one or more basic human needs. He grants that traditionally property provided *security* to enjoy the fruits of labor, but this is no longer unconditionally true, nor is it necessary: "Property is the instrument, security is the object, and when some alternative way is forthcoming of providing the latter, it does not appear in practice that any loss of confidence is caused by the absence of the former."[56]

The chief problem arises that, as modern industry is increasingly characterized by absentee ownership, property loses its function and starts to "undermine the creative energy which in the earlier ages property protected." As a result, nationalization of industry is desirable but not as an end in itself. When the "question of ownership has been settled, the question of administration remains." And it is at this juncture that Tawney raises the issue of "workers control":

> Of the abolition of functionless property transferred the control of production to bodies representing those who perform constructive work, (employee) associations which are now purely defensive would be in a position not merely to criticize and oppose but to advise, to initiate and to enforce upon their own members the obligations of the craft.[57]

It was through industrial restructuring along such lines that Tawney expected social needs to be best satisfied as well as promising the release of "a degree of energy, which while it can be stimulated by economic incentives, yields results in excess of any which are necessarily merely to avoid the extreme of hunger and destitution."[58] But at the same time, he keeps reminding the reader "that no change of system or machinery can avert those causes of social malaise which consist in egotism, greed or quarrelsomeness of human nature." All we can do is "to create an environment in which those are not the qualities which are encouraged." And he concludes that "society" must so organize that the instrumental character of economic activity is emphasized by its subordination to the social purpose for which it is carried on."[59]

E. F. SCHUMACHER (1911-1977)

The late E. F. Schumacher has to be seen as one of the more recent attempts to contribute to an economics centered around the human standard, in his own words, an economics "as if people mattered." Schumacher, after a career actively involving him with British and international postwar policy issues relating to full employment policy and international finance, joined the National Coal Board in 1950.[60] In that capacity he was invited to visit Burma as an economic advisor. That experience reoriented his economics toward small-scale, labor-intensive development projects. He traveled all over the world to advise governments on relying more on indigenous technology, an intermediate technology, that goes today under the label of "appropriate technology." He saw it as the prime task to create "millions of new workplaces in the rural areas and small towns of Third World countries." For this, he proposed four basic requirements:

- That workplaces have to be created in areas where the people are living now, and not primarily in metropolitan areas into which they migrate.
- The workplaces must be, on the average, cheap enough so that they can be created in large numbers with little capital.
- Production methods must be relatively simple minimizing skill requirements relating to production, organization, finance, and marketing.

- Production should be mainly from local materials for local use.[61]

In 1971, after having experimented with Buddhism, he converted to Roman Catholicism and two years afterward published his best-seller book, *Small is Beautiful*, making him, in Theodore Roszak's words, "the Keynes of postindustrial society."[62] In it, he not only advocated and refined Gandhi's thoughts on development, but also a human scale enterprise, cooperative and social ownership, Tawney's meaningful work, and resource conservation for the industrialized world. His basic premise was that work, technology, and ownership patterns should be on a human scale.

The immense success of his book (it was translated into fifteen languages) attests to the fact that humanistic economics is as "alive and well" today as it had been in Sismondi's times.

The Unity of the Humanistic School in Economics

The thought of the earlier teachers of human economy reaching back to the second decade of the nineteenth century was articulated during widely different periods in an ever-changing socio-economic context. Figure 1, on the following page, lists the names discussed in temporal sequence.

Obviously, there was plenty of diversity in the basic questions that were asked and the solutions offered. So, for example, the prime problem for Sismondi was the emergence of the new industrial system in France, which he saw as a menace threatening the independence of craftsmen and family farmers and so sought to slow down. But above all, he was preoccupied by the recurring business cycles which threatened the very livelihood of the new class of the industrial proletariat. When Ruskin wrote during the latter half of the eighteenth century, industrialization in England was an accomplished fact, but there was now the clearly manifest problem of the industrial workers toiling in dehumanizing jobs. It was a period of mounting industrial warfare

Figure 1
The Humanistic School in Historical Perspective

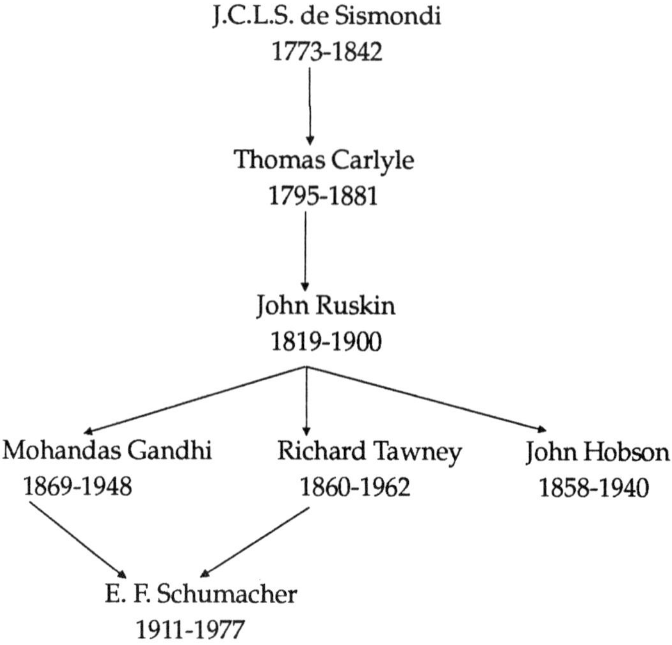

and strikes fueled by a growing antagonism between labor and capital, with professional economists standing on the sidelines not showing much inclination to dispute the dominant ideology that the common welfare would best be served by the unregulated play of individual self-interest. Ruskin saw no more important task than to throw himself against the tide, especially against its very core: an abstract and pretentious economics that proceeded by ignoring the social and creative aspects of human nature and threatening and diminishing the human spirit.

John Hobson and Richard Tawney witnessed the rise of organized labor during the first half of the twentieth century. They explored, among other things, the possibilities of converting the large-scale enterprises already dominating the industrial landscape in Britain and elsewhere into more humane and democratic institutions.

Mohandas Gandhi finally found himself surrounded by the hopeless poverty and misery in colonial India. His primary problem was to formulate a development strategy that would be more geared to benefit the millions of peasants and craftsmen struggling for subsistence.

Yet, in spite of all these differences in terms of time periods and culture, they were all united by a basic attitude and approach which we here characterize as the "humanistic perspective." Let us then follow up this historical survey with a brief articulation of some of the basic elements constituting a contemporary humanistic perspective in economics.

Criticism of Both Capitalism and Bureaucratic Socialism

All the thinkers surveyed shared a basically negative attitude toward the prevailing capitalist institutions under which they lived. Their criticism was not sporadic or focusing on merely trivial aberrations of the system, but it aimed at the very heart of the system: the private owners of capital with power over an increasing army of workers and making decisions with social and human consequences. At the same time, however, there was limited sympathy for a socialist alternative, particularly not for the Marxian/communist brand of socialism.

In sum, there was basic agreement on the paramount importance of individual freedom and political democracy, especially of the participatory kind, and the utility and morality of private property within a framework of democratic social control over business. Most of the criticism voiced by these economists on the status quo were meant to re-integrate the social and human "noneconomic" aspects into the decision-making process in the economy.

The Measuring Rod of Human Personality

The criticism arising out of a perception of fundamental human *problems* was grounded in certain positive human values. These human values were readily derived from a strongly held common sense idea of what constitutes human nature, particularly the distinctively human element. Man had inborn needs not only for biological survival, but also a need for developing personality as fully as possible. In a way, the human economy school centers on human personality, where "personality" and "personality growth" need to be understood in a social or cultural context: a well-structured society being an essential ingredient for a well-ordered personality. Clearly, there is a natural interdependence between individual and social institutions. Change one, and you will also affect the other. Through the issue of meaningful work, so central to Ruskin and Hobson, and its effect on mental health and wholeness, we get a certain amount of economic determinism, at least as long as laissez-faire prevails over social control. The links are straightforward: economic motive → technology → quality of work → quality of personality. At the same time, however, we are free to change this cycle by moderating and controlling the economic motive, and by delegating decisions about technology and working methods to the most affected: the workers themselves. In this perspective, the preferred strategy is to foster higher consciousness and more community, instead of the accumulation of wealth, as the guiding force in a human economy.

NEED FOR EFFECTIVE SOCIAL CONTROL OF THE MARKET

Already implied under the first two points is a persistent ideological aversion to laissez-faire. All humanists discussed were in agreement that to let the competitive forces of industry and commerce alone run our economic affairs is nothing less than a death certificate for all kinds of vital human aspirations. It atomizes and antagonizes the population, as well as impoverishing its weakest segment for the apparent benefit of the most privileged groups. In an economic world where "might is right," self-regarding tendencies start to dominate individual consciousness and selfishness naturally emerges as a defensive "virtue." The nature of production and work will be dictated by the urgency of individual greed to the virtual neglect of human needs, whether they be survival or higher needs.

What is needed is an explicit instrument of social control constraining individual self-interest for the sake of the common good: sufficiency and dignity for all. Although there is a predisposition for participatory over-representative democratic government and the maximum possible amount of decentralization compatible with the nature of the particular problem, the humanistic school has never identified with libertarian anarchism, but leaned more strongly in the syndicalist direction, a sort of "organized anarchy" that also recognized the need for certain highly centralized government activity, in the case of Hobson stretching even to some sort of world government. The principle underlying the determination of the proper scope of government can be represented by the need of *correspondence* between economic action and government control. Community self-government in economic matters implies corresponding community political control over its economy. If one sphere is more extensive, it will quite naturally dominate the others, and so undermine the type of wholistic integrated social self-determination which has been at the very heart of scholars from Sismondi to Gandhi.

Anti-maximizing Economic Man

There has always been the widely shared conviction that academic economic theory resting on such atomistic abstractions as Economic Man helps to give legitimacy to the inhuman policies crated by the actual industrial and commercial system. Economics, by refusing to open itself to considerations of ethical or *right* conduct emerges as some sort of evil force molding individual consciousness and speeding up social decay and the human suffering. Not surprisingly, our humanistic critics focused much of their work and writings on attacking the prevalent economic theories propounded in their time. Moreover, they did so—at least as much as they were capable of—in the language of economic parlance. It is probably fair to say that their impact on changing the mainstream economic thought was relatively minor, but it *also* seems true that the critics more informed with economic theory, such as Sismondi and Hobson, had a far greater impact on social thought and theory than the less economically trained Carlyle, Ruskin, and Tawney, although Gandhi's success would have to be seen as the major exception to this general rule.

The Possibility of Objective Social Evaluation

We have to briefly address one other common feature that, although controversial, never seemed to be regarded as warranting any explicit defense. The members of the humanistic school acted upon some sort of deep conviction that the human values underlying their work was, at least as far as they could ascertain, normatively *objective*. The ethics of vital human needs was *not* regarded as only valid within their particular country at a particular point in time; it was supposed to reflect *absolute*, not relative truth. In this respect, they differed from the members of the German "historical school" who felt that it was the (neglected) task of economic theory to incorporate the particular ethics observed to dominate in a culture.

The centering around human values deemed to be universally true is a double-edged sword. Analytically, it gives a thinker greater power and elegance in building a comprehensive system to recommend public and social policy, but it also makes its proponents vulnerable to accusations of being absolutist, elitist, and dogmatic. Such charges are, more often than not, the product of misunderstanding. Let me try to demonstrate this to the extent possible.

First, the humanistic school has to be understood as a movement that arose in direct protest to the claims of scientific mainstream economics. Now, is it not true that the normative, prescriptive element in conventional economics has rarely, perhaps only once or twice at the hands of Bagehot and Leslie, been presented as only valid in a particular social and temporal context? Was it not one of the very strengths of classical political economy to promote its discovered economic laws of society as objectively valid, and that it was not only futile but wrong to interfere with this natural mechanism? So, the argument against trade unions or minimum wage legislation was not couched in terms of subjective opinion, but in relevance on the classical wage-fund doctrine, as a factual scientific truth commanding universal respect. A similar story could be told about the argument against trade protection. And finally, the goal of maximum consumer satisfaction, as measured by willingness and ability to pay, is generally pictured as one commanding universal assent. It determines what is allocatively efficient and what is positive "waste."

In throwing themselves against such prescriptions, it is only human, perhaps natural, that the humanists sought to fight fire with fire, to come up with an alternative perspective that was similarly unambiguous in its goals and statements. Counter arguments were offered in the name of sound, or as Hobson put it, "enlightened common sense." Such common sense was seen in the way proposed by moral philosopher Thomas Reid, as the sense of the common, of what is common to all. In this light, they all argued from the common sense perspective of what is human nature. Above all, they believed it was noncontroversial to accept as axiomatic the belief that human life is intrinsically valuable and with it the satisfaction of the inborn biological survival needs that make life possible: food and shelter. What is true for the eskimo is also true for the cave dweller or the Wall Street broker and will be true as long as there are human beings.

It is hard to assail this perspective as subjective and unscientific, and I know of nobody who has successfully made such a case. Basic material needs are objective; if they are not fulfilled, the consequences with respect to health and life can be readily observed. To this extent, the norm chosen by the humanistic economists is empirically falsifiable and yet seemingly quite robust. Much of the humanistic economic proposals for alleviation of poverty through taxing monies that would otherwise have been spent on luxuries stands firmly on such basis.

Next is the appeal to common sense that besides material survival and animal-type instincts relating to acquisitive, predatory behavior, there are also higher reaches of human personality shared by all of humanity. These higher reaches relate to Man's self-awareness, moral capacity, and social consciousness. All this may not be necessarily grounded in laboratory research, but it does have immense appeal to just about everybody not indoctrinated by the science game confined to naturalistic methods and creeds.

What is bound to be more controversial is the humanistic belief that a wholistic policy science should explore the interrelation between the human mind and social institutions. This view brings us to the most controversial humanistic faith, particularly two questions: First, how can attainment of a more distinctly human, moral character be attained and, second, what is the specific content of these higher needs? Let us look at these in turn.

Moral Character Partially Dependent on Economic Institutions

First, the reader will recall that the humanistic perspective puts much stress and emphasis on economic security and fairness. Once again, the appeal here is to common sense. That it has been widely accepted is, for example, amply evident in how U.S. society has tended to structure the institutions that are vitally important, such as the disinterested administration of justice and the disinterested search for truth. Not surprisingly, we are well accustomed to the institution of lifetime job tenure in academia and the courts. The American Alexander Hamilton, in the *Federalist Papers* (1982), explicitly recognized such lifetime tenure (called "the standard of good behavior") as "the citadel of public justice," and the key "to secure a steady, upright and impartial administration of the laws."

Hamilton amplifies this concept in these words:[63]

> The standard of good behaviour for the continuance in office of the judicial magistracy is certainly one of the most valuable of the modern improvements in the practice of government. In a monarchy it is an excellent barrier to the despotism of the prince. In a republic it is a no less excellent barrier to the encroachments and oppressions of the representative body. And it is the best expedient which can be derived in any government, to secure a steady, upright and impartial administration of the laws. (p. 393)

> . . . nothing can contribute so much to its [the judiciary's] firmness and independence, as permanency in office; this quality may therefore by justly regarded as an indispensable ingredient in its constitution, and in a great measure as a citadel of public justice and public security. (p. 394)

> Next to permanency in office, nothing can contribute more to the independence of judges than a fixed provision for their support. (p. 400)

Lifetime job security makes absolutely no sense from the Economic Man point of view that informs conventional economic thinking, but it is quite reasonable to expect that some minimum provision against potentially negative consequences will facilitate the quest for justice and truth, especially when either requires actions that are unpopular with the power centers in society. Is it not also equally reasonable to expect that a worker will be more committed to excellence and behavior benefitting more the common good than his or her own immediate advancement if there is no prevailing climate of "good guys finish last"? In that sense, the concern with security is very much linked with a general assurance, often based on trust, that others will reciprocate fairly rather than betray the trust extended to them. Any giving of oneself to an organized group or society is made that much easier if there is a perception that others will not exploit one's generous advances. Trade unions will moderate their wage demands if they feel that others do likewise, yet in a climate of "might is right" we cannot expect much self-restraint.

If this sounds "metaphysical," arbitrary, and dogmatic, the humanistic point of view as a whole would seem vulnerable to the same change. If the foregoing logic makes sense, on the other hand, then our intentions would seem to confirm the humanistic logic.

What about the content of the higher needs? Here we are apt to encounter the most difficult questions, many of which have led to the ridicule of utopians throughout the ages, and quite rightly so. The humanistic economists surveyed here believed to be moving on firmer ground when they claimed that meaningful work (defined broadly as work that commands intrinsic interest) and economic democracy are objectively desirable, even if not actually observable as strongly demanded by the working classes. Today there is much empirical evidence coming from the relatively new field of industrial psychology to back up such claims, but in earlier periods it was argued primarily on enlightened common sense.[64]

The Question of "Absolute Truth"

So much for the logical backbone for humanistic value standard as it emerged in its one-hundred-fifty-year history. But, before we leave this subject, it is important to point out that the nonrelativistic/transcultural ethics of humanistic economics is not meant to be absolutely true in the sense of precluding any further debate on the issue. Instead, it is believed to be the best possible approximation so far to some transcendental truth. As such, it claims to be "true" until somebody else comes up with a better picture of socio-economic reality. Also, we may add that although the basic human needs (food, shelter, etc.) are absolute in their nature, their particular manifestation is heavily culture-dependent. So, for example, a hungry eskimo may eat fish while a hungry stockbroker might generally prefer something quite different. They both have to eat, but they will do so in the cultural context they are accustomed to. The same pertains to the need for shelter and clothing, as well as a higher need for affection, social contact, and esteem. But it seems counterproductive to focus so much on the differences as to lose sight of the more fundamental commonalities.

Contemporary Humanistic Economics

Although the humanistic tradition can pride itself on historical roots that are at least in length comparable to its neoclassical and Marxist counterparts, it continues to evolve by responding to the ongoing panorama of newly emerging problems and developments. One of these developments is the changes in mainstream economic theory which need to be critically confronted and reassessed. Other changes pertain to the new developments in related disciplines, such as psychology and moral philosophy, and finally there are the new developments in actual economic reality, particularly the problems associated with global economic integration and Third World development.

THE PERSPECTIVE OUTLINED IN THE CHALLENGE OF HUMANISTIC ECONOMICS

It was in the context of many such changes that there seemed to arise a new need for a comprehensive rearticulation of a human economy alternative. *Challenge of Humanistic Economics* published in 1979 attempted to do just that.

In retrospect, it seems that its significance was essentially twofold. It took the traditional human standard of personality interpreted in the new light of Abraham Maslow's humanistic psychology and, second, it employed that author's famous hierarchy of basic needs to provide a systematic analysis of the status of needs in economic theory and in the economy at large. The move in such a direction seemed particularly promising due to the fact that Maslow's theory was developed scientifically, i.e., empirically, by clinical research and by comprehensive surveys of American society. It was especially reassuring to discover that Hobson's security postulate was independently derived and confirmed as catalyst for the growth of personality. Moreover, Maslow's landmark book entitled *Personality and Motivation* (1954) promised to offer much that was relevant with respect to the economist's perennial concern with labor productivity. Once again, so much of Hobson's writings on the subject seem to be validated.

Utility and Needs

For us, perhaps one the most exciting discoveries was a 1954 paper by the well-known economist Nicholas Georgescu-Roegen focusing on another problem that had also occupied Hobson: how we choose between qualitatively different needs.[65] We were particularly impressed by his "thought experiment" proving the economist's conception of one-dimensional commensurability based on "utility" to be counterfactual. Instead, it established the opposite claim, long held by humanistic economists, of fundamentally irreducible needs or basic wants:

> In support of the Irreducibility of Wants, one may refer to many everyday facts; that bread cannot save someone from dying of thirst, that living in a luxurious palace does not constitute a substitute for food, etc. But there is another important argument in favour of the irreducibility. If all wants were reducible we could not explain why in any American household water is consumed to the satiety of thirst—and therefore should have zero "intensity" of utility at that point—while since water is not used to satiety in sprinkling the lawn, it must have a positive "final degree of utility." Yet, no household would go thirsty—no matter how little—in order to water a flower pot.[66]

In other words, a flesh-and-blood consumer will, in this example, be *in equilibrium* when his marginal utility of drinking water is zero while his marginal utility of watering flowers is significantly positive. Now, to further illustrate the problem, imagine a sudden water shortage compelling our consumer to cut back her water consumption. Where can we expect the reduction to be made? According to standard economic theory, assuming as it does the reducibility of all wants to a single uniform quality, rational behavior implies cutting back those units of water with the least marginal utility: in our case, the "low-utility" water used for drinking. We wonder, why does Economic Man go thirsty in order to water a flower pot? Answer: because he neither has nor cares for a real life.

The point of Georgescu-Roegen's illustration is simply to indicate that people do have different kinds of wants yielding different kinds of utility. Such structured wants, being as they are incommensurable, resist being calculated, quantitatively compared, and balanced against each other. Accordingly, the economists' treatment of utility as a one-dimensional abstract concept is, for purposes of describing real human behavior, a highly misleading one. This piercing example produced by a renowned expert on utility theory clearly suggests that human beings do not conform to the economist's assumption of reducible needs.

Neither are the consequences simply too insignificant to warrant the "conspiracy of silence" with which this disturbing piece of analytical insight was received. According to its author, "the hierarchy of wants throws overboard any ophelimity index" of the kind that economists axiomatically assume in order to do their work. True, the hierarchy conception does allow for an ordering of all commodity combinations, but the order is a special kind (called lexicographic) that lacks the property of commensurability and therefore denies representation by the conventional indifference curve approach so central to economic theory today.

A New Challenge in the Making

More generally, *Challenge of Humanistic Economics* may have been reasonably successful in introducing many students and even some teachers of economics to the history of economics, competition, freedom, work, welfare state, economic democracy, and steady state economics, all from the humanistic tradition. But at the same time, we realized that the power of its argument depended to a large extent on the reputation of Maslow's hierarchy of basic needs, a concept that was increasingly questioned during the 1970s and particularly in the 1980s. Soon we learned (as had Abraham Maslow himself in his later work) to de-emphasize the importance of his multi-level hierarchy in favor of just two types of needs: deficiency needs and growth needs. Deficiency needs relate to all needs in the hierarchy except self-actualization and self-transcendence, these latter making up the "growth needs" or "meta-needs." He related these two type of needs to the basic duality of the human being, "the predicament, of being simultaneously merely creaturely and godlike, strong and weak, limited and unlimited, merely animal and animal-transcending, . . . yearning for perfection and yet afraid of it, being a work and also a hero."[67] In short, "the human being is simultaneously that which he is and that which he yearns to be."[68]

The Perspective of a Dual-Self

Psychologically, the growth of personality now must be seen in a somewhat different light. According to Maslow:

> If we define growth as the various processes which bring the person toward ultimate self-actualization, then this conforms better with the observed fact that it is going on *all* the time in the life history. It discourages also the stepwise, *all* or none, saltatory conception of motivational progression toward self-actualization in which the basic needs are completely gratified, one by one, before the next higher one emerges into consciousness.[69]

In other words, instead of an organism instinctively progressing step-by-step through the hierarchy, the new view regards the human person as dual as well as conscious of this duality. That the human self is dual is not only more in accord with empirical test results,[70] but is also broadly consistent with other personality theories advocated by prominent psychologists, particularly Carl Rogers, Gordon Allport, and Eric Fromm. Janet T. Spence, in her 1985 Presidential Address to the American Psychology Association, referred to the "duality of human existence" as an important concept in understanding achievement motivation.

At the same time, we realized that this dual-self theory was also consistent with the earliest beginnings of Classical Humanism in philosophy. It was the very basis for Pico della Mirandola's fifteenth-century *Oration on the Dignity of Man*. According to Pico, this dignity rests in Man's freedom, his capacity and need to direct and shape his own life. A list of nine hundred questions that Pico had posed for debate along with his oration, was declared heretical by the Church, and they only allowed him to publish their introduction. In it, the Deity addresses Adam:

> We have made you a creature neither of heaven nor of earth, neither mortal nor immoral, in order that you may, as the free and prouder shape of your own being, fashion yourself in the form you may prefer. It will be in your power to descend to the lower, brutish forms of life; you will be able, through your own decision, to rise again to the superior orders whose life is divine.[71]

This double nature of the person, its "dual-self," is the essence of what has come to be called Classical Humanism. According to this view, we have within us both the higher and the lower, the noble and the base, and our freedom lies in our capacity to choose between the two.

Similarly, there is much in German philosophy, especially Immanuel Kant's de-ontological theory of morality where the two-self model manifests itself in the tension between the actual (phenomenological) self and the ideal (noumenal) self. The image of duality has survived into modern existentialism, particularly in Martin Buber's distinction between the I of the I-It and the qualitatively different I of the I-Thou.

As a result of all these new realizations, we felt it wise to rebuild our foundation by replacing some specifics of the more controversial humanistic psychology with more permanent pieces of the less vulnerable "humanistic" *philosophy*, or better, "philosophical anthropology." While retaining Maslow's security need as the door in the wall leading from the domain of the deficiency needs to the stairway of personality growth, there is now even more emphasis on Hobson's two other "catalysts"—meaningful work and a degree of basic fairness in the economic system.

The Dual-Self and Choice Theory

In the book entitled *Humanistic Economics: The New Challenge* (Lutz & Lux, 1988), this new way of looking at the humanistic tradition was proposed. Much of the emphasis is now on self-interest and the possibility of recognizing non-self-interested or "disinterested" or—what amounts to the same thing—"higher self-motivated" economic behavior. Above all, we were now able to get a better grasp on Economic Man, an abstraction often portrayed by some as tautologically true, by others even as a self-evident postulate. A prominent example of the latter can be found in modern economics: Lionel

Robbins (1984) claimed as a main postulate of the theory of nature that "individuals can arrange their preferences in an order, and in fact do so," is "so much the stuff of our everyday experience that [it has] only to be stated to be recognized as obvious." To him, the postulate was "merely a convenient formal way of exhibiting certain permanent characteristics of man as he *actually is*."[72]

From a modern humanistic point of view, such characterization now emerges as only a half truth. We do, of course, have preferences underlying choice and/or manifested in choice, but as postwar developments in the philosophy of action increasingly recognize, *we also have preferences about our preferences.*[73] An alcoholic may resent his drinking, a smoker his wanting to smoke, TV addicts often wish they would spend more time otherwise. But such attitudes do not only pertain to these common afflictions, but may also pertain to one's behavior in all affairs of life: I wish I would not always brag, I wish I would not always tend to act in a way that compromises my integrity, etc.[74] According to Frankfurt (1971), freedom of the will necessitates the conceptual framework of second-order preferences, which is to have the preferences one wants to have. In doing so, one avoids a contradiction between the higher and lower preferences.[75] Exercising free will in this fashion is equivalent with maintaining our moral integrity. The second-order self, or the "higher self," has been allowed to take control of the lower self, i.e., the (lower) self exercises "self-control."

Modern economic man, with his one-dimensional preferences, fits Frankfurt's description of a rational "wanton" lacking higher-order preferences:

> What distinguishes the rational wanton from the rational agent is that he is not concerned with the desirability of his desires themselves. He ignores the question of what his will is to be. Not only does he pursue whatever course of action he is most strongly inclined to pursue but he does not care which of his inclinations is the strongest.[76]

Moreover, and most significant for a humanistic point of view, he would resemble more an animal than a person:

> Many animals appear to have the capacity for what I shall call "first-order desires" or "desires of the first order" which are simply

> desires to do or not to do one thing or another. No animal other than man, however, appears to have the capacity for reflective self-evaluation that is manifested in the formation of second-order desires.[77]

In a similar vein, the recent president of the American Economic Association, Amartya Sen (1977), maintains that "*purely* economic man is indeed close to a social moron. Economic theory has been much preoccupied with this rational fool decked in the glory of his *one* all-purpose preference ordering."[78] We need not dwell on the point. Whether modern economic man is more of an "infrahuman" wanton or a foolish social moron, both images are probably quite accurate descriptions of something that is less than fully human.

Maximization Behavior Attacked

Armed with these new insights, we could better appreciate another essential limitation of the very bedrock of economics: the idea of reducing all human behavior to maximization behavior. To begin with, the claim that "all is maximization" does not make much sense from a linguistic or logical point of view. As Leibenstein (1979) put it: "Words have to be used in such a way that they do not contradict their essential meaning. Thus, in using the word "maximization," we must of necessity assume that non-maximization is meaningful in the same context."[79]

In brief, what the postulate assumes does not make logical or semantic sense.

The realization that there must be such a thing as deliberate "non-maximization" of behavior is the very starting point, not only for humanistic economic psychologists, but for anybody striving for a more real and meaningful economics. It follows directly from our departure from "one-dimensional" man. Besides the calculating, utilitarian ego engaged in *unrestrained* self-regarding or maximization, there also exists what we may label "*restrained* maximization." The restraining factor is an agent's aspirational self, the real world proxy for the higher self. Needless to say, the restraint is an inner or a psychological one and, for this reason, restrained "maximization" is intrinsically non-maximization. A mainstream utilitarian may counter that we are simply incorporating a "taste for restraint" into our now more complex function to be maximized. Maximization would then be more complex yet still apply. To this, we answer—in following Leibenstein (1979, pp. 416-17)—that when an agent behaves in accordance with an alleged "taste for non-maximization," it would lead to a logical contradiction: A person is maximizing when he is not maximizing.[80]

In other words, we are restrained by our innermost personal values, articulated by our higher order, moral preferences. The restraining higher self, according to which the higher preferences are formed, resembles in many ways the classic Freudian concept of super-ego. Yet, such resemblance is somewhat superficial.

Unlike the super-ego, the authentic higher self is not externally imposed by parental authority or some other "socialization process." From a humanistic perspective, it is an inborn essence of our human nature.[81] Of course, guidance by our self or conscience is anything but infallible. Well-intended actions may have deplorable consequences. Through a critical and open-minded attitude, we learn to continuously reform or "retune" our intuitions; in the same process, even strongly held cultural values are constantly critically reevaluated.

Postulating restrained maximization merely amounts to recognizing "inner obligation" or moral commitment. We are often bound by such considerations or obligations whether it maximizes our "utility" or not; in such cases, we act by an inner necessity, an inner need for personal integrity, self-respect, self-actualization, or ego transcendence. And it is precisely this capacity, this free choice of whether or not to let ourselves be guided by the (higher) self that gives us dignity as human beings. In this view, realization of the self, our "God-like quality" or the Kantian "noumenal self," is what elevates us above nature and so conveys dignity.

Conflict of Interest Recognized

Agents being imbued with two basic interests, one self-regarding, the other responding to an interest beyond one's (empirical) self, to an ideal or compelling moral principle now opens the door to being able to understand the common legal notion of "conflict of interest."

Mention the concept conflict of interest to an economist and he (she) will understand it like Robert Axelrod (1970) as "the state of incompatibility of the goals of two or more actors, in other words, a conflict between people." Such an interpretation follows directly from the fundamental assumption underlying the theory of choice: one-dimensional human beings with one-dimensional preference scales, each one having only *one* goal in mind. By this view, it is easy to conflate the issue with the notion of opportunity cost: every action has potential alternatives and we will have to choose. And such choice, according to economics, can be resolved by means of calculation. There is no real loss; in the choice between a nickel and a dime, we do not really suffer *any* loss when we go for the dime—quite the contrary. The reason is that the losing alternative (for the nickel) is commensurable and compensated by taking the dime.

Yet, in both ordinary and legal language the concept refers to an incompatibility between the "public" or "common" interest and the private (usually pecuniary) interest within an individual. We have a conflict within ourselves between two levels of motives (say, personal advantage versus the public good). That such conflicts are very real and frequent any minimally alert observer of the daily news will readily confirm. This is not a nickel versus dime type of choice. Instead, we pit two incommensurable qualities or ends against each other. Choosing one means we are depriving ourselves of the other. Conflict of interest constitutes a basic reality in our psychological makeup and it readily permeates our own daily activities. It must seem rather odd that economists as practitioners of their "science of choice" cannot account for it when analyzing human actions. This is particularly so since such inner conflict involves the purest of pure individual choice: are we to maximize our utility or are we to restrain self-interest by responding to a moral motive? Given the framework of modern economics, we have to question whether such human action and inner conflict can be described or explained within such an economics. Not surprisingly, we are also told that recognition of inner conflict and struggle is either irrelevant or (particularly for a follower of the so-called "Austrian School") impossible. Either way, the issue is not dealt with. This type of neglect is not only counterfactual, but unnecessarily confining and so also counterproductive.

At least the issue of conflict of interest allows us to perceive the essence of the (mistaken) philosophy of economics: there is only one goal, one interest in analyzing human behavior; everything else is means to that single purpose. Yet, we do have more than one end, and selecting the right end is a choice that needs to be addressed somehow.

Within our richer humanistic framework, the choice between individual utility and a public or common purpose is central. We can, within the limitations of our moral strength, choose to restrain our maximization impulse and overcome self-interest, and to freely decide to be bound by considerations of moral principle or altruistic love. Clearly, we are graced with the distinctly human capacity of free will. By being able to overcome "inner contradiction," by following our inner conscience, we gain moral and personal integrity and affirm the human dignity that goes with it. Within a Maslowian framework, this is what the growth needs of genuine self-esteem, self-actualization, and self-transcendence are all about. And to repeat what is critical for economic policy considerations, a certain assurance of gratification of our deficiency needs does help to render a free-will choice less heroic.

Having established that the person is not one-dimensional as manifest in matters of conflict of interest dilemmas, we can proceed to argue the relevance of a dual-self point of view for economics—already dealt with concerning such topics as the prisoner's dilemma, self-motivation, a philosophy of government as articulator of the common or higher self, and an analysis of the effect of wage labor on human dignity. This last point has been argued elsewhere,[82] but it is of a large enough significance to briefly comment on further here.

The Human Value of Economic Democracy

It will be remembered that for humanistic economists, especially the later ones but also earlier for Sismondi, a great value has been placed on self-determination and control over production and work. One common element characterizing this type of economics has always been a deeply felt aversion to absentee ownership and control, whether in free-enterprise capitalism or bureaucratic socialism. It was always considered sensible that workers should also be owners of enterprise, one way or the other. Is this long-held ideal just a particular opinion grounded in individual taste and preference *or* can it be presented in the same way as biological need satisfaction: an *objective* value? Hobson, Tawney, and Gandhi no doubt treated it often in this way, although Hobson was not convinced that it was sufficiently practical. The arguments offered for self-management and worker ownership were, however, primarily implicit and ad hoc in nature, thereby lacking any great power of persuasion. As a result, worker cooperatives remained a relatively weak link in the axiology of human economy.

The most recent work by American economist David Ellerman, featured in *Humanistic Economics: The New Challenge,* must therefore be seen as a most welcome strengthening and refinement of the general vision. It attacks the wage system, depicted as a degrading, self-rental system that treated employees as mere means or instruments toward the goal of company profit.[83] In contrast, an alternative approach to production centered around the person is a system of workers self-determination and management. This approach treats him or her as an end with value of its own, and so respects that person's dignity. Unlike a rental situation where they yield or give up the power to make decisions over their labor, they *delegate* that power to a more expert manager or managing board. Similarly, they now can claim and appropriate the whole fruits of their labor for which they are legally responsible. As owners of a rental tool, on the other hand, they would not be legally responsible for their actions costing and benefiting their company.

The idea that a person is not a *thing*, and should not be treated as such, is a theme deeply rooted in humanistic thought of the last few centuries. Accordingly, Ellerman's penetrating demonstration that *only* worker ownership is compatible with this ideal adds a powerful philosophical dimension in favor of economic democracy. Moreover, as is shown in *Humanistic Economics,* the idea of inherent human dignity fits exceptionally well the new dual-self concept for integrating human economy.

Besides establishing a sound normative basis for worker ownership and cooperatives, Ellerman's pioneering work also suggests radically new ideas on how to make them effective competitors in the marketplace. Although it is heartening to learn about and appreciate the success of the cooperative forms created in Spain's Mondragón, we have discussed those matters elsewhere and need not repeat it here.[84]

Global Economic Aspects

There are other highlights in *Humanistic Economics* that serve to illustrate the evolving nature of the humanistic paradigm. Among them is one pertaining to a new interpretation of Gandhian economics where Amritananda Das, an Indian scholar, has been able to translate Gandhi's economic philosophy into a rigorous and analytically powerful development strategy for Third World countries.

Another development relates to the perennial question of free trade in a new global economy. Although it is a problem that already occupied the talented mind of Adam Smith two hundred years ago, it has only recently become an issue that pertains to the everyday life of most citizens.

John Hobson, when discussing a global economy seven decades ago, did endorse free trade, but only within a context of some adequate global governance structures. What he and many after him tended to overlook was the increasingly threatening reality of free trade without such structures. In these new circumstances, modern humanistic economics will have to take a stand for or against international free trade. In *Humanistic Economics*, it is argued that a "principle of correspondence" enabling social control of the market will—in the absence of any realistic prospect for such a world government and a body of an effectively enforceable international law—have to insist on a harmonization of the economic and political domains by cutting back the thrust of economic forces and confining them within national borders where they can be restrained and subordinated to overall social policy goals. Accordingly, a satisfactory welfare state, full employment, and a sustainable cooperative movement can in the long run only be enabled by social control of trade among nations. This means meaningful tariffs, or better, following American economist Culbertson, a policy of bilaterally balanced trade through nontariff trade agreements.[85]

It should not come as a surprise that the traditional anti-laissez-faire stance of humanistic economics would by the same logic also apply to both national and international trade alike. But, the economist will point to the crucial difference captured by the doctrine of comparative advantage. And in theory that is true, but *only* if the assumption of factor immobility is realized. In the real world of increasingly perfect capital mobility, however, comparative advantage collapses into absolute advantage, meaning wage competition, and/or dysfunctional competition of lowering workplace or environmental standards in order to attract capital investment.[86]

We will refrain from discussing humanistic development economics here but refer instead to a veritable textbook presenting the very core of a development strategy in time with human values: a book by Amritananda Das, *Foundations of Gandhian Economics*.[87]

Conclusion

Let us conclude our survey of contemporary humanistic economics by restating its essential nature.

Humanistic economics continues to be a doctrine fundamentally critical of mainstream economic theory, particularly its normative branch: welfare economics. It does so by applying the human standard of personality. In this process, it reaffirms the primary of physiological need satisfaction for all, and it adds to this another criteria, claimed to be objective: human dignity interpreted as the need to treat human beings as ends, not as means.

Policy issues as diverse as poverty relief in advanced economies, development in Third World countries, the new international economic order, the need for economic security and democracy, can all be discussed in a much more meaningful way and many solutions to them can also be derived. All said, humanistic economics emerges as new and *prescriptive human* welfare economics compatible with purely *descriptive* neoclassical insights, even the *descriptions* embodied in the Marxian causal framework.

It is no doubt an ambitious, perhaps even a superhuman, task to articulate such a comprehensive normative social theory, but its construction has, historically speaking, been a collective effort reaching a high watermark in the synthesizing work of John Hobson some fifty to one hundred years ago. As the world continues to change, new problems appear and new solutions within the existing framework may be found. The publication of *Humanistic Economics* was meant to address many of these issues. Nevertheless, and needless to say, the final chapter on humanistic economics remains to be written. At this time, another installment has appeared, emphasizing human dignity (Lutz, 1995) and rationality (Lutz, 1993).[88] We too build the road as we travel. The way to approach that goal is by means of a highly critical open mind and an open heart.

Prospects for a Vital Alternative Economics

Humanistic economics, ever since Sismondi, has been a response to serious social problems encountered in an economic system. This alone can be valuable, especially when the mainstream economists do not think it worthwhile to address or even admit the existence of some obvious problems, including alienation, consumerism, persistent trade deficits, etc. It may very well be that the strength of a humanistic perspective will grow in proportion to such unresolved problems. Somebody, and he or she better be in economics, will have to address the problems of depletion of vital natural resources, the mounting new insecurity of uninsured workers, the continued erosion of community, persistent alienation among the work force, the high unemployment among the young, the farm crisis, the irreversible environmental destruction, regional deindustrialization due to globalization of trade, and nuclear proliferation. The list is long and could easily be further lengthened. There certainly seems to be ample material there to keep open-minded economists busy for decades to come.

Different Types of Alternative Economics

Yet, assurance about the future prospects of human economy says nothing about its quality and beneficial impact. Much of the answer to that question depends on the kind of alternative economics we choose to pursue.

Most commonly found is an approach that seeks to address the general crisis by centering on particular problems and dealing with them on a case-by-case, more fragmented basis. This method is certainly tempting for anybody who has a heart, ample time, and adequate writing skills, but it also does have serious limitations. Lacking a more sweeping, universal framework, it will often not be able to deal with the intricate context influencing a particular problem, e.g., the farm crisis. As a result, the analysis may often be seen as dealing more with manifestations than with deeper causes. For the same reason, the solutions will often be seen as similarly lacking, consisting often in no more than moral exhortations, pleas for a change in consciousness, and sermons about "personal empowerment." Such prescriptions, occasionally supplemented by a small experiment, cannot really be expected to have much impact. They will often be alien to statesmen, ignored by academia, and soon forgotten by the very groups targeted for relief. Political correctness does not mean political acceptance, and empowerment may or may not entail actual gains in power.

The humanistic tradition described in this chapter has always been keenly aware of such pitfalls and errors. To that extent, it has also been more effective in changing the world. Sismondi's concern with poverty, recurrent slumps, demise of craftsmen, unemployment, and so forth led him to take an in-depth look at the entire economic system, how it operated, and on what principles it should operate. The same is true for Hobson when he witnessed the phenomenon of imperialism, with European powers scrambling for territory in the southern hemisphere, and he analyzed it as the result of surplus accumulation due to lopsided income distribution. To curtail this, imperialism would for him require a major surgical procedure—reforming the basic socio-economic system dominating England and a handful of other countries on the Continent.

To focus on specific social problems from a more general, contextual perspective requires the existence of some general, alternative tool of analysis. That tool needs to penetrate to the very core of the economic system from which all the problems located around the periphery can be seen in a truly new light. We have to recognize, for example, that many problems at their basic underlying level are created and accumulated through an economic force that appears to many as cold and impersonal and disembedded from its social and cultural context. This force, fueled by egoism of all sorts and parading as the so-called "invisible hand" in a laissez-faire economy, may even lull and numb people into some quasi-intoxicated state that may effectively prevent them from realizing that they can "self-empower" themselves. So many people keep themselves so busy with shopping or TV entertainment that they are not even motivated to look at the very books promising new ideas for helping them, whether the remedy is "voluntary poverty," "solar power," or more effective energy conservation.

Whether we like it or not, we have to find social means to control or discourage excessive egoism. Individual or group empowerment can only be effective by mutual respect and a healthy dose of compassion. Overall, remedial action then will have to consist predominantly of social activism aiming at new social legislation. Humanistic economics, before and after Gandhi, has always been in the forefront and ready to wrestle with the serpent of politics in order to help restructure a socio-economic system that degrades and hurts its people. Holding to an interactionist model of social institutions and individual behavior would also discount the doctrine that individual change ought to be a prerequisite of social change. No, we perfect ourselves in the very struggle for social reform.

To the extent that the above comments and reflections bear any truth value, the strength of the humanistic paradigm becomes more apparent. It will be seen not only as a more ambitious, but also a more general, sweeping, and serious alternative. Trying to be more scholarly and respectable, we hope to be treated with more respect by academics and politicians, and as a result also have more impact on opinion leaders in social philosophy, social theory, and law. In fact, we venture to assert that it is to a significant extent because of people like Sismondi, Ruskin, and Hobson that we have today a greater amount of human welfare than could be taken for granted one or two centuries ago.

Humanistic economics has been presented here as a school of thought, although one with "open walls." How viable and effective it will be in the years ahead, only time will tell. But the track record does encourage us to expect some results, provided, of course, we continue to honor the principles and methods that have emerged from its tradition. With humanity at the brink of ecological disasters or self-destructive "free" global trade under the WTO, can anybody really afford to withhold wholehearted encouragement and commitment, regardless of immediate results and academic applause? At the same time, we cannot forget that with a goal as ambitious as progress of humanity in an environmentally sustainable economy, we can only expect to do as much as is humanly possible, while entrusting the rest faithfully to the workings of a higher will, whatever that may be.

Similarly, it is important to remember that humanistic economics is rooted in the present age, the "Age of the Economist," of materialism, false individualism, and sterile consumerism. Its basic direction is not "left or right," but rather aimed at transforming and elevating. It takes its stand by peacefully and constructively confronting these forces. If this warrants the popular label "New Age Economics," so be it. But the New Age we are fighting for *in* the world cannot really be expected to come by some "cosmic conversion" as foretold thousands of years ago, or by intervention of some other miraculous supernatural force. We have to do the work ourselves; we take the world as we find it in the *"here"* and *"now,"* with all its ugliness and all its beauty. Similarly, there is no appeal to spirits or some other impersonal spiritual dimension, while at the same time there is no denial whatsoever of the potential importance or relevance of the spiritual. Rather, it banks on the spiritual as that which is common to us all, in the higher self, and in a deep faith that life is ultimately meaningful through its service to some higher purpose—genuine Community, Justice, Beauty, and Truth.

The French Revolution was fought for liberty, equality, and brotherhood. Capitalism embraced the first goal, socialism the second. But neither can be realized without the third. What needs to be done is a greater focus on the more elusive goal of brotherhood and sisterhood. And for that we need a recentered economics progressing in the direction of Sismondi, Ruskin, Hobson, Gandhi, and Tawney. This is the urgent task inspiring contemporary human economy.

NOTES

1. J. C. L. Simonde de Sismondi, [1826] 1994, *New Principles of Political Economy*, 2nd ed., New Brunswick, New Jersey: Transaction Publishers , p. 8.

2. *Ibid.*, p. 7.

3. *Ibid.*, p. 140.

4. *Ibid.*, p. 127.

5. *Ibid.*, p. 148.

6. *Ibid.*, p. 222.

7. *Ibid.*, p. 50.

8. John Ruskin, [1864] 1988, *Unto This Last*, New York: John Wiley & Son, pp. 17-19

9. *Ibid.*, p. 19.

10. *Ibid.*, p. 28.

11. John Ruskin, 1880, "Letters on Political Economy" in his *Arrows of the Chace*, vol. 2, Boston: Colonial Press, p. 282.

12. John Ruskin, quoted in James C. Sherbourne, 1972, *John Ruskin or the Ambiguity of Affluence*, Cambridge, Massachusetts: Harvard University Press.

13. John Ruskin in *Manchester Examiner Times*, October 2, 1860; quoted in Adam Smith, 1973, *The Wealth of Nations*, New York: McGraw-Hill, p. 224.

14. John Hobson, [1866] 1938, *Confessions of an Economic Heretic*, New York: Macmillan Co., pp. 38-39, 42.

15. Kadish, 1990, "Rewriting the 'Confessions': Hobson and the Extension Movement" in Michael Freeden, ed., *Reappraising J. A. Hobson*, New York: Routledge, Chapman & Hill, pp. 116-66.

16. Hobson, [1866] 1938, *Confessions, op. cit.*, p. 84.

17. John Hobson, 1901, *The Social Problem*, London: Nisbet, p. 38.

18. John Hobson, [1914] 1968, *Work and Wealth: A Human Valuation*, New York: Augustus M. Kelley, p. 1.

19. John Hobson, 1929, *Economics and Ethics*, London: D.C. Heath, p. 77.

20. Hobson, [1914] 1968, *Work and Wealth, op. cit.*, p. 13.

21. *Ibid.*, p. x.

22. *Ibid.*, p. 71.

23. *Ibid.*, p. 73.

24. *Ibid.*

25. *Ibid.*, p. 74.

26. *Ibid.*, p. 46.

27. Hobson, 1929, *Economics and Ethics, op. cit.*, p. 266.

28. *Ibid.*, p. 267.

29. *Ibid.*, p. 300.

30. John Hobson, [1909] 1969, *The Industrial System: An Inquiry into Earned and Unearned Income*, New York: Augustus M. Kelley.

31. Hobson, 1929, *Economics and Ethics, op. cit.*, p. 199.

32. *Ibid.*, p. 284.

33. *Ibid.*, p. 45.

34. *Ibid.*, p. 234.

35. Hobson, [1914] 1968, *Work and Wealth, op. cit.*, p. 298.

36. *Ibid.*, p. 300.

37. *Ibid.*, p. 88.

38. *Ibid.*

39. John Hobson, [1922] 1981, *Incentives in the New Industrial Order*, Westport, Connecticut: Hyperion Press.

40. *Ibid.*, p. 110.

41. *Ibid.*, p. 111.

42. Hobson, 1929, *Economics and Ethics, op. cit.*, p. xxxi.

43. *Ibid.*, p. 121.

44. Hobson, [1914] 1968, *Work and Wealth, op. cit.*, p. 331.

45. *Ibid.*, p. 341.

46. Mohandas Gandhi, 1927, *An Autobiography*, Ahmedabad: Navajivan

Publishing House, p. 22.

47. A. M. Huq, reprinted in R. Diwan & M. Lutz, 1985, "Welfare Criteria in Gandhian Economics," *Essays in Gandhian Economics,* New Delhi: Gandhi Peace Foundation, pp. 66-75.

48. Gunnar Myrdal, 1972, *Against the Stream,* New York: Random House, p. 233.

49. Quoted in G. R. Madan, 1966, *Economic Thinking in India,* Delhi: Chand Publishing Co., p. 137.

50. For a rigorous interpretation of Gandhian economics, see the book by Amritananda Das, 1979, *Foundations for Gandhian Economics,* New York: St. Martin's Press. A more philosophical approach is contained in R. Diwan & M. Lutz, 1985, *Essays in Gandhian Economics,* New Delhi: Gandhian Peace Foundation.

51. Quoted in R. H. Terrill, 1973, *Tawney and His Times,* Cambridge, Massachusetts: Harvard University Press, p. 36.

52. R. H. Tawney, 1920, *The Acquisitive Society,* New York: Harcourt, Brace & Co., p. 8.

53. *Ibid.,* p. 39.

54. *Ibid.,* p. 85.

55. R. H. Tawney, 1931, *Equality,* London: Allen & Unwin, pp. 46-47.

56. Tawney, 1920, *Acquisitive Society, op. cit.,* p. 81.

57. *Ibid.,* pp. 117, 154.

58. *Ibid.,* p. 159.

59. *Ibid.,* pp. 180, 184.

60. For an excellent history of his career as an economist, see C. Hession, 1986, "E. F. Schumacher as Heir to Keynes' Mantle," *Review of Social Economy* (April), pp. 1-25.

61. E. F. Schumacher, 1973, *Small is Beautiful,* New York: Harper & Row, p. 165.

62. *Ibid.*, p. 5.

63. Alexander Hamilton, 1982, *Federalist Papers*, New York: Bantam, pp. 393-94, 400.

64. See, for example, the evidence in K. Lux and M. Lutz, 1986, "Economic Psychology: The Humanistic Perspective" in A. J. MacFadyen, ed., *Economic Psychology*, New York: New Holland, pp. 383-424.

65. Nicholas Georgescu-Roegen, 1954, "Choice, Expectations and Measurability," *Quarterly Journal of Economics* 68:4 (November), pp. 503-34.

66. *Ibid.*, p. 516.

67. Abraham Maslow, 1968, *Toward a Psychology of Being*, New York: Van Nostrand Reinhold, p. 174.

68. *Ibid.*, p. 160.

69. *Ibid.*, p. 26.

70. See M. Wahba and L. Bridwell, 1976, "Maslow Reconsidered: A Review of Research on the Need Hierarch Theory" in *Organizational Behavior and Human Performance*, pp. 212-40.

71. Quoted in *Manas* XXXII, no. 5 (January 1980), p. 2.

72. Lionel Robbins, [1932] 1984, *An Essay on the Nature and Significance of Economic Science*, London: Macmillan, p. 79, emphasis added.

73. See Harry Frankfurt, 1971, "Freedom of the Will and the Concept of the Person," *Journal of Philosophy* 68:1, pp. 5-20; and R. Jeffrey, 1974, "Preferences Among Preferences," *Journal of Philosophy* LXXI: 13, pp. 377-91.

74. For a recent discussion of the prevalence of second-order preferences, see Steven Rhoads, 1985, *The Economist's View of the World*, Cambridge: Cambridge University Press, ch. 9.

75. Also, according to Abraham Maslow (1962, *Motivation and Personality*, New York: Harper & Row), self-actualizing persons "spontaneously tend to right because that is what they *want* to do, what they *need* to do, what they enjoy, what they approve of doing, and what they will

continue to enjoy" (p. 159). They "find duty and pleasure to be the same thing" (p. 163). And he realizes that such behavior "means control, delay, limits, renunciation, frustration, tolerance and discipline" (p. 164).

76. Frankfurt, 1971, "Freedom of the Will," *op. cit.*, pp. 5-20.

77. *Ibid.*, p. 7.

78. Amartya Sen, 1977, "Rational Fool: A Critique of the Behavioral Foundations of Economic Theory," *Philosophy and Public Affairs*, no. 6, pp. 317-44.

79. Harvey Leibenstein, 1979, "A Branch of Economics Is Missing: Micro-Micro Theory," *Journal of Economic Literature* XVII (June), pp. 495-96.

80. For a recent discussion of this issue, see Mark Lutz, 1993, "The Utility of Multiple Utility," *Economics and Philosophy* 9:1 (April), pp. 145-54.

81. Maslow, 1962, *Motivation and Personality, op. cit.*, pp. 6-7.

82. See Mark Lutz and Kenneth Lux, 1988, *Humanistic Economics: The New Challenge*, New York: The Bootstrap Press, ch. 6.

83. *Ibid.*, ch. 8.

84. *Ibid.*, chs. 8 and 12.

85. See J. M. Culbertson, 1984, *International Trade and the Future of the West*, Madison: 21st Century Press (P.O. Box 5010, Madison, WI 53705).

86. For two recent pieces arguing along these lines, see Mark Lutz, 1993, "Cardinal Issues in the Future of Social Economics: A Humanistic View," *Review of Social Economy* 51:4 (Winter), pp. 455-75; and Lutz, 1995, "Doubt and Competition" in Ed O'Boyle, ed., *Essays in Social Economics*, London: Routledge.

87. Das, 1979, *Foundations*, *op. cit.*

88. Mark Lutz, 1995, "Centering Social Economics on Human Dignity," *Review of Social Economy* 52, pp. 1-24; and Lutz, 1993, "The Utility of Multiple Utility," *op. cit.*

BIBLIOGRAPHY

Culbertson, J. M., 1984, *International Trade and the Future of the West,* Madison, Wisconsin: 21st Century Press.

Das, Amritananda, 1979, *Foundations of Gandhian Economics,* New York: St. Martin's Press.

Diwan, Romesh, and Mark A. Lutz, 1985, *Essays in Gandhian Economics,* New Delhi: Gandhi Peace Foundation.

Frankfurt, Harry G., 1971, "Freedom of the Will and the Concept of the Person," *Journal of Philosophy* 68:1, pp. 5-20.

Freeden, Michael, ed., 1990, *Reappraising J. A. Hobson: Humanism and Welfare,* New York: Routledge, Chapman & Hall.

Gandhi, Mohandas, 1927, *An Autobiography,* Ahmedabad: Navajivan Publishing House.

Georgescu-Roegen, Nicholas, 1954, "Choice, Expectations and Measurability," *Quarterly Journal of Economics* 68:4 (November), pp. 503-34.

Hamilton, Alexander, 1982, *Federalist Papers,* New York: Bantam

Hession, Charles, 1986, "E. F. Schumacher as Heir to Keynes' Mantle," *Review of Social Economy* (April), pp. 1-25.

Hobson, John A., 1901, *The Social Problem,* London: Nisbet.

__________, [1909] 1969, *The Industrial System: An Inquiry into Earned and Unearned Income,* New York: Augustus M. Kelley.

__________, [1914] 1968, *Work and Wealth: A Human Valuation,* New York: Augustus M. Kelley.

__________, [1922] 1981, *Incentives in the New Industrial Order,* Wesport, Connecticut: Hyperion Press.

__________, 1929, *Economics and Ethics,* London: D.C. Heath.

_________, [1866] 1938, *Confessions of an Economic Heretic,* New York: Macmillan Co.

Huq, A. M., 1985, "Welfare Criteria in Gandhian Economics," reprinted in R. Diwan and M. Lutz, *Essays in Gandhian Economics,* New Delhi: Gandhi Peace Foundation.

Jeffrey, R., 1974, "Preferences Among Preferences," *Journal of Philosophy* LXXI:13, pp. 377-91.

Kadish, 1990, "Rewriting the 'Confessions': Hobson and the Extension Movement" in Michael Freeden, ed., 1990, *Reappraising J. A. Hobson,* New York: Routledge, Chapman & Hall, pp. 137-66.

Leibenstein, Harvey, 1979, "A Branch of Economics Is Missing: Micro-Micro Theory," *Journal of Economic Literature* XVII (June), pp. 495-96.

Lutz, Mark A, 1993, "Cardinal Issues in the Future of Social Economics: A Humanistic View," *Review of Social Economy* 51:4 (Winter), pp. 455-75.

_________, 1993, "The Utility of Multiple Utility," *Economics and Philosophy* 9:1 (April), pp. 145-54.

_________, 1995, "Centering Social Economics on Human Dignity," *Review of Social Economy* 52, pp. 1-24.

_________, 1995, "Doubt and Competition" in Ed O'Boyle, ed., *Essays in Social Economics,* London: Routledge.

Lutz, Mark A., and Kenneth Lux, 1979, *The Challenge of Humanistic Economics,* Menlo Park, California: Benjamin Cummings.

_________, 1988, *Humanistic Economics: The New Challenge,* New York: The Bootstrap Press.

Lux, Kenneth, and Mark A. Lutz, 1986, "Economic Psychology: The Humanistic Perspective" in A. J. MacFadyen, ed., *Economic Psychology,* New York: New Holland, pp. 383-424.

Madan, G. R, 1966, *Economic Thinking in India,* Delhi: Chand Publishing Co.

Maslow, Abraham, 1962, *Motivation and Personality,* New York: Harper & Row.

_________, 1968, *Toward a Psychology of Being*, New York: Van Nostrand Reinhold.

Myrdal, Gunnar, 1972, *Against the Stream*, New York: Random House.

Pheby, John, ed., 1994, *J. A. Hobson after Fifty Years: Free Thinker of the Social Sciences*, New York: St. Martin's Press.

Rhoads, Steven, 1985, *The Economist's View of the World*, Cambridge: Cambridge University Press.

Robbins, Lionel, [1932] 1984, *An Essay on the Nature and Significance of Economic Science*, London: MacMillan.

Ruskin, John, 1880, "Letters on Political Economy" in his *Arrows of the Chace*, vol. 2. Boston: Colonial Press.

_________, [1864] 1988, *Unto This Last*, New York: John Wiley & Son.

Schumacher, E. F., 1973, *Small is Beautiful*, New York: Harper & Row.

Sen, Amartya, 1977, "Rational Fool: A Critique of the Behavioral Foundations of Economic Theory," *Philosophy and Public Affairs*, no. 6, pp. 317-44.

Sherbourne, James C., [1827] 1972, *John Ruskin or the Ambiguity of Affluence*, Cambridge, Massachusetts: Harvard University Press.

Simonde de Sismondi, J. C. L., [1826] 1994, *New Principles of Political Economy*, 2nd edition, New Brunswick, New Jersey: Transaction Publishers.

Smith, Adam, [1776] 1973, *The Wealth of Nations*, New York: McGraw-Hill.

Tawney, R. H., 1920, *The Acquisitive Society*, New York: Harcourt, Brace & Co.

_________, 1931, *Equality*, London: Allen & Unwin.

Terrill, R, 1973, *R. H. Tawney and His Times*, Cambridge, Massachusetts: Harvard University Press.

Wahba, M., and L. Bridwell, 1976, "Maslow Reconsidered: A Review of Research on the Need Hierarchy Theory" in *Organizational Behavior and Human Performance*, pp. 212-40.

III

BEYOND ECONOMISM: TOWARD A THEORY OF ANOTHER DEVELOPMENT

Björn Hettne

The Crisis in Development Theory

Throughout the 1980s, the field of development studies was challenged by a fundamentalist, monodisciplinary trend in the academic world, and a neoconservative trend in politics. Both trends reduce the "development problem" in a highly simplistic way, thus neglecting the insights achieved in the field during three decades of empirical and theoretical explorations into previous unknown territories.

Some looked upon this as an "impasse" in theorizing on development[1] and a search for new directions "beyond the impasse" started.[2] Others have gone to the extreme of declaring the whole development project an "intellectual ruin," referring primarily to what can be described as "the mainstream paradigm" or "actually existing development." The argument is that at a time when development has evidently failed, "it has been of paramount importance to liberate ourselves from its dominion over our minds."[3]

The field of development studies experiences *internal* challenges as well, because many established truths and conventional wisdoms have been questioned and abandoned in the course of its development. This has given rise to a wave of self-criticism and erosion of confidence. To quote Robert Chambers, "it is alarming how wrong we were, and how sure we were that we were right."[4] In another retrospective essay, John Toye makes the observation that real development, as opposed to the expectations of leading development economists of the 1950s and 1960s, contains a strong element of surprise not at all accounted for in development theory.[5]

Put differently, the pioneering years were thus also a time of optimism, as Paul Streeten observes: "It is not easy to convey, in the present atmosphere of gloom, boredom and indifference, surrounding discussions of development problems, what an exciting time of fervent these early years were."[6]

Many examples can be given of this atmosphere of gloom, most of them referring specifically to development economics. In an essay entitled "The Rise and Fall of Development Economics" Albert Hirschman complains:

> Articles and books are still being produced. But as an observer and longtime participant I cannot help feeling that the old liveliness is no longer there, that new ideas are ever harder to come by and that the field is not adequately reproducing itself.[7]

Undoubtedly a certain amount of cynicism is creeping into the field. Any rethinking, however, is in itself a healthy phenomenon, if established concepts and theories are found to be deceptive and irrelevant. I personally think that the debate in development studies during the last decade has been fruitful and vital from the point of view of breaking through deceptive concepts and theories. The problem is where to go from here.

The reorientations in development theory go in different directions. In my view, the search for an alternative theory will have two major characteristics: it will go beyond economism, and it will be normative. Economics is an aspect of human behavior usually concerned with individual maximization and problems of choice in situations of scarcity. In spite of all interdisciplinary attempts, the economistic bias has marked the whole project of "development studies" and led it to the crisis referred to above. The old and almost forgotten ideas of Karl Polanyi will be relied on in pursuing this point.

To search for alternatives is to be normative since there can be no "positive" studies of what does not yet exist. This trend is summarized in the concept of "Another Development," popularized by the 1975 Dag Hammarskjöld report "What Now," prepared on the occasion of the Seventh Special Session of the United Nations General Assembly. Subsequent contributions can be found in the magazine *Development Dialogue*. Sometimes the concept "Alternative Development" is preferred, as in the dossiers of the International Foundation for Development Alternatives (IFDA). The journal *Alternatives*, published by the Institute for World Order (New York), and the Centre for the Study of Developing Societies (Delhi) have also contributed significantly to this trend.[8]

On this point, I draw on the normative trend in development theory during the 1970s, interrupted by the new realism of the 1980s. This chapter is thus devoted to contributions which deal with development not in terms of how it actually takes place but rather how it *should* take place. Normative theories are important, since visions of the good society influence actual development, to the extent that development is affected by political actions and human will, rather than being a "natural history." In the world of "actually existing development," sixty percent of the world's population belongs to a periphery of stagnation, marginalization, and poverty. This is "the true drama to which an alternative development responds."[9] It is the perspective of the excluded. Alternative development is a cry for visibility, participation, and justice.

In what follows, we shall first analyze the alternative approach from a metatheoretical perspective in order to grasp its significance and avoid a premature dismissal of it as utopianism. Even if it is true what Samir Amin has said[10] about the green currents being symptoms rather than solutions to the crisis, they will become more and more practically important as the crisis deepens. Therefore, we shall try to put these currents in an historical and sociological perspective. After that, we shall summarize the emerging approach in terms of five major themes: egalitarian development, self-reliant development, sustainable development, territorial development, and ethnodevelopment. These themes sum up the criticism against the conventional development paradigm, and to my mind they also provide foundations for an alternative theory.

The Roots of Anotherness

From a positivist point of view, the concept of Another Development is a development ideology without relevance for understanding development as it actually takes place. It must be recognized that whatever development which is occurring today is in fact more consistent with the conventional modernization paradigm than with the set of ideals implied in what we, for lack of a better term, call Anotherness. Why, then, this interest in Another Development?

One way of explaining this ideological trend would be to look upon it primarily as a phenomenon of overdevelopment rather than underdevelopment. The paradox to be explained is why the concept of Another Development, implying small-scale solutions, ecological concerns, popular participation, and the establishment of community, have met with relatively more enthusiasm in the rich countries.

The reasons for the lack of interest in the poor countries are not far to seek. Small may be beautiful, but it does not entail *power* (social power, state power, military power). The masses in the Third World will never reach the material standard of living at present maintained in the West, and by Third World elites, but some urban middle classes in some areas may, at least theoretically, achieve this. Consequently, those chosen to become "modern" do not intend to be fooled into some populist *cul-de-sac*.

Why then this interest for Another Development in the North? One answer to this would be that the collective consciousness of the industrially advanced countries now is going through a process of transformation. Let us suggest a framework within which this transformation can be analyzed.

Western development thinking can be analyzed as a dialectical process between a *Mainstream* (or dominant development paradigm) and its *Counterpoint*. Mainstream development thinking can be analyzed along a continuum running between two ideological antipoles, "socialism" (i.e., state interventionism) vs. "capitalism" (i.e., the rule of the market). Much of the political debate in the West has been concerned with state vs. market, and the relative merits of development strategies within the Mainstream Western tradition: the liberal model, the state capitalist strategy, the Soviet model, Keynesianism, and now we have to add neoliberalism. The development strategies are varieties of the basic paradigm, expressing different historical possibilities and constraints. They vary mainly with regard to means, that is, the relative role of state and market, but as far as ends are concerned, they are basically all similar.

Opposed and dialectically related to the predominant development paradigm, there has been a Counterpoint, articulating antimodern interests in different historical contexts. The Counterpoint protest was increasingly reduced to a more or less ideological phenomenon, as the modern complex was institutionalized in structures, such as the state and the bureaucracy, the industrial system, the urban system, the market system, the techno-scientific system, and the military-industrial complex.

A society organized according to Counterpoint ideals would, in negation of the modern complex, be *physiocratic*, in the sense that the earth and the natural resources constitute the ultimate precondition for human existence; *ultrademocratic*, in the sense that people exercise control over their own situation; and *structurally undifferentiated*, in the sense that the division of labor will be located within rather than between individuals. This tradition is rooted in the "Gemeinschaft" type of society, whereas the dominant thinking in the West rationalizes the "Gesellschaft" model. Below, various historical manifestations of the Counterpoint are briefly summarized:

- *Conservative romanticism* was a reaction against the nineteenth-century bourgeois society, articulating the interests of a threatened traditional elite. However, the criticism of industrialism had a universal character, transcending the more immediate situation of class struggle because of the wider relevance of this criticism. It is that particular dimension of conservatism which is of interest here, not the European counter-revolution in general. In daily parlance, conservatism means being against change, but it would be equally appropriate to think of conservatism as preserving what is valuable from the point of view of certain values. When the planet is threatened we all tend to become conservative.

- *Utopian Socialism* was a complex and at the same time rather inconsistent ideological trend. It is recognized as a distinct ideology simply due to the fact that Marx and Engels described the works of the three major proponents (Saint-Simon, Owen, Fourier) as examples of "pre-scientific socialism." One could regard Saint-Simon as fairly "Mainstream" because of his association with Comte's ideas, his firm belief in Progress, and his worship of "le système industriel." Owen's strong commitment to small-scale organization makes him a truer representative of the Counterpoint, but on the other hand he was in fact an industrialist who believed in industrialism. Fourier, who criticized the dullness of industrial production and stressed the importance of "passions," comes closer to the Counterpoint. It is significant that his contribution is the only one to have experienced a revival in our time.[11]

- *Anarchism* was above all a reaction against statism in its various dimensions but, like romanticism, it favored a decentralized and multifaceted social structure which made individual self-realization possible. Like the utopian socialists the anarchists were, to say the least, a mixed lot, many of them rather eccentric. In fact some anarchist traditions were very close to early radical liberalism, whereas others tended to be more collectivist. Of course, this had much to do with specific national patterns of culture—Russian anarchism, for instance, tending toward anarcho-communism, American toward anarcho-capitalism. As a political movement, anarchism was particularly strong in Spain where the Civil War, and what followed after it, put an end to this peculiar tradition. Modern anarchism retains its hatred of the centralized state but has also discovered ecology.[12] Ecologism stands out as a new synthesis of traditional anarchist thinking about the necessity for decentralized social, economic, and political organization.

- *Populism* has been a contested concept,[13] tending to create confusion due to its different connotations in different political contexts. I would regard the Russian populism as the classical case, which has made its reappearance in contemporary Third World contexts.[14] It is an extremely well-articulated populist ideology, mainly because it attracted a number of Russian intellectuals in the late nineteenth century. The narodniks argued against industrialism as a large-scale and centralized form of production but did not oppose all kinds of technological progress.The narodniks were furthermore antistatists, which is natural in view of the form Russian industrialization took. Their views on the state, however, contained many nuances.[15] Perhaps their most interesting contribution to the Counterpoint was the criticism of the idea (and ideal) of division of labor. They refused to accept the sacrifices in terms of human personality recognized but considered unavoidable by both Adam Smith and Emile Durkheim to get a more differentiated complex and efficient society.[16]

- *The Green Ideology* can be seen as a synthesis of neopopulist and neoanarchist ideas, which were revived in the 1960s forming part of the new left movement in the U.S. and Europe, later to merge with ecology and peace movements. These ideas bear a certain resemblance to the classical populism and anarchism in urging for a community ("Gemeinschaft") and in their distaste of industrial civilization. However, there are significant new elements of which the most prominent are ecological consciousness, encompassing the total global ecological system, and a strong commitment to a just world order. The historical movements were more parochial.

As the Green movements transform themselves to parties (or exploit party politics as one arena of struggle), there is a need for a new "green" economics which, as Paul Ekins points out,[17] stands out as a Counterpoint to the assumptions of formal economics:

- Much formal economic activity is harmful and much is the wasteful result of having to remedy those harms.

- The most important work in society is done outside the formal economy.
- Money can be a useful economic means but is a totally inappropriate economic end.
- The local economy matters far more to people than the national aggregate.

The Green critics of industrial society are of middle-class origin and it may be as true of them as what Marx once said about the utopian socialists: "they all want the impossible, namely the conditions of bourgeois existence without the necessary consequences of those conditions."[18] As a matter of fact, this is true about all the historical manifestations of the Counterpoint discussed above. The antisystemic articulations of protest are typically parochial, rejecting specific historical class interests. The criticism as such may nevertheless be more universally valid, transcending class positions and informing later protest movements in the continuous resistance against an inhuman system.

In fact, the old Russian populism, contemporary Third World populism, and the present upsurge of green movements in the West may be seen as an example of intellectual interaction between "developed" and "developing" societies. It is a most significant fact that there exists one intellectual trend which is rooted both in Western and non-Western traditions, and that this type of development thinking is drawing on contributions from both Western and Third World thinkers. The Green perspective has the potential of bridging the North-South dualism in development thinking and becoming truly transnational. Since market exchange is the dominant mode of economic integration on the world level, it is not unreasonable to expect worldwide antisystemic movements in support of specific communities.[19]

In the case of the Counterpoint, I cannot identify such established, visible *structures* as industrialism, urbanism, professionalism, militarism, and other Mainstream structures. Since the Counterpoint is an emerging phenomenon, the supporting structures are also emerging—only partly visible and partly understood.

It is obvious that a certain mode of institutionalization corresponds to a certain set of ideas, a social paradigm. The Mainstream development paradigm is rooted in an institutional structure with manifestations such as industrialism, statism, and professionalism, whereas the Counterpoint has expressed itself mainly on the ideological level. This is precisely the weakness of the contemporary manifestations of the Counterpoint which lacks an institutional base from which "modernity" can be opposed. The inherent attractiveness of the Counterpoint, whatever it may be, does not provide a sufficient base for social change in the desired direction. Only in the wake of traumatic failures of Mainstream development—various "development catastrophes" in the poor world and technological setbacks (the Challengers and Chernobyls to come) in the rich—will provide the pedagogical showcases for rethinking.

The Substantive Approach

We now come to the theoretical and methodological problem of seeing in society, not only what exists (positivism) but what could exist (normativism) and what is emerging (futurism).

Mainstream social science is subordinated under the "Zweckrationalität" of the present society. Theories based on the "Wertrationalität" of human survival are consequently dismissed as non-scientific and too value-loaded to be accepted in the academic world. It is a world which has its own modes of institutionalization, recruitment, socialization, negative sanctions, and rewards. Mainstream economics, for instance, is an expression of the "Zweckrationalität" of market exchange, and the major alternative—Marxist theory—is historically linked to state intervention and the command economy.

Any third approach—"green" economics in contradistinction to "blue" and "red"—is hard to discover in contemporary social science for the simple reason that it hardly exists in the real world of modern economic life, and this fact, then, becomes an argument against taking any notice of it. Positive social science deals with what *is*, not with what *ought* to be. This is a dilemma for economists trying to develop a New Economics.[20]

One way out is to marry history and social science, as has been discovered and rediscovered repeatedly. A major contribution in this respect is the substantive approach of Karl Polanyi. Some of his ideas will be drawn upon here in an attempt to relate the Mainstream-Counterpoint contradiction to the institutional level. The fundamental problem is to understand the *substantive* character of market exchange, and what possible substitutes there are in the existing modes of the institutionalization of economic life.[21]

The concept of "market" has two meanings, one concrete, namely, the *market place*; the other abstract, referring to the *market system*. Market places are a more or less universal phenomenon, as we can learn from history and anthropology. They all operate in accordance with the same basic logic, regardless of how the society at large has chosen to institutionalize economic life. The prices of goods exchanged on the market fluctuate according to supply and demand conditions, and determine "profits" of different commodities in the short run and resource allocation between production of different commodities ("investment") in the long run.

The crucial point is that societies completely dominated by the market principle, which implies that also land, capital, and labor have been commodified, is a recent phenomenon. Historically there has been two other possible economic integration mechanisms: *reciprocity* and *redistribution*.

The former refers to socially embedded forms of exchange in small-scale symmetric communities; the latter to politically determined distribution in stratified societies, marked by a center-periphery structure. Both modes of distribution were undermined by the growth of market exchange. However, as the market principle penetrated all spheres of human activity, thereby eroding social structures, redistribution had to be reinvented in order to provide people with the necessary social protection. This was the origin of the welfare state. Thus, modern industrial societies are typically distinguished by a market-redistribution mix. Depending on the nature of this mix, we call some "capitalist" and other "socialist." In neither system did reciprocity play any role in economic transactions outside the family.

In the present economic crisis, there are those who tend to rely on redistribution and the public sector (the Keynesians), whereas others look to the market principle for guidance (the neoliberals). These are the two Mainstream solutions. There is, however, also a Counterpoint solution stressing the role of symmetric exchange and new forms of cooperation at the local level. This solution presupposes a revitalization of the reciprocity principle.

At present, there are signs that the legal and illegal informal economy is growing in importance. To a large extent, it is due to various attempts at surviving in a situation of economic stagnation, but there are also examples of more positive and ideologically conscious efforts to apply the principle of reciprocity to new systems of production.

In the long historical perspective, the market principle has gradually assumed more importance at the cost of the two competing principles, particularly redistribution. The latter overtook the principle of reciprocity, which lost its relevance as larger political formations emerged. This contradiction between the redistribution and market principles can also be seen as a competition between the polity and the economy. The typical situation in economic history seems to have been "politics in command."

Capitalism meant an enormous strengthening of both state and market at the cost of the autonomy of local communities. In spite of the state/market contradiction—*the* ideological controversy of our time—both these institutions were intimately related during the rise of capitalism. Under mercantilism, national markets were created through the subordination of local economic systems under absolute state power. At the same time, the foundation was laid for a world market controlled from Europe and the new nation states which typically became colonial states. The strongest of them all was Great Britain, which in fact was hegemonic enough to allow the market principle to determine economic transactions on the world level and to force other states to apply free trade principles, at least until the crisis of the 1870s.

The decades before this crisis as well as the decades before the crisis of the 1930s were periods of more or less complete market dominance. Economic Man was thus born in an institutional setting where men and women themselves were commodified. The market society was a utopia in the making but, as happens with utopias, reality overtook it in the form of recurrent crises. Politics took command in the form of fascism, communism, and welfareism (social-democratic reformism based on Keynesian economics). In the post-war world, welfareism was established in most of Western Europe and communism in Eastern Europe as two varieties of the Mainstream paradigm. Both systems are today in crisis. The Green current is one of the responses.

The new trends, the future relevance of which we can only speculate about, are no longer confined to the ideological level. There is a structural counterpart at the more concrete socio-economic level in the emergence of "the informal economy."[22]

There are several synonyms or partly overlapping concepts: unofficial economy, underground economy, parallel economy, black economy, hidden economy, informal sector, etc. The proliferation of concepts indicates a phenomenon that is relatively unexplored and it is uncertain if the concepts always refer to the same phenomenon. It exists in both in North and South, both in East and West, but there must obviously be some crucial differences involved here. What makes it possible to deal with them in the same context is simply that they are responses to crises in the three "worlds," in the system of market exchange as well as in the system of redistribution.

In a Third World context, the formal/informal distinction was first used in the 1972 ILO Report on Kenya. No less than seven criteria were used: easy as opposed to difficult entry to the economic system; reliance on indigenous rather than foreign resources; family in contrast to corporate ownership; small as against large scale of operations; labor-intensive and adapted versus capital-intensive and imported technologies; informally rather than formally acquired skills; and unregulated and competitive as opposed to protected markets.

Since this approach is difficult to translate into operational terms, in practice simplified dichotomies are employed, such as small/large, self-employment/wage employment, registered/unregistered, and the like. The problem with these is that the two resulting sectors are not qualitatively distinct due to the variety of transitional forms between the two poles.[23] This indicates that the distinction is a transitory phenomenon, perhaps toward a "new economics."

In the industrialized world ("first" and "second"), informal economy has even more complex connotations. In a capitalist market system, "informal" can imply also production, distribution, and consumption networks that emerge outside, or at least on the periphery, of the market nexus. In planned socialist economies, "informal" would rather refer to the non-regulated economic activities that usually take the form of market exchange, but *nota bene* in the substantive rather than the formal sense of the word—exchange in the *market place* not in the *market system.*

A system of market places is qualitatively different from a market system and perfectly compatible with the more balanced pattern of integrative principles which must be the solution to the present crisis. However, the institutionalization of new economic patterns will hardly take place without political interventions. The state no longer has the key, as was the case in the previous crisis, neither has it the same legitimacy. It nevertheless remains a potential crucial actor in putting social limits to market exchange and permitting the emerging reciprocity structures to operate, even if this means stepping down from its role of omnipotence.

The self-regulating market was a political arrangement. The maintenance of this system on the world level has presupposed strong, hegemonic states. In order to protect less developed societies against the market, the state grew stronger and stronger, until the societies needed protection not only from the market but also from the state. The state must be distinguished from the society, and the re-embedding of the economy in the society presupposes not only a reduced role for the market but also for the state. This implies the rise of reciprocity. It also implies a new form of politics.

Marc Nerfin associates the "new politics" with what he calls *The Third System.* Thus we can speak of the new political movements as "Third System Politics," a system of power representing people who act through voluntary institutions and associations. It is the main bearer of new values and visions and thus the most important source of change. The First System is a system of power comprised by the governing structures of terrirorial states, i.e., the state system, whereas the Second System is associated with economic power: the market and market forces such as corporations and banks.[24]

Egalitarian Development

No development strategy explicitly aims for inegalitarian development, but most conventional strategies implicitly assume inequality (social or regional) as a necessary price for growth. In contrast, egalitarian strategies give a higher priority to redistribution than to growth. One such strategy is the Basic Needs Approach (BNA).

In the early 1970s, it was widely agreed that economic growth did not necessarily eliminate poverty. Rather the growth that actually took place in most developing countries went together with increases in absolute poverty. In response to this, the Basic Needs Approach favored a *direct* approach, i.e., a straight relationship between development strategy and elimination of poverty, rather than waiting for the "trickling down" effects of growth.[25]

The diverse background of the various elements constituting the BNA, and the resultant complexity of the concept, explains some of the confusion that has characterized the debate on the approach, as well as the concept as such. Thus a first distinction should be made between the discussion centered on the viability of the strategy and the more philosophical debate on human needs, partly stimulated by the strategy discussion.

In what follows, we will be more concerned with the general basic needs (or human needs) discussion. Here a distinction has been made between, on the one hand, a universal and objective interpretation of "needs" and, on the other, an interpretation that is subjective and relativistic.[26] The former school defines human needs as something that applies to all human beings and that could be quantified and measured; the latter takes human needs to be historically relative and therefore to be seen in the context of specific social systems. The first school refers to those needs that in all societies are necessary for physical reproduction, whereas the second approach has more to do with what makes life worth living in different cultures. In the first view, basic needs are quantifiable and a universally valid definition is possible. According to the second view, basic needs is a qualitative concept that partly falls in the realm of philosophy and religion. It covers also transcendental values and is relative with respect to different cultures. A universal definition is therefore impossible.

The first approach belongs to the positive; the second to the normative approach in development theory. The former is closely related to the redistribution with growth strategy of the World Bank, one important difference being that it implies channeling particular resources to particular people.[27] In this context of Another Development, we are primarily concerned with the second approach but, as will become clear, the two interpretations are not easily separated in practice.

The Basic Needs concept conforms to a general tendency that can be noted in development theory; key concepts such as "unified approach," "self-reliance," "ecodevelopment," and "basic needs" tend to take on more and more dimensions and end up as full-edged development philosophies. This naturally irritates down-to-earth planners, trained in positivist social sciences. The theoretical polarization today is perhaps not so much between liberals and Marxists, as between positivists and normativists (or between Mainstream and Counterpoint tendencies). According to the Another Development School, basic needs refers to ways of life rather than the preconditions for survival.

Manfred Max-Neef,[28] working in the Another Development tradition, makes the important distinction between *needs* and *satisfiers*, a distinction that bridges the universal and the specific in the human needs debate. For instance, housing and food are satisfiers of the need of subsistence; education is a satisfier of the need of understanding. From this point of view, fundamental human needs are finite, few, and classifiable. They are also the same in all cultures. What changes (over time and through cultures) is the form or the means by which these needs are satisfied. Following Mallman of the Bariloche Foundation in Argentina, Max-Neef lists examples of needs that in his view form a system: subsistence, protection, affection, understanding, participation, leisure, creation, identity, and freedom. The satisfiers are infinite, but failure to make the distinction between needs and satisfiers will only lead to a "cosmetic improvement of the economistic view of development."

It is interesting to note that the debate on basic needs, starting in the Third World and then subject to conservative reabsorption in the West, now creates some suspicion in its place of origin. It is thus very common to look upon the BNA as an alleviationist strategy, a concoction by enemies of the NIEO in the industrial countries.[29]

In the early 1980s, the BNA had already lost its appeal, as had the NIEO some years earlier, and in the 1981 Cancun top-level meeting on development, quite different (but not really new) signals were given. Now the relevance of the "simple" BNA is rather to provide arguments against a regression to a development philosophy of the 1950s, a return which is in fact favored also by the ruling elites in the Third World. The "complex" BNA will nevertheless remain an important component in the Another Development paradigm.

Self-Reliant Development

Another key concept, forming part of the normative trend during the 1970s but later removed from the center of the debate, was Self-Reliance (SR). The popularity of this approach was obviously a corollary to the breakthrough of the dependence paradigm, self-reliance being the antithesis to dependence. This approach had earlier been discussed in the context of individual national experiences, such as India in the days of Mahatma Gandhi, Tanzania after the Arusha declaration, and China under Mao Zedong. The concept of self-reliance was brought to the international scene by the non-aligned countries at their 1970 meeting in Lusaka, to be further elaborated at their 1972 conference in Georgetown. Thus SR emerged as a strategic concept in the international discussion just before the concept of NIEO, which in contrast provided a perspective of international cooperation rather than withdrawal.

In this way, two perspectives—one stressing more symmetric

relations and mutual benefits from trade and cooperation, the other reliance on one's own resources—converged in the international debate on development in the mid-1970s. Self-reliance should, according to the NIEO philosophy, not be pushed too far in case a more just international economic order really began to take shape. On the other hand, it was something to fall back on if the rich world refused to cooperate. This more cautious attitude may be found in the so-called Cocoyoc Declaration, adopted by the participants in a 1974 UNEP-UNCTAD symposium in Mexico. A typical passage from this document reads:

> We believe that one basic strategy of development will have to be increased national self-reliance. It does not mean autarchy. It implies mutual benefits from trade and co-operation and a fairer redistribution of resources satisfying the basic needs. It does mean self-confidence, reliance primarily on one's own resources, human and natural, and the capacity of autonomous goal-setting and decision-making. It excludes dependence on outside influences and powers that can be converted into political pressure.

This formulation, which clearly emphasizes the potential value of trade and cooperation, was restricted to *national* self-reliance. Furthermore, it emphasized the economic and political aspects of the strategy. As was indicated above, the approach can be widened into a fulledged and more radical development strategy, providing guidelines for almost all fields of action on different levels of society.[30]

The rationale for self-reliance as a comprehensive development strategy has been summarized by Johan Galtung in the following hypotheses:

- Priorities will change towards production for basic needs for those most in need.
- Mass participation is ensured.
- Local factors are utilized much better.
- Creativity is stimulated.
- There will be more compatibility with local conditions.

- There will be much more diversity of development.
- There will be less alienation.
- Ecological balance will be more easily attained.
- Important externalities are internalized or given to neighbours at the same level.
- Solidarity with others at the same level gets a solid basis.
- Ability to withstand manipulation due to trade dependency increases.
- The military defence capability of the country increases.
- Today's center and periphery are brought on a more equal footing.[31]

This list of the benefits of self-reliance contains a certain flavor of utopianism and Galtung is at pains to point out that the thirteen rationales should be seen as hypotheses about positive effects.

Self-reliance is not merely an economic policy; if consistently applied, it implies fundamental structural transformations. This becomes clear as soon as one leaves the level of rhetoric and penetrates further into the implications of the concept. Since a complete withdrawal from the international economic order is a realistic option for very few countries, our subsequent discussion will be in terms of *qualifications* of the concept, focusing upon the problems of *size, level,* and *degree.*

The problem of size in economic development has been neglected in both liberal and socialist development theory. The recommendations of the development strategies implied in these two orthodoxies are either to specialize and reap the benefits from comparative advantages and economies of scale, or to develop toward national autarchy through the establishment of heavy industries, making the maximum use of the domestic market.

Original contributions to the discussion on size and self-reliance have been a theoretical field of special concern for Caribbean economists, which possibly could be accounted for by geographical factors. One major contribution to the analysis of the policy options open to small countries was that of W. G. Demas who saw *structural transformation* as the essential ingredient of self-sustained economic growth.[32] As such a transformation—implying among other things a reduction of dualism between the productivity of different sectors, elimination of subsistence production, and the establishment of a national market—is hard to achieve in a small economy, Demas advocated integration of the region in a common market system. Such a policy (the creation of CARIFTA—the Caribbean Free Trade Association) was not very successful, however, for reasons largely connected with the problem of dependence. Clive Thomas[33] therefore rejected regional integration under capitalism as viable, and instead developed a strategy for planned transition to socialism with special reference to small dependent economies. In accordance with the dependency school, he considered the essence of underdevelopment to be the externally induced cumulative process of divergence of the pattern of resource use, domestic demand, and the needs of the broad mass of the community. Thus the fundamental objective of a strategy for self-reliance must be to revert this process and to achieve a *convergence* of domestic resource use and domestic demand.

The convergence of resource use and demand is the first ironclad law of transformation, the second being the convergence of needs with demand. The strategy of convergence should not only lead to a shift toward production for basic needs, but should also rationalize agriculture through the spread of industrialization techniques and shift the balance in favor of industry. There is no conflict between industry and agriculture since "industrialization is a social process necessary to enable society to master the material environment in the service of its own needs."[34]

A strategy of comprehensive planning requires the domestic production of those *basic materials* that are required as primary inputs for the manufacture of the *basic goods* of the community. It is necessary to ensure that these basic materials are substantially derived from domestic resources. This constitutes the necessary condition for the growth of an *indigenously oriented technology*. The scope for structural transformation will be heavily dependent on the resource configuration in each and every society. Economies of scale (at present completely misguiding) should be judged from the point of view of a *critical minimum* rather than idealized optimum levels.

Thomas' strategy is *national*. SR should, however, not be mixed up with national autarchy, but should be seen as a precondition for genuine cooperation based upon the principle of symmetry. This utopian image necessitates self-reliance on a number of societal levels. We may distinguish between *local, national,* and *regional* levels. It is with reference to the local and regional level that we find new theoretical contributions, whereas national self-reliance is an old political goal.

An ambitious form of regionalization is the Third World *collective* level, but this project seems less realistic today. The implementation of the NIEO would go a long way to achieve Third World collective self-reliance, but there is no guarantee that this would be a better world for the bulk of the population in developing countries.

There is, of course, nothing wrong with trade union action on the part of Third World countries in order to impose concessions on the industrial countries. Higher level self-reliance is, however, not sufficient for lower level self-reliance:

> Given the present world structure the center-periphery gradients are all there to be used by the strongest among today's poorer countries. Thus, regional self-reliance might protect the Third World against dependence on the First and Second worlds (and for that reason be strongly resented by them), but would not offer any protection against penetration by the Brazils, the Irans and the Indias, and (still to come) the Nigerias. The sub-imperial connections of today may become the raw material for forging the imperial connections of tomorrow.[35]

A certain degree of state power may be a precondition for self-reliance on the local level: some economic planning will always be necessary even in an extremely decentralized economy, the national center should provide a good infrastructure for any cooperation between the local units, the state may have to intervene in order to correct imbalances in resource endowments, and the local units must be protected from external penetration, for example, by the multinationals.

Thus, in order to achieve self-reliance in the radical sense of the word, distinguished from the traditional preoccupation with merely economic and military strength of the nation-state, it is necessary to combine all three levels "with the development of human beings everywhere as the goal."[36]

Most spokesmen for the strategy of self-reliance emphasize that SR must not be confused with autarchy. Rather it is seen as a precondition for meaningful (i.e., symmetric) cooperation. This is implicit in our discussion on levels and size, but there is nevertheless reason to discuss the problem of *degree* more specifically.

To change an economic system from a dependent to a self-reliant one necessarily implies deep structural changes. Hence the emphasis on *participation* in strategies of SR. This will serve as a check on too dramatic crash programs for self-reliance which, if imposed on the people, tend to backlash on the government.

As was emphasized in the Dag Hammarskjöld report referred to above, a strategy of self-reliance will also necessitate selective participation in the international system: "Selective participation of Third World countries in the international system is a prerequisite for the application of new development strategies, for strengthening internal sovereignty and for reinforcing self-reliance."[37]

It is further underlined in the report that the concept of selective participation is a flexible one. Different conditions among Third World countries will require a variety of selections, not only by different countries but also by any country at different times. The only general guidelines that can be formulated are the following ones:

- There is a minimum degree of links required to sustain the development process.
- There is a maximum degree of links beyond which no effective sovereignty can be maintained.
- There are affirmative links which reinforce self-reliance.
- There are regressive links which weaken self-reliance.

It is a task of alternative development theory in the years to come to provide the necessary theoretical and empirical base for the *strategy of selective participation* with the purpose of promoting self-reliance on all levels: the local, the national, and the regional. This will require knowledge of the development process in individual countries and about the international context, a theory about which links are productive and which are counterproductive, and futuristic studies of the possible outcome of various counterstrategies which obviously will be undertaken by the dominant centers.

Sustainable Development

One fundamental incentive behind the current search for another development paradigm is the new environmental consciousness that emerged in the 1970s expressed in the report of the World Commission on Environment and Development: *Our Common Future.*[38] Consequently, this ecological orientation constitutes an important dimension in Another Development.

First to be discussed in this section is the recent preoccupation with scarcity in the social sciences, a concept which fits badly with the orthodox paradigm. Secondly, we ask how well prepared the social sciences are for dealing with these issues. Thirdly, the problem of the relationship between development and environment is explained.

Modern growth and modernization theory has been relatively unconcerned with the problem of *scarcity*. This optimistic streak is different from the classics for whom the problem of scarcity was a major preoccupation in political economy, not only in the Ricardian (relative) but also in the Malthusian (absolute) sense. That most of the pessimistic prophecies of the "dismal science" fortunately turned out to be wrong, or at least exaggerated, allowed later generations of economists (the exception of Jevons and the "coal question" proves the rule) to be much more relaxed on this issue. The warnings came from other quarters, whereas typically the economists have been trying to maintain an optimistic spirit.[39]

In Mainstream Marxist theory, scarcity is socially determined by the shackles imposed on the forces of production by the capitalist system, whereas communism is defined by an *abundance* which removes conflict over resource allocation and eliminates the role of economics.[40]

To point out this bias in Marxism, which by the way is subject to some rethinking in the era of "new scarcity," is not to deny that scarcity takes a particular and probably more severe form under capitalism where misery and affluence coexist in an outrageous fashion.

We are told that in a transition from a capitalist to a socialist ecology the mastery of nature should:

- Benefit all people and not just a small ruling class;
- Maintain the dialectical balance of natural ecology in harmony with human needs; and
- Be qualified by a theoretical understanding and an aesthetic appreciation of nature.[41]

This kind of transition is yet to be seen.

However, absolute scarcity does exist and this necessarily implies "limits to growth."[42] The problem is what limits to what kind of growth, and in what time perspective. These crucial questions may have been unsatisfactorily answered until now, but that is certainly no reason to deny, suppress, or neglect the problem of scarcity.

The first alarm on the physical limits to growth was the 1972 report from the Club of Rome, which then set the framework for the discussion in the 1970s, much of which happened to be highly critical of the report. Perhaps the obsession with physical limits, implying a sudden apocalyptic end of the world, was its main weakness. The *fact* of relative scarcity will, of course, make itself felt in a number of ways long before a society approaches any absolute limits. Some of the resultant changes may relieve the scarcity problem through technological innovations, others will aggravate it through intensive competition and political/military struggle on various levels of the world system.

Recently the relationship between environmental degradation and conflict has drawn the attention of researchers and activists. For instance, an Earthscan report[43] argues that diminishing natural resources have become an important cause of violent human conflicts both between states and within states (riots, military coups, and revolutions).

The relationship as such is obvious since the changing environment provides the context in which varying types of conflicts emerge, but the actual cause-effect problem has not been the subject of systematic research. The problem of environmental refugees in Africa, the Indian subcontinent, Central America, and the Caribbean shows the undeniable connection between environment, conflict, and security.

So far the experiences suggest that the marriage between ecology and the social sciences does not come about easily. Is there some hidden contradiction or incompatibility beween, for example, economic and ecological thinking? Kenneth Boulding identifies several similarities in their methodological approaches, but also significant differences:

> In their underlying value systems, ecologists often tend more toward Hindu or Buddhist values, in which man is seen as only part and perhaps not even a very important part of a vast natural order. Economics, however, emerged out of a civilization, part of Western Europe, that was created largely by Christianity and which regarded man as the measure of all things and the universe as existing mainly for his pleasure and salvation.[44]

The distinction in terms of values goes much deeper than a contrast between the economic and ecological disciplines. It corresponds to that dualism in Western thought we earlier referred to as Mainstream versus Counterpoint. Economics is certainly the most Mainstream of the social sciences but the difference is one of degree. It is true that in economics the controversy as to whether or not natural resource scarcity and economic growth are fundamentally antagonistic is a classical one. The dominant line of thought among economists, however, takes an optimistic view of technological progress and regards natural resources as a highly dynamic concept. The ecological movement is consequently placed within the realm of "metaphysical naturalism."[45]

In the late 1960s, however, there was an animated debate partly stimulated by E. J. Mishan's *The Costs of Economic Growth*.[46] As was pointed out by Mishan himself, one had to separate two questions: whether the continued economic growth is physically possible and whether it is desirable. If a specific future is undesirable, we do not have to bother about its viability. Both questions are, however, difficult to answer within the strict limits of economics.

As far as the possibility of future growth is concerned, we have to distinguish between the scarcity of natural resources in the physical sense, and the ecological or environmental functions that different ecosystems provide.[47] To understand when such functions are threatened, we need help from the ecologists.

Until recently the problem of interactions between ecology and society has been conspicuous by its absence from the other social sciences as well—with the exception of social anthropology, where the man/environment relationship and its ramifications have been more difficult to hide than in social sciences mainly dealing with industrial, functionally organized societies, and macro-structures. It is well known that anthropologists, generally in vain, have emphazised the local interests of populations in connection with dams or other large-scale constructions. "Progress" most often had its way.

However, rethinking has started in several social sciences. Political scientists like Karl Deutsch discovered *ecopolitics*: the political challenge produced by the growing interplay of man's economic activities and the environment.[48] This challenge is not only the concern of nation-states. Environmental interdependence transcends political borders, thereby increasing the importance of international actors and institutions.

Thus ecology also provided a new context for international relations, what Dennis Pirages has called "global ecopolitics."[49] The new scarcity, or the problem of planetary finality, poses new issues in world politics, reminding us of the basic oneness of the world from an ecological point of view. This also implies a normative bent in international relations theory: The *is* of power politics is being replaced by the *ought* of ecopolitics. Furthermore, there are now a vast range of actors apart from the states that create the substance of world politics which tends to be so much more than the "high politics" of national security.

One should expect spatially and resource-oriented disciplines like human geography to shoulder a particular responsibility in forging the ecosocial system and the issue of development into an analytical whole. Harold Brookfield, for example, has observed that development studies and the study of changes in man's use of environment together provide theoretical elements to be used in the task of generating a dynamic man/environment paradigm.[50]

The new discipline of human ecology, now emerging as a transdisciplinary field of training and research, could possibly contribute to such a paradigm, provided it is firmly established as a combined study of man living in two systems, the ecological and the social, held together by a high degree of interdependence.

Sustainability is a normative concept that has appeared in development theory as a consequence of the environmental concerns from the early 1970s and onwards. It is particularly associated with Lester Brown and the Worldwatch Institute,[51] and also stands out as a key concept in *Our Common Future*. The main message it carries is that neither the old nor any new international economic order would be viable unless the natural biological systems that underpin the global economy are preserved. This ecological imperative, in turn, calls for a redirection of the development process itself.[52]

Lester Brown underlined four problematic areas from the point of view of sustainability:

- *The Lagging Energy Transition.* Although the depressed world economy has made the development of energy demand less dramatic than projected, the transition to new sources of energy is still a necessity. Both nuclear energy and coal create sustainability problems of their own, and the development of renewable energy sources has proved to be a slow process.

- *The Deterioration of Major Biological Systems.* The deterioration of the four major biological systems—oceanic shoals, grasslands, forests, and croplands—is another serious problem, since their "carrying capacities" are exceeded. Thus not only non-renewable but also renewable resource bases are shrinking.

- *The Threat of Climate Modification.* Climate changes occur both as long-term cyclical processes and as a result of human activities (deforestation, pollution of the atmosphere, etc.). The effects of even minor decreases or increases in temperature may have catastrophic effects upon the productivity of various ecosystems.

- *Global Food Insecurity.* A transfer of cropland from subsistence production to cash-crop production and a shift from a variety of indigenous food crops to imported foods like wheat and rice has created a global food insecurity. These ecological threats to human security are clearly related to the Mainstream paradigm of development of a functional type and can only be countered if this paradigm of development is reconsidered.

The problem of development in the context of ecological constraints is something the social sciences will have to deal with in spite of their lack of preparedness. The orthodox view of unlimited economic growth as some kind of natural law must be replaced. On the other hand, a general hostility toward growth because it threatens the ecological balance must also be avoided. There is no point in substituting one myth for another. The road forward goes somewhere between growthmania and ecologism.

At the so-called Earth Summit, or the UN Conference on Environment and Development (UNCED) in Rio in June 1992, representatives of one-hundred-eighty countries attended. There were also thousands of activists of citizen movements from all over the world, making it the largest meeting ever held on our planet. Many participants were strongly committed to a fundamental change in the pattern of development, and the interlinked problems of pollution, global warming and sea-level rise, soil erosion and desertification, population growth and poverty.

Different environmental problems get different priorities in the North than in the South, and in the South the now living generation receives more attention than future generations. Intragenerational and intergenerational equity cannot so easily be separated. The "greening of the capital" has become a new strategy of the TNCs.[53] The environmental demands in the North are now described as a new form of imperialism in the South. Nature has become part of the bargaining game between North and South, which in a way is a recognition that it, after all, has a price.

Territorial Development

Another Development is a process that is more "territorial" and less "functional." This distinction refers to two different paradigms in regional planning:

> The territorial force derives from common bonds of social order forged by history within a given place. Funtional ties are based on mutual self-interest. Given inequalities at the start, a funtional order is always hierarchical, accumulating power at the top. Territorial relationships, on the other hand, though they will also be characterized by inequalities of power, are tempered by the mutual rights and obligations which the members of a territorial group claim from each other.[54]

The problem is how to reduce the dominance of function over territory, and how a "recovery of territorial life" can be brought about. To some extent, this already takes place when people react in their own way and as best as they can to the challenges of the crisis of the world economy, taking the local space as their point of departure. The point, however, is to make the territorial principle part of a planned transition toward a more sustainable development.

According to the dominant *functional* principle, development is an abstract process related to an artificial "national economy," an aggregate of production data and other indicators of development. Behind this abstraction we can observe the concrete socio-economic "worlds" that most people identify with and depend upon. When this relationship is disturbed and threatened by "modernization," conflicts occur over the goals and means of development. Smaller territorial units, however, lack autonomous power in the functional system, typically organized as a center-periphery structure. The revitalization of territorial life would therefore not be possible without a transfer of power to local communities, while the state level assumes the function of coordinator. The territorial principle is implicit in the theorizing around the concept of ecodevelopment, defined as:

> . . . [A] style of development that, in each ecoregion, calls for specific solutions to the particular problems of the region in the light of cultural as well as ecological data and long-term as well as immediate needs.

> Accordingly, it operates with criteria of progress that are related to each particular case, and adaption to the environment plays an important role.[55]

From this perspective there are no models to emulate. A "backward" country should not look for the image of its own future in the "advanced" country but in its own ecology and culture. Development has no universal meaning. There is no development *as such,* only development of *something,* which in this case would be a certain ecoregion. A development strategy informed by this territorial perspective must make efficient use of those resources which happen to exist in that particular area, and in a way that both sustains the ecological system (outer limit) and provides the people living there with their basic human needs (inner limit).

Territorial development thus necessitates a development strategy which differs radically from conventional strategies with their *universal* elements: capital, labor, investment, etc. An ecodevelopment strategy, in contrast, consists of *specific* elements: a group of people with certain cultural values living in a region with a certain set of natural resources. The goal of territorial development, then, is to improve *that specific situation,* not to bring about "development" in terms of GNP or some other abstraction.

Ethnodevelopment

A development that concerns "people not things," as expressed by Julius Nyerere, will for all practical purposes have to deal with ethnic and indigenous groups, since "people" consist neither of individuals, nor of nation-states. Conventional development thinking does not exclude the idea of victims of progress: "It is generally recognized that tribal peoples are being drastically affected by civilization and that their cultural patterns and, in many cases, the peoples themselves disappear as civilization advances."[56]

One of the more unexpected and still not very well-understood outcomes of the Mainstream development process is an explosion of ethnic violence. The way ethnic movements and ethnic conflicts relate to the development process is highly complex, but the different outcome of growth, as well as stagnation, on different social groups and regions must obviously have an impact on ethnic relations.

In what follows, we shall first exemplify with some recent incidents of ethnic disturbances, secondly discuss how these cases may relate to various patterns of development, and finally explore the preconditions for an "ethnodevelopment," i.e., a model of development that brings out the potential inherent in different ethnic groups, rather than leading them into feuds with one another.

Ethnic conflicts are worldwide but have been particularly intense in South Asia during the 1980s. Pakistan was divided once on the ethnic issue. Today the city of Karachi is often paralyzed due to ethnic wars between Pathans and Mohajirs and, on the national level, the Punjabi dominance is challenged both from Sind and Baluchistan. Bangladesh itself today experiences ethnic conflicts between Buddhist Chakmas from the hill-tracts and Muslim Bengalis from the overpopulated plains. History thus ironically repeats itself in the form of new patterns of internal colonialism. Similar conflicts take place in India between tribals and the Hindu population, for instance, in Bihar. In Assam, the "sons of the soil" defend their primary right (as they conceive it) to resources and employment against immigrants from Bangladesh, West Bengal, and Bihar. "Sons of the soil" organizations are active in many states, for example, Maharashtra and Karnataka. In Guyarat, the higher castes attack lower castes because of the policy of protective discrimination. In Kashmir and Andhra Pradesh, Muslims and Hindus kill each other; in Punjab, Hindus and Sikhs; and in Sri Lanka, the Sinhalese-Tamil conflict borders on civil war.

In all these conflicts, there is an economic factor of varying importance but never absent. However, there is no uniform cause behind ethnic conflicts. For the forest tribes in different parts of India their mobilization is a matter of physical survival. For the Sikhs in Punjab the economic interests involved are harder to specify. The economic relations between the Sinhalese and the Tamils in Sri Lanka are also complex, and from the perspective of class it is necessary to distinguish between several subgroups within the two communities.

However, the reality of ethnic conflicts can no longer be disregarded by theorists and practitioners of development, since the rise of ethnopolitics must be related to economic development one way or the other. The problem is that we do not really know how. I therefore agree with Stavenhagen, when he says that the neglect of the ethnic question in development thinking is not an oversight but a paradigmatic blind spot.[57] In order to build a theory of Another Development, one must explore the ethnic factor in development within a rather simple framework to start with. The time for generalizing and theorizing will come later. The basic departure from conventional theory is that people are divided in different ways than being consumers and producers, sellers and buyers, employers and employees, and the like.

In what ways can conflicts between specific social groups be related to different patterns of economic development? The range of economic problems that may influence ethnic relations is great indeed: struggle for scarce resources, regional imbalances, infrastructural investments with a great impact on indigenous economic systems, labor market conflicts, distributional conflicts, and so forth.

Most of these problems affect all societies, but in multi-ethnic societies they are more severe and tend to become permanent. There may be so-called spread effects within ethnic groups, but definitely less so between them. In order to provide some order, one could work with the following tentative distinctions:

- Conflicts relating to the control of natural resources;
- Conflicts relating to major infrastructural projects affecting local ecological systems;
- Conflicts stemming fron secular but uneven trends, such as commodication, proletarianization, urbanization, et cetera;
- Conflicts relating to the principal content of development strategies; and
- Conflicts of distribution.

Conflicts relating to natural resources can be exemplified by the way forest wealth is used by jungle tribes, on the one hand, and urban middle-class populations on the other. For the former, a forest represents a way of life; for the latter, a forest may represent building materials or paper for the newspaper industry. Urban groups may not even be aware that a forest is inhabited by human beings and, if they are, they may not consider these beings as human. The conflicts resulting from such clashes of interest are fundamental and represent two different paradigms of development: growth and modernization versus ethnodevelopment or, in spatial terms, functional versus territorial development. The same applies to the second type: infrastructural projects affecting local ecosystems.

The third type of conflict has to do with the unevenness of development, which means that certain regions are placed in more advantageous positions than others and consequently attract more investment and skills. Such centers usually become the bases for nation-building, whereas people in the backwash regions are reluctant citizens. Their protests are often expressed in ethnic terms. The state usually develops common interests with the most commercialized regions, since they provide the type of free-floating resources upon which various state functions depend. Furthermore the "state class" is often recruited from the same ethnic group that reinforces the bias.

Most of the options we have referred to so far are more or less explicitly reflected in the development strategy carried out by a particular regime, but in some cases the ethnic issue is part and parcel of the development strategy itself and therefore directly intervening in the ethnic struggle. This, for instance, is the case with the *bhumiputra* policy of the Malaysian government.

Finally, government directly intervenes in the ethnic struggle by the way it distributes public works, education, employment, and patronage. As is the case with the policy of protective discrimination by the government of India, the allocation of education and public employment opportunities by quotas even makes it necessary to belong to a certain community and remain a loyal member of it.

In this context, our distinction between functional and territorial principles of development is of help. According to the former principle, development is basically a result of specialization and an advanced division of labor between regions; according to the latter, it is the regions themselves which are to be developed, not the functional system.

It is easy to see the connection between these two principles and ethnic conflicts. Ethnic groups are most often locally based and their cultural identity is closely related to the ecological particularities of the region and to a certain mode of exploiting the natural resources. A process of "development" that threatens the ecological system of a region is therefore also a cultural threat against the ethnic group for which this region is the habitat. Obviously such a process cannot be regarded as development for the ethnic group thus threatened, even if this is considered to be development in the macro–system, or functional system. As Rodolfo Stavenhagen has suggested, a development process appropriate for a particular ethnic group can be termed "ethnodevelopment."[58]

This is a radical concept since it turns the table of the conventional conception of ethnicity as an obstacle to modernization.[59] There is in most social science literature an inbuilt bias against ethnic identification and in favor of national identification, regardless of how unrealistic a particular nation-state project may be. But the re–emergence of ethnicity may be seen as a "reaffirmation of a long-existing ethnic identity *in* the process of positive development — as an *integral part* of development, where the state (or at least certain aspects of it), not ethnicity, is an obstacle to development."[60]

I would consider ethnodevelopment as a basic component in Another Development, together with egalitarian development, self-reliant development, sustainable development, and territorial development. They are all complementary and mutually supportive. Egalitarian development implies development consistent with basic needs and self–respect; self–reliant development is based on the principle of autonomy; and sustainable and territorial development refer to the habitat where ethnic groups live. Thus territorial development and ethnodevelopment are two aspects of the same thing in cases where ethnic identity is territorially based.

In the case of dispersed ethnic groups this, of course, does not apply, and the principle of ethnodevelopment would rather coincide with the protection of cultural, religious, and linguistic rights, in the framework of a functional system. The concept of culture is, however, basic to the two situations (the territorial and the functional).

The cultural dimension in development is another neglected dimension. Sometimes it is asserted that a development strategy must take the culture of a specific country into consideration. The "national" culture is, however, often rather artificial compared to regional and ethnic cultures, unless one particular subnational culture is elevated as *the* national culture. Thus, in any case, ethnodevelopment is a challenge to the nation-state. It is development within a framework of *cultural pluralism*, based on the premise that different communities in the same society have distinctive codes of behavior and different value systems.[61] This conception of culture could be contrasted with a hegemonic concept of culture as diffused downwards resulting in a shared national culture.

Overcoming State-Centrism

It was stated in the introduction to this chapter that an alternative development theory must go beyond economism and be normative. If this is taken seriously, the question of actors in development must also be raised. So far development strategies have been formulated by economists and implemented by governments. This is what development has been about. The principles of Another Development suggest other types of actors: ethnic and territorial groups, local communities, but also supranational bodies involved in issues which go beyond the capacity of individual states, for instance many of the requirements for sustainable development. Thus Another Development implies not only a movement beyond economism but beyond all state-centered paradigms.

The structures of the social sciences is, to a degree, hard to understand, determined by the process of state-formation and our perceptions of the world as "citizens" of nation-states. The concept of development is primarily related to a specific territory together with its population claimed by a state, and its purpose has been defined as to coincide with the purpose to consolidate the position of the state *vis-à-vis* other states.

The concept of security, which for any human being would contain a sense of being in control of one's own destiny, has from the state-centric perspective been defined as a degree of militarization corresponding to the militarization in the "external world," i.e., other nation-states also worried about their "security," and consequently harboring an inbuilt tendency toward militarization.

Problem-solving on these and many other issues will have to go beyond the nation-state, which means that our current social sciences are patently inadequate. My prognosis is that the "softer" disciplines will adapt quicker to the new realitites than the "harder." This spells problems for economics in particular.

NOTES

1. D. Booth, 1985, "Marxism and Development Sociology: Interpreting the Impasse," *World Development* 13, no. 7, pp. 761–87.
2. F. J. Schuurman, ed., 1993, *Beyond the Impasse: New Directions in Development Theory*, London: Zed Books.
3. W. Sachs, ed., 1992, *The Development Dictionary*, London: Zed Books, p. 5.
4. R. Chambers, 1985, "Putting 'Last' Thinking First: A Professional Revolution," *Third World Affairs 1985*, London: Third World Foundation.
5. J. Toye, 1987, "Development Theory and the Experience of Development: Issues for the Future" in L. Emmerij, ed., 1987, *Development Policies, op. cit.*
6. P. Streeten, 1981, *Development Perspectives*, London: MacMillan.
7. A. Hirschman, 1981, "The Rise and Fall of Development Economics" in Hirschmen, ed., *Essays in Trespassing: Economics and Politics and Beyond*, New York: Cambridge University Press, pp. 1-24.
8. "What Now. Another Development," The 1975 Dag Hammarskjöld

Report, *Development Dialogue,* no. 1/2.

9. J. Friedmann, 1992, *Empowerment: The Politics of Alternative Development*, Cambridge, Massachusetts: Blackwell, p. 30.

10. Quoted in H. Addo et al, eds., 1985, *Development as Social Transformation*, Tokyo: United Nations University Press.

11. K. Taylor, 1982, *The Political Ideas of the Utopian Socialists,* London: Frank Cass.

12. M. Bookchin, 1980, *Toward an Ecological Society,* Montreal: Black Rose Books.

13. G. Ionescu and E. Gellner, 1969, *Populism: Its Meanings and National Characteristics,* New York: Macmillan.

14. B. Hettne, 1976, "The Vitality of Gandhian Tradition," *Journal of Peace Research* XIII, no. 3.

15. I. Berlin, 1979, *Russian Thinkers*, New York: Viking Penguin, p. 217.

16. A. Walicki, 1969, *The Controversy over Capitalism: Studies in the Social Philosophy of the Russian Populists,* Oxford: Clarendon Press, p. 53.

17. P. Ekins, ed., 1987, *The Living Economy: A New Economics in the Making,* London: Routledge.

18. G. Kitching, 1982, *Development and Underdevelopment in Historical Perspective: Populism, Nationalism and Industrialization,* London and New York: Methuen, p. 32.

19. M. Friberg and B. Hettne, 1985, "The Greening of the World: Towards a Non-Deterministic Model of Global Processes" in H. Addo et al, eds., *Development as Social Transformation, op. cit.*

20. Ekins, 1987, *op. cit.*

21. K. Polanyi, 1957, *The Great Transformation,* Boston: Beacon Press; and 1977, *The Livelihood of Man* (H. Pearson, ed.), New York: Academic Press.

22. J. I. Gershuny, 1979, "The Informal Economy: Its Role in Post–Indus-

trial Society," *Futures* (February).

23. R. Sandbrook, 1982, *The Politics of Basic Needs: Urban Aspects of Assaulting Poverty in Africa,* London: Heinemann, p. 16.

24. M. Nerfin, ed., 1977, *Another Development: Approaches and Strategies,* Uppsala: The Dag Hammarskjöld Foundation.

25. L. Emmerij, 1988, "Peace and Poverty: Europe's Responsibility" in B. Hettne, ed., *Europe: Dimensions of Peace,* London: Zed Books.

26. K. Lederer, ed., 1980, *Human Needs: A Contribution to the Current Debate,* Oelgeschlager, Gunn & Hain/Verlag Anton.

27. P. Streeten, 1979, "A Basic-Needs Approach to Economic Development" in K. P. Jameson and C. K. Wilber, eds., *Directions in Economic Development,* Notre Dame: University of Notre Dame Press.

28. M. Max-Neef, 1987, "Human Scale Economics: The Challenges Ahead" in P. Ekins, ed., *The Living Economy, op. cit.*

29. R. Prebisch, 1980, "Toward a Theory of Change," *CEPAL Review,* no. 9, p. 187.

30. J. Galtung, P. O'Brien, and R. Preiswerk, eds., 1980, *Self–Reliance, A Strategy for Development,* London: Bogle-L'Ouverture.

31. *Ibid.,* pp. 25-26.

32. W. G. Demas, 1965, *The Economics of Development in Small Countries with Special Reference to the Caribbean,* Montreal: McGill University Press.

33. Thomas Clive, 1974, *Dependence and Transformation: The Economics of the Transition to Socialism,* New York: Monthly Review Press.

34. Demas, 1965, *Economics of Development, op. cit.,* p. 181.

35. Galtung et al, eds., 1980, *Self-Reliance, op. cit.,* p. 361.

36. *Ibid.*

37. "What Now," *op. cit.,* p. 67.

38. World Commission on Environment and Development, 1987, *Our Common Future*, Oxford: Oxford University Press.

39. W.Beckerman, 1974, *In Defence of Economic Growth*, London: Jonathan Cape.

40. A. Nove, 1983, *The Economics of Feasible Socialism*, London: George Allen & Unwin.

41. H. L. Parsons, 1977, *Introduction to Marx and Engels on Ecology*, Westport and London: Greenwood Press, p. 67.

42. H. Brookfield, 1975, *Interdependent Development*, London: Methuen.

43. L. Timberlake and J. Tinker, 1984, *Environment and Conflict: Links Between Ecological Decay, Environmental Bankruptcy and Political and Military Instability*, London: Earthscan (Brieng Document no. 40).

44. K. Boulding, 1966, "Economics and Ecology" in F. Fraser–Darling and J. D. Milton, eds., *Future Environments of North America*, New York: Natural History Press, p. 230.

45. H. J. Barnett and C. Morse, 1963, *Scarcity and Growth: The Economics of Natural Resource Availability*, Baltimore: John Hopkins University Press.

46. E. J. Mishan, [1967] 1993; *The Costs of Economic Growth*, rev. ed., Westport, Connecticut: Greenwood Publishing Group; also, A. Weintraub, El. Schwartz, and J. R. Aronson, eds., 1973, *The Economic Growth Controversy*, New York: International Arts and Sciences Press.

47. R. Hueting, 1980, *New Scarcity and Economic Growth*, Amsterdam: North-Holland.

48. K. W. Deutsch, 1977, *Eco-Social Systems and Eco-Politics*, Paris: UNESCO.

49. D. Pirages, 1978, *The New Context for International Relations: Global Ecopolitics*, North Scituate; Massachusetts: Duxbury Press.

50. Brookfield, 1975, *Interdependent Development*, *op.cit.*

51. L. R. Brown, 1981, *Building a Sustainable Society*, New York and

London: W. W. Norton.

52. M. Redcliff, 1987, *Sustainable Development: Exploring the Contradictions*, London and New York: Methuen.

53. W. Sachs, ed., 1992, *The Development Dictionary, op. cit.*; and 1993, *Global Ecology: A New Arena of Political Conflict*, London: Zed Books.

54. J. Friedmann, and C. Weaver, 1979, *Territory and Function: The Evolution of Regional Planning*, London: Edward Arnold, p. 17.

55. I. Sachs, 1974, "Ecodevelopment," *Ceres* (November-December), p. 9.

56. J. H. Bodley, 1982, *Victims of Progress*, Palo Alto: Mayfield Publishing.

57. R. Stavenhagen, 1986, "Ethnodevelopment: A Neglected Dimension in Development Thinking" in R. Anthorpe and A. Kráhl, *Development Studies: Critique and Renewal*, Leiden: E. J. Brill, p. 77.

58. *Ibid.*

59. D. K. Thompson and D. Ronen, 1986, *Ethnicity, Politics and Development*, Boulder: Lynne Rienner, p. 7.

60. *Ibid.*, p. 6.

61. P. Worsley, 1984, *The Three Worlds: Culture and World Development*, London: Weidenfeld & Nicolson.

BIBLIOGRAPHY

Addo, H. et al, eds., 1985, *Development as Social Transformation*, Tokyo: United Nations University Press.

Barnett, H. J., and C. Morse, 1963, *Scarcity and Growth: The Economics of Natural Resource Availability*, Baltimore: John Hopkins University Press.

Beckerman, W., 1974, *In Defence of Economic Growth*, London: Jonathan Cape.

Berger, P. L., 1977, *Pyramids of Sacrifice: Political Ethics and Social Change*, Harmondsworth: Penguin.

Berlin, I., 1979, *Russian Thinkers*, New York: Viking Penguin.

Bodley, J. H., 1982, *Victims of Progress*, Palo Alto: Mayfield Publishing.

Bookchin, M., 1980, *Toward an Ecological Society*, Montreal: Black Rose Books.

Booth, D., 1985, "Marxism and Development Sociology: Interpreting the Impasse," *World Development* 13, no. 7, pp. 761–87.

Boulding, K., 1966, "Economics and Ecology" in F. Fraser–Darling and J. D. Milton, eds., *Future Environments of North America*, New York: Natural History Press.

Brookfield, H., 1975, *Interdependent Development*, London: Methuen.

Brown, L. R., 1981, *Building a Sustainable Society*, New York and London: W. W. Norton.

Chambers, R., 1985, "Putting 'Last' Thinking First: A Professional Revolution," *Third World Affairs 1985*, London: Third World Foundation.

Demas, W. G., 1965, *The Economics of Development in Small Countries with Special Reference to the Caribbean*, Montreal: McGill University Press.

Deutsch, K. W., 1977, *Eco-Social Systems and Eco-Politics*, Paris: UNESCO.

Ekins, P., 1988, "Green Ideas on Economics and Security and Their Political Implications" in M. Friberg, ed., *New Social Movements in Western Europe*, United Nations University European Perspectives Project 1986-87, Gothenburg University Padrigu Papers, Tokyo: United Nations University Press.

Ekins, P., ed., 1987, *The Living Economy: A New Economics in the Making*, London: Routledge.

Emmerij, L., 1988, "Peace and Poverty: Europe's Responsibility" in B. Hettne, ed., *Europe: Dimensions of Peace*, London: Zed Books.

Emmerij, L., ed., 1987, *Development Policies and the Crisis of the 1980s*, Paris: OECD.

Friberg, M., and B. Hettne, 1985, "The Greening of the World: Towards a Non-Deterministic Model of Global Processes" in H. Addo et al, eds., *Development as Social Transformation*, Tokyo: United Nations University Press.

Friedmann, J., 1992, *Empowerment: The Politics of Alternative Development*, Cambridge, Massachusetts: Blackwell.

Friedmann, J., and C. Weaver, 1979, *Territory and Function: The Evolution of Regional Planning*, London: Edward Arnold.

Galtung, J., P. O'Brien, and R. Preiswerk, eds., 1980, *Self-Reliance, A Strategy for Development*, London: Bogle-L'Ouverture.

Gershuny, J. I., 1979, "The Informal Economy: Its Role in Post–Industrial Society," *Futures* (February).

Hettne, B., 1976, "The Vitality of Gandhian Tradition," *Journal of Peace Research* XIII, no. 3.

Hirschman, A., 1981, "The Rise and Fall of Development Economics" in Hirschman, ed., *Essays in Trespassing: Economics and Politics and Beyond*, New York: Cambridge University Press.

Hueting, R., 1980, *New Scarcity and Economic Growth*, Amsterdam: North-Holland.

Ionescu, G., and E. Gellner, 1969, *Populism: Its Meanings and National Characteristics*, New York: Macmillan.

Kitching, G., 1982, *Development and Underdevelopment in Historical Perspective: Populism, Nationalism and Industrialization,* London and New York: Methuen.

Lederer, K., ed., 1980, *Human Needs: A Contribution to the Current Debate,* Oelgeschlager, Gunn & Hain/Verlag Anton.

Max-Neef, M., 1987, "Human Scale Economics: The Challenges Ahead" in P. Ekins, ed., *The Living Economy: A New Economics in the Making,* London: Routledge..

Mishan, E. J., [1967] 1993, *The Costs of Economic Growth,* rev. ed., Westport, Connecticut: Greenwood Publishing Group.

Nerfin, M., ed., 1977, *Another Development: Approaches and Strategies,* Uppsala: The Dag Hammarskjöld Foundation.

Nove, A., 1983, *The Economics of Feasible Socialism,* London: George Allen & Unwin.

Parsons, H. L., 1977, *Introduction to Marx and Engels on Ecology,* Westport and London: Greenwood Press.

Pirages, D., 1978, *The New Context for International Relations: Global Ecopolitics,* North Scituate; Massachusetts: Duxbury Press.

Polanyi, K., 1957, *The Great Transformation,* Boston: Beacon Press.

_________, 1977, *The Livelihood of Man* (H. Pearson, ed.), New York: Academic Press.

Prebisch, R., 1980, "Toward a Theory of Change," *CEPAL Review,* no. 9.

Redcliff, M., 1987, *Sustainable Development: Exploring the Contradictions,* London and New York: Methuen.

Sachs, I., 1974, "Ecodevelopment," *Ceres* (November-December).

Sachs, W., ed., 1992, *The Development Dictionary,* London: Zed Books.

________, 1993, *Global Ecology: A New Arena of Political Conflict*, London: Zed Books.

Sandbrook, R., 1982, *The Politics of Basic Needs: Urban Aspects of Assaulting Poverty in Africa*, London: Heinemann.

Shuurman, F. J., ed., 1993, *Beyond the Impasse: New Directions in Development Theory*, London: Zed Books

Stavenhagen, R., 1986, "Ethnodevelopment: A Neglected Dimension in Development Thinking" in R. Anthorpe and A. Kráhl, *Development Studies: Critique and Renewal*, Leiden: E. J. Brill.

Streeten, P., 1979, "A Basic-Needs Approach to Economic Development" in K. P. Jameson and C. K. Wilber, eds., *Directions in Economic Development*, Notre Dame: University of Notre Dame Press.

________, 1981, *Development Perspectives*, London: MacMillan.

Taylor, K., 1982, *The Political Ideas of the Utopian Socialists*, London: Frank Cass.

Thomas, Clive, 1974, *Dependence and Transformation: The Economics of the Transition to Socialism*, New York: Monthly Review Press.

Thompson, D. K., and D. Ronen, 1986, *Ethnicity, Politics and Development*, Boulder: Lynne Rienner.

Timberlake, L., and J. Tinker, 1984, *Environment and Conflict: Links Between Ecological Decay, Environmental Bankruptcy and Political and Military Instability*, London: Earthscan (Brieng Document no. 40).

Toye, J., 1987, "Development Theory and the Experience of Development: Issues for the Future" in L. Emmerij, ed., 1987, *Development Policies and the Crises of the 1980s*, Paris: OECD.

Walicki, A., 1969, *The Controversy over Capitalism: Studies in the Social Philosophy of the Russian Populists*, Oxford: Clarendon Press.

Weintraub, A., E. Schwartz, and J. R. Aronson, eds., 1973, *The Economic Growth Controversy*, New York: International Arts and Sciences Press.

"What Now. Another Development," The 1975 Dag Hammarskjöld Report, *Development Dialogue,* no. 1/2.

World Commission on Environment and Development, 1987, *Our Common Future,* Oxford: Oxford University Press.

Worsley, P., 1984, *The Three Worlds: Culture and World Development,* London: Weidenfeld & Nicolson.

IV

HUMAN AND ECONOMIC DEVELOPMENT: THE CHANGING CONTEXT

Willis W. Harman

Prologue

In the following, I wish to place myself in the position of not so much theoretician as reporter. The present world economic system did not result from someone's theory about how it should be. Rather, its basic pattern evolved at a time of dramatic societal change in Western Europe, and the theories came later. Expanding commerce and changing metaphysical assumptions and a new industrial ethos were creating a new society; the evolution of the economic system was part of that overall system change.

Some such sea change is taking place again. This time it is worldwide, equally profound, and happening faster. The changing face of economics is a part of that, and if we are to understand the part we must understand the whole. Thus the early portion of the following discussion will not be about economics at all, but about that changing context.

We shall be attempting to interpret the historical present, say, the last third of the twentieth century. The signs indicate that the global context for human and economic development is changing in a favorable direction. In the latter portion of the chapter, we will explore a few of the implications for the shape of a future and, in some respects, better world.

The Broader Context of Development

Let us focus on three aspects of this broader context: (1) the emerging "information society," (2) the spread of a global perspective, and (3) changes in value perspectives and underlying beliefs. What is happening in each of these three areas constitutes such a major shift that it alone would result in profound change in the world's economic and political institutions. The three together help to define a system change of consummate proportions.

After exploring briefly these three facets of change, we will explore some further reasons for considering the change to be so fundamental.

CHARACTERISTICS OF "INFORMATION SOCIETY"

Over half the labor force in the United States, and an increasing fraction of economic activity, are now involved primarily with information-handling activities. Less than a quarter of the work force is now occupied with the sort of activities that shaped the economic system in its present form, mainly the growing, extraction, and production of commodities, materials, and things. Statements similar to these would hold true for other highly industrialized societies such as Western Europe and Japan. Further trends are bringing changes in all the developed countries with implications that are both controversial and not well understood. The circumstances leading to the present situation are reviewed briefly below.

As is well known, a key feature of the period following the industrial revolution was a dramatic reduction of the fraction of the work force involved in agricultural production, which in the United

States dropped from close to ninety percent in the early 1800s to a few percent by the 1980s. Observing the beginning of this trend, one might possibly have argued that as labor productivity rose and costs decreased, demand for agricultural products would rise, so that the employment of human labor might be maintained at close to its former levels. But that did not occur. Instead, the demand for agricultural products saturated, and there was a major displacement of labor from agricultural to industrial production.

There was a similar shift from handicrafts to machine production. The displacement of handicraftsmen by textile machinery in the early nineteenth century led to the notorious Luddite riots in England, and to concern about the labor-replacing effects of advancing technology. This concern was short-lived, however, partly because new industries were rapidly springing up which absorbed the displaced labor, and partly because of massive migrations of workers to new opportunities in less crowded territories.

Following the Great Depression and World War II, concern about unemployment was again high in the major industrialized countries. War production was dropping off, as was employment in the military forces. For the time being, the problem was "solved" by two remarkable shifts in values that were especially visible in the United States. One was the outmoding of frugality in favor of a mass-consumption society. America became a "throwaway society," the word "consumer" became part of the economic vocabulary, and frugality was frowned upon as bad for the economy. The second shift was an overthrowing of the ethic that forbade a nation to manufacture arms for other than its own defense. The instruments of war became a major factor in the economies of a number of nations, where salesmen in and out of uniform contributed to the world's embarking on an unprecedented arms race.

Later on, as the possibilities of computer-guided automation of production processes became apparent in the early 1960s, there arose again a great fear of technological disemployment. Automation was termed "the silent revolution" and viewed with dread in some quarters. Most forecasts, however, anticipated continued increases in industrial production of diverse kinds of goods, and increases in consumption of that product. However, that did not happen. Instead, employment in goods-producing industries peaked and started downwards. Demand for these products did not rise sufficiently to counteract labor productivity increase and maintain industrial employment levels.

Further, the new information-related activities created employment at a totally unanticipated rate—a rate so high that in the United States, the majority of the work force are now involved with information-related activities. Once again, we hear the reassurances that somehow demand for these information-related services will increase at such a rate that we need not fear the further job-displacement effects of computer technology, artificial intelligence, and robots. Never mind that mindless consumption of information services may not be the choice of thinking people, anymore than was boundless consumption of food or manufactured goods.

We tend to overlook how basic is this shift to the "information society." The fundamental concepts of business and labor, of employment and welfare theory, of liberal and Marxist analysis, are all based in a production-focused society. It may have seemed to make sense in the past to think of economic production as the defacto goal of society; to think of an ever-increasing fraction of overall human activity being treated as commodities in the mainstream economy; to assume that the individual's primary relationship to society is related to a mainstream-economy job (i.e., having one, being married to someone who has, or in training for one); to have social thinking dominated by concepts of scarcity, commercial secrecy, and money exchange. However, that is not necessarily the case in the future. The primary resource of future society is information, knowledge, learning, and wisdom. But knowledge is not a commodity like tomatoes or automobiles; it cannot be priced and distributed in the same ways and it does not behave according to the same "laws." Thus the present signs of the inadequacy of past thinking should not be surprising. There is no reason to expect the old concepts to fit the new situation.

For an assortment of reasons (most probably international competition), implementation of artificial intelligence and robots and attendant job displacement will occur very rapidly—much more rapidly than job creation by any new industries on the horizon. There are, in general, three basic responses to such a situation:

- Attempt to create jobs by stimulating economic growth, using transfer payments to take care of those left out (in other words, continue the same old thinking);
- Treat work opportunity as a scarce commodity that has to be rationed through work-sharing plans, a shortened work week, etc. (Considering how much useful work might be directed toward benefiting humankind, this tactic is not too sensible when you think about it); and
- Adopt an entirely different mode of thinking, wherein the widespread elimination of human labor through use of machines is taken as a stimulus to re-examine the basic assumptions of production-focused society—including the assumption that income distribution must be tightly linked to jobs in the mainstream economy.

The last is by far the most promising in the long run; however, societies tend to find rethinking most uncomfortable, and to avoid it except as a last resort. The rethinking needs to start with a basic question: *What is the next phase after the production-focused society?* When a society has become so technologically advanced that production of all the goods and services people can reasonably need or want (or all that the planet can stand) can be accomplished with ease, employing only a fraction of the potential work force, what then substitutes for economic production as the central goal of society?

The fundamental problem is not how to stimulate more demand for information services, nor how to create more jobs in the mainstream economy. It is, rather, a basic problem of meaning. *What is the central meaning of advanced human society now that economic production is no longer a challenge and does not provide central meaning to such societies (and because focusing on economic production in the long run does not lead to a viable global future)?*

Most of the above comments relate to industrialized societies. But, as we shall see below, the industrial paradigm generates a similar fundamental question for the developing countries.

Spread of a Global Perspective

It may have been feasible in the past to ignore the global-system aspects of much social and economic activity. That is no longer the case. Most medium-sized and large business organizations are now transnational, at least in some sense. So also are the problems confronting us. These range from acid rain, toxic chemical concentrations, and deteriorating water supplies, to widespread maldevelopment and long-term soil degradation by industrialized agricultural methods and an assortment of economic ailments, including spreading and possibly chronic unemployment and precariousness of the world financial system. Another new factor is the presence of an international labor market, with implications yet to be revealed. And enveloping all of this, made possible by a global communication system, is a global climate of public opinion.

It is now clear that the complex of global environmental, resource, and species-extinction problems, contributed to by increasing industrialization throughout the world, must be taken seriously. The 1980 U.S. *Global 2000* report was followed by similar reports from a number of nations, all reiterating more or less the same message. The problems are becoming progressively more severe. They are highly interconnected with one another and with industrialization and population concentration. Without major changes in the present trends, the problems will become intolerably grievous by the end of the century.

These problems are now generally recognized to be systemic in nature and characteristic of the global system, even though specific manifestations may appear to be localized. Some of the environmental and resource problems are consequences of widespread poverty and hunger, bringing strains on the natural environment that include overgrazing, deforestation, soil erosion, and surface water pollution. Other aspects of environmental degradation and resource exploitation stem from the economic activities of the rich nations that must overconsume to keep their economies "healthy."

These problems will not be resolved by some "technological fix" or improved management. A much more fundamental system change will be required, including a change in the overall network of economic incentives. While individual conclusions and recommendations in the various analyses can no doubt be challenged, the swing of informed public opinion is clearly toward considering the problems to be real.

Another threat taken far more seriously in recent years is that of the nuclear "balance of terror." The nuclear weapons had been around for decades, but the new mood was probably triggered as much as anything by the perceived combativeness of the Reagan Administration and talk of "limited nuclear war." Jonathan Schell's book, *The Fate of the Earth,*[1] struck a nerve by persuasively arguing that there is no conceivable solution to the nuclear dilemma other than to "reinvent the world." (A short-lived hope was kindled in some circles by the fanciful "Star Wars" proposal to provide a protective shield over certain favored regions of the globe.) The unsolvability of the nuclear dilemma is perhaps the major factor making the public tolerant toward the possibility of a major restructuring of the global system.

At least equally significant with these two aspects of the new global perspective is the change in thinking taking place within the "sleeping giant" known as the developing world. The giant is awakening. Those who had for so long accepted the role of deprivation, inferiority, and servility are less and less willing to do so. For the two decades following World War II, political liberation and economic development were the two chief themes. Development was defined as "modernization" and thought to be synonomous with industrialization. Increasingly, however, cultural leaders in the developing countries have come to see that the best development for them is not necessarily abandonment of their own cultural roots and adoption of the alien culture of Western industrial society. Cultural diversity has come to be seen as an endangered planetary resource, somewhat as species diversity in an ecological system is a precious resource. Thus there have been in recent years not only growing insistence on a different international economic order, but also on exploring alternative development paths.

Basic Needs and Equity

One key dimension of the global development issue is that of needs satisfaction and equity. In a series of documents from the International Labour Organization and other United Nations agencies relating to demands for a "New International Economic Order," a set of universally felt human needs has been defined as being in essence:

- Basic human needs (adequate food, shelter, health care, education, employment, and personal security;
- A sense of the dignity of being human;
- A sense of becoming (a chance to achieve a better life);
- A sense of justice or equity; and
- A sense of solidarity, of belonging to a worthy group, and of participation in decisions that affect the group's, and one's own, destiny.

National-level programs aimed at guaranteeing the right to satisfaction of these universal needs have been adopted by over one-hundred-twenty countries, in most cases within the past three decades. In some of the countries, including the United States, the programs were preceded by years of debate over the appropriateness of such guarantees and the kinds of programs and payments involved. Behind the rhetoric of the demands for a new economic order is the proposition that a concept of welfare that has thus far been accepted and applied within a majority of individual nations should now be extended to the entire family of humankind. Despite inevitable opposition, ultimate acceptance of this proposition appears likely, in that it is an extension of an already accepted basic trend.

It should be clear that this amounts to much more than a mere adjustment of the existing economic institutions for more equitable distribution. It implies no less than a restructuring of international society around a newly recognized fundamental right, as profound in its ultimate implications as the concept of democratic government two centuries ago.

The Development Dilemma

Whether or not the pressure for a new economic order grows or declines, the basic situation remains. It is by no means obvious that the global system in anything like its present form is viable in the long term, or that it leads toward an ecologically sustainable global society or a satisfactory resolution to the plight of the poorest peoples. Nor is it clear how basic a change would be required for it to do so.

The global dilemma can be simply stated. *Of the easily imaginable paths of global development, those that appear to be economically feasible do not look to be ecologically and socially plausible, and those that appear ecologically feasible and humanistically desirable do not seem economically and politically feasible.*

To illustrate, imagine that all the developing countries were somehow to be successful in following the examples of the industrialized and newly industrializing countries (as was assumed in the 1950s and 1960s to be the "normal" course of development). The planet would be hard-pressed to accomodate six to eight billion people living high-consumption lifestyles, and it is easy to imagine intense political battles over environmental and quality-of-life issues. We may try to picture another path where the presently high-consumption societies remain so, but the poorer countries also remain at the low level (i.e., poor), with low per-capita demands on resources and environment. It is hard to see how a global system with such a persisting disparity of income and wealth could avoid vicious "wars of redistribution," with terrorism as one of the main weapons. A third conceivable path in which high-consumption societies voluntarily cut consumption to ameliorate some of the problems is equally difficult to make plausible, partly because of the severe unemployment problems those societies would face. A path to global socialist hegemony is apparently attractive to some developing nations, but totally unacceptable to the major capitalist nations.

What all this comes to is a basic challenge to past assumptions about the future of the globe. No consensus exists today on what constitutes a viable pattern of global development. It is increasingly clear that present trends do not. The Western industrialized paradigm appears in the end to be incompatible with a wise relationship to the earth and her resources; to systematically produce marginal people who have no meaningful roles in the society; to result in a society that habitually confuses goals with means (i.e., economic and technological achievement); and to persistently endanger the future of the human race with arms races which are an intrinsic aspect of the system. Thus present economic, corporate, and social policies are, by and large, inconsistent with viable long-term global development, and are being made without a picture of a viable global future in mind.

CHANGES IN VALUE PERSPECTIVES AND UNDERLYING BELIEFS

The third aspect of world change to explore is a shifting value emphasis visible throughout the industrialized world, particularly the English-speaking portion, and a far more profound, long-lasting, and consequential shift in underlying beliefs.

Basically, this is a change in attitude toward our inner, subjective experience, affirming its importance and its validity. Indications of a recent strengthening of "inner-directed" values (ecological, humane, spiritual), and a corresponding weakening of economic and status values, are fairly well documented by now. It appears that the fraction of U.S. adults whose choices are predominately motivated by inner-directed values has grown from negligibility twenty years ago to something like a fifth to a quarter in the early 1980s. Similar, if less pronounced, shifts have been observed in the other industrialized countries. Underlying this value shift is a more subtle but more fundamental shift in beliefs away from the confident scientific materialism of the earlier part of the century, and toward some form of universal transcendantalism.

Paralleling this value-and-belief shift in the developed world is a related shift in values and beliefs in the developing countries. This is again partial and indistinct; however, its direction is clearly away from Western materialism and toward a reassertion of the validity and truth in native cultural roots. In both developed and developing countries, this shift represents a striking reversal of centuries-long trends.

Both of the above statements require qualification. In a typical industrialized country, such as those of northern Europe or North America, one can easily identify at least three broad groups of people who are associated with three conflicting tendencies:

- Those who anticipate that the future will be more or less a continuation of past trends—e.g., social problems solved through continued economic and technological growth, continued emphasis on material progress and the prevalence of economic rationality, continued nationalistic tendencies, and "realistic" or hard-nosed approaches to international politics;

- Those who are keenly aware of a weakening of traditional values, and seek to strengthen these through a recommitment to fundamentalist beliefs and value emphases; and

- Those who seek a whole-system change through redefining the socially dominant vision of reality.

We focus on the smallest of three, namely, the last group which we will further identify below as being involved with a "new heresy." This group comprises a new force in history. As recently as a quarter of a century ago, it was hardly to be found; even a few years ago it was still weak and barely visible. We shall attempt to make the case below that this group is worthy of special attention because of its potentiality for being the nucleus of major societal change.

Similarly, in the developing world, we can typically find at least three groups associated with different anticipations for the future:

- Those who conceive of "development," much as it was viewed for the two decades following World War II, and seek their destiny in the world economy, aspiring to economic goals and the material allurements of the rich capitalist countries;
- Those who are threatened by the impact of "modernization" on traditional values and seek a return to fundamentalist beliefs and practices; and
- Those who are disillusioned with the materialistic nihilism reached by Western civilization and see a possibility for an alternative development based on indigenous cultural roots, but concerned with progress in wholesome human development, broadening of knowledge, matters of equity and opportunity, and fruitful interchange with the rest of the world.

Again, we focus on the smallest and last of the three because of its potentiality for alignment with the "new heresy" group in the developed world and for becoming a nucleus of worldwide fundamental change.

The Changing View of Consciousness

Central to the shift we are attempting to identify is a changing view of human consciousness. Why this topic should be so important will require further discussion.

Throughout history, individuals and communities seem repeatedly to have come upon the creative factors and forces of the human psyche. Great philosophies and great religions have time and again come into being as an outcome of such discoveries, and for a while have profoundly influenced the course of human events. But as often as the discoveries have been made, they have been lost or become inaccessible, at best preserved within some esoteric group. For the past several centuries, the power and prestige of the Western influence has caused a weakening of this element of traditional cultures. With the vogue of positivistic science in the earlier part of this century, the religious meanings associated with deep inner experiences were rather thoroughly debunked, and serious exploration of the creative unconscious processes was discouraged.

Recently, however, in the highly industrialized countries, there has been a resurgence of interest in the creative aspects of consciousness. This has shown up both in the broader society in various meditative disciplines and religious philosophies, and in the scientific community in research on consciousness. This latter development is well summarized in the following quotation from Nobel laureate Roger Sperry's lead paper in the 1981 *Annual Review of Neurosciences*:

> Social values depend . . . on whether consciousness is believed to be mortal, immortal, reincarnate, or cosmic . . . localized and brain-bound or essentially universal. . . . The new interpretation [in science] gives full recognition to the primacy of inner conscious awareness as a causal reality. . . . Recent conceptual developments in the mind-brain sciences rejecting reductionism and materialistic determinism on the one side, and dualisms on the other, clear the way for a rational approach to the theory and prescription of values and to a natural fusion of science and religion.[2]

No scientist of comparable stature had previously made such a claim, and it would be naive to imagine that Dr. Sperry's colleagues are in full agreement. Nevertheless, there existed in 1986 a field of consciousness research in a sense that none existed a quarter of a century ago, and there is a clear corresponding shift in cultural beliefs.

At the same time, one can discern in developing societies, existing simultaneously with the rush to acquire the technological goodies of the Western world, a rediscovering and re-honoring of the wisdom inherent in the traditional culture. A portion of the Westernized elite in these countries is experiencing the same disillusionment with Western materialism and the same search for lost meaning that one finds in the U.S. and northern Europe.

The practical significance of this shift in basic premises may not be immediately apparent. Modern industrialized society, like every other in history, rests on some set of largely tacit, basic assumptions about who we are, what kind of universe we are in, and what is ultimately important to us. The scientific materialism, which so confidently held forth its answers to these questions a couple of generations ago, is a dying orthodoxy. Its basic premises are being replaced with some sort of transcendalist beliefs that include increased faith in reason guided by deep intuition. In other words, a respiritualization of society is taking place, but one more experiential and noninstitutionalized, less fundamentalist and sacerdotal, than most of the historically familiar forms of religion. With this change comes a long-term shift in value emphases and priorities.

Alternative Visions of Reality

Because these indications of shifting basic assumptions are potentially so important, let us dwell on them a bit longer.

It will help make the key point if we think of the final third of the twentieth century as similar to the period of the seventeenth century in Western Europe.

Impact of the "Scientific Heresy"

Few of us would doubt that the scientific revolution of the seventeenth century was one of the important watersheds in Western history—for that matter, in the history of the planet. The world perceived by the educated person of the year 1600 was still the world of the Middle Ages. The earth, seat of change, decay, and Christian redemption, was perceived to be at the center of the cosmos, while above it circled the unchanging planets and stars, signaling and influencing human events by their locations and aspects. The world was "enchanted" and imbued with purpose; everything in it was seen as wondrous and alive. The cosmos was a place of "belonging"; personal destiny was bound up with the destiny of the whole, and this relationship gave meaning to life.

By 1700, the educated person perceived a very different reality; the earth was but one of many planets, orbiting around one of many stars. But the change was far more fundamental than that. It essentially consisted of a shifting of allegiance from the scholastic authority system of the late Middle Ages to the authority system of empirical science. By 1700, the tacit metaphysical assumptions of medieval thought were in the process of being replaced by the metaphysical assumptions of modern science. This is essentially a dead universe, perhaps constructed and set in motion by the Creator, but with subsequent events accounted for by mechanical forces and lawful behaviors. Divine purpose was an anthropocentric notion, or if it existed was unknowable and played no part in the scientific understanding of the world. Reports of such phenomena as the working of enchantments, the occurrence of miracles, and the existence of witches and others with supernatural powers, for which there had once seemed to be overwhelming evidence, were now to be dismissed as the results of charlatanry and delusion.

At the heart of this change was the "scientific heresy." It was directed against the traditional way of thinking and education known as Scholasticism. The latter assumed a world created and guided by God for man's benefit. Its understandings were largely arrived at by citing authorities, either philosophical or scriptural. The primary function of this knowledge was to rationalize sense experience with revealed religion. In contrast, the new way was to be empirical: what is true is what is found by scientific inquiry to be true. Ultimate authority lies in experiment and disciplined observation, rather than tradition.

It was certainly not apparent in the middle of the seventeenth century that the "scientific heresy" would change everything and that no institution in society would remain unaffected. The "scientific revolution," the rising influence of "practical" economic values, the concept of material progress, the capitalist revolution, and the "invention" (with the Treaty of Westfalia) of the autonomous nation-state were all aspects of a single, comprehensive, and fundamental change of mind.

The Peculiarity of the Scientific World View

The remarkable achievements of the scientific method of inquiry, as well as the perplexities it has encountered in some areas such as the study of consciousness, are related to a set of underlying assumptions at a metaphysical level. These include in particular:

- *Objectivism:* The assumption that there exists a real, objective world which can be (scientifically) known with ever-increasing precision;
- *Positivism*: The assumption that what is (scientifically) real is what is physically measurable; and
- *Reductionism*: The assumption that (scientific) understanding is to be found in the reducing of phenomena to more elemental ones (e.g., explaining heat in terms of molecular motion, or behavior in terms of response to physical stimuli).

The metaphysical bias represented by these assumptions, totally alien to the belief systems of *all* of the world's traditional cultures, came to characterize early science for a number of practical and political reasons. It distinguished scientific explanations from such prescientific explanations as the whims of the gods, or the intervention of Divine grace, or "natural tendencies" (like bodies seeking to come to rest near the center of the universe or nature abhorring a vacuum). The physicalism and empiricism of science were a reaction to the authoritarianism of the Scholastics. Reductionism seemed to lead to a more fruitful kind of explanation than the medieval concepts of ruling spiritual forces. Objectivism accelerated scientific progress and, equally important, avoided a territorial clash with the institutions of religion, which has come to view the soul and spirit as their special domain.

As science gained prestige, these assumptions became increasingly influential in the institutions of society. When Western Europe and North America came to put more and more emphasis on industrializing economic production, there was a natural tendency to support research into knowledge that would improve the abilities to predict and control, and hence to generate new technologies. This strengthened still further the positivistic and reductionistic bias in science.

All the same, there remained a feeling on the part of many scientists (as well as non-scientists) that something important was being left out. After all, the only experience of reality that we have directly is our own conscious awareness. There seemed something unnatural about a science that appeared to deny consciousness a causal reality when one's everyday experience affirmed it as a most important casual reality. In such areas as psychosomatic illness—the effects of the mind on healing, or on the functioning of the body's immune systems—neither the positivistic premise nor the reductionistic one seemed to fit. (The concept of health, for example, is not reductionistic but holistic.) Besides, there were a vast range of anomalies, including the so-called "psychic" phenomena, that were not supposed to happen but apparently sometimes do. There are phenomena in which one's state of mind seems to have effects in the physical world, directly as in the reported instances of dramatic healing or indirectly as in the cases of presumed telepathic communication.

Only in very recent years has there been much awareness that Western science might be a cultural artifact, a view of reality from a particular position, not necessarily asymptotically approaching a totally accurate depiction of reality.

THE "NEW HERESY" AND TRADITIONAL KNOWLEDGE

Each of us exhibits resistance to the discovery that our own view of reality is conditioned and parochial. Often, we are spared the discomfort of that discovery by the fact that most of those around us were conditioned by the same cultural matrix and affirm the same picture of reality. Thus our collective resistance is even stronger; even more determinedly do we resist discovering that our own society's view of reality is a cultural artifact—and hence, in a sense, arbitrary.

The well-demonstrated fact that our perceptions of reality can be altered by hypnotic suggestion should be the main clue. In demonstrations of hypnosis, the extent to which this is true can be startling. By changing the inner, and largely unconscious, belief structure through hypnotic suggestion, a person can be led to perceive what actually is not there, or to fail to perceive what *is* there. Through hypnotic suggestion a person can be led to exhibit a strength or ability that he/she normally does not seem to possess; or, on the other hand, to fail to have strength or ability that is ordinarily present. What we perceive is far less a matter of "what is there," and far more a matter of our internalized beliefs than most of us would comfortably recognize.

Collectively, in "cultural hypnosis" a similar thing occurs. Through constant exposure to the cultural suggestion of how to perceive the world, persons brought up in a particular culture experience the world the way it is experienced in that culture. One may know, abstractly, that the world as seen by other cultures is a different reality; yet one's own way feels unquestionably right—and furthermore, one can argue, it has successfully passed the tests for validity for many generations.

The World of Traditional Cultures

It is important to note some of the most significant differences in reality as experienced through the lens of Western science and through the eyes of traditional cultures. Present in medieval Christianity and carried over into the modern age is the deep-seated conviction that all of nature exists for the benefit of the human race. It seems perfectly reasonable to modern man to allow the extinction of hundreds of species of plants and animals because they have no value in the economy; to destroy native habitat because it is in the way of economically profitable activities; and to discount the future at an appropriate rate (depending on interest and inflation rates)—i.e., to formalize that the future well-being of humans as well as other creatures is not a factor in present decision making.

Because of the way they perceive reality, practically all traditional cultures instill a different attitude toward nature. In their realities, the natural world was not created for the benefit of human beings, but for itself. Other creatures are not alien to us, but close relatives. One would not have the right, for example, to raise pigs and chickens in little boxes with no chance to exercise in even a fenced-in yard.

The relationship to land, too, is different. In the modern world, land is a form of capital. It is a factor in production, a source of sustenance *and* profits. Rights of use, on which the medieval economy rested, have given way to rights of ownership—the right to buy and sell. Land can be exploited, soil can be mined, one can do whatever can be economically justified. By contrast, in most non-Westernized societies only rights of land use are recognized. Land is not a possession, but an inheritance handed down by the ancestors, to be held in trust for the unborn.

"Development" is a word that has been used by the modernized nations to signify industrial and technological change in the pattern pioneered by them. But traditional peoples often have a very different concept of the desirable future; it may have more to do with religious ceremony than with economic growth and high-tech gadgets. To them, what is called development in the Westernized world may mean the destruction of their culture and subjugation by an alien culture.

The modern world has been quick to put down other views of reality as "primitive" and "prescientific." But those other views of reality *worked*, or they would not have lasted for thousands of years. The modern view of reality, in an important sense, is *not working*. That is precisely why it is increasingly held up to question.

Jacob Needleman succinctly expressed the Western crisis in science in the Introduction to *A Sense of the Cosmos*:

> Once the hope of mankind, modern science has now become the object of such mistrust and disappointment that it will probably never again speak with its old authority. The crisis of ecology, the threat of atomic war, and the disruption of the patterns of human life by advanced technology have all eroded what was once a general trust in the *goodness* of science. And the appearance in our society of alien metaphysical systems, of "new religions" sourced in the East, and of ideas and fragments of teachings emanating from ancient times have all contributed doubt about the *truth* of science. Even among scientists themselves there are signs of a metaphysical rebellion. Modern man is searching for a new world view.[3]

CULTURAL RELATIVITY AND SCIENCE

It has been humbling for scientists to come to recognize that science is in a sense a cultural artifact. A different society with a different "cultural hypnosis"—for example, different unconscious assumptions about reality—would have created a different science.

This observation poses a perplexing puzzle. There is apparently a dual relationship between experienced "reality" and the science that is developed. There is no doubt in anyone's mind that the scientific knowledge that has been gained influences the way we perceive the world. *But, the way the world is experienced in our culture influences what kind of science gets developed.* As Western society after the Middle Ages became increasingly secular, it created a science based on the positivistic assumption that only what can be physically measured is scientifically real. Then this science found that everywhere it looked in the universe there was nothing save that which was measurable! A basic tenet of the new science was that scientific explanations are deterministic and reductionistic; science then peered out into the universe and discerned nothing resembling purpose!

This thought—that a society's basic experiencing of reality shapes its science as well as the reverse—may be quite disturbing as one pursues its implications. When the shift took place from medieval to modern society, it was not a matter of the medieval paradigm having been proved wrong. Rather, the gradual secularization of values which had been taking place over several centuries had brought the culture to the point where an empirical science served its needs better than the outmoded Scholisticism. Similarly, if the adequacy of the scientific/economic authority system is being challenged today, it is not a matter of its being right or wrong so much as a question of whether the needs of persons, societies, and the planet are being well served.

There are two main reasons that the underlying assumptions of Western industrial society are being challenged, and probably are shifting. One is the accumulation of evidence, reminding us that the contemporary scientific world view does not jibe with the totality of human experience —in particular, with the experienced realm of deep inner experience, from which all individuals and societies eventually get their primary value commitments. The other is the many ways in which the consequences of the modern paradigm are not good for people, and not good for the planet. The serious problems of our day—from the threat of nuclear weapons and toxic chemical concentrations, to systemic hunger and poverty and environmental deterioration, to insults to the earth's life-support systems—are the direct consequences of the Western industrial mindset that began to dominate the world several centuries ago.

But if the assumptions that shaped the modern world are no longer serving it well, what are the replacement assumptions? It is not easy for us in modern society to imagine that a change in basic assumptions might be under way, as fundamental and as thoroughgoing in its eventual impacts as was the scientific revolution. The characteristics of science, which we identified above as objectivism, positivism, and reductionism, seem so identified with "scientific method" that it seems heretical indeed to suggest that they might be giving way. Yet one has only to listen to the conversation around one to realize that a number of related topics are discussed seriously today that a quarter of a century ago would never have been mentioned with serious intent—e.g., altered states of consciousness, insight through near-death experiences, meditation, yoga, synchronicity, "channeling," past lives, karma, the actuality of psychic phenomena.

If "consciousness as causal reality" is somehow going to be dealt with in the prevailing picture of reality, how will this be reconciled with science as we have known it? There appear to be two main answers: a new version of dualism and a dramatically different kind of assumption that makes "physical reality" less fundamental than consciousness itself.

The Prospects for a New Dualism

It has been increasingly clear that besides the science of measurable information, quantified descriptions, deterministic models, and reductionistic explanations, these consciousness-related aspects of human experience seemed to call for another kind of knowledge. It is the kind of knowledge found useful in guiding human development—making value choices, humankind's search for meaning, and understanding the universe. It is concerned with purpose and volition; it places emphasis on value issues and teleological explanations; it uses models and metaphors involving holistic concepts like health, purpose, love, trust; it places value on explorations of alternate states or "levels" of consciousness, particularly the "deep intuition."

Thus one possible way of resolving the perceived incompleteness of science in its present form is to think in terms of a complementary body of knowledge. This dualistic approach has been proposed by a number of eminent scientists, including Nobel laureates Roger Sperry and Sir John Eccles. Ultimately, in this approach, there are two basic kinds of "stuff" in the universe. One is matter-energy stuff, explored so competently by science in its present form. The other is mind-spirit stuff, not physically measurable but "real" in human experience. Complementing science in its present form is a second kind of knowledge-seeking, one resembling science in its open spirit of inquiry and public validation of knowledge, but resembling the humanities and religion in being concerned with values, purposes, and meanings.

A Third Kind of Metaphysical Assumption

Besides this dualistic alternative there is yet a third possible kind of metaphysical assumption. To see how this gets into the picture, we need to draw upon a finding from the field of comparative religion.

It turned out that when scholars looked carefully into the world's many different spiritual traditions, an important common thread appeared. The various religious traditions tend to have both exoteric or public versions, and also esoteric "inner-circle" understandings. The latter typically involve some sort of spiritual or meditative discipline; they place primary emphasis on the indiviual's own inner access to the sources of wisdom and enlightenment. The exoteric versions of the world's religions are obviously very different, one from the other. However, the esoteric versions appear to be essentially the same, and to represent a valuable body of experience it would not be prudent to ignore.

Whereas the exoteric versions are often dualistic, the esoteric forms assert a monistic point of view: The ultimate stuff of the universe is consciousness. Mind or consciousness is primary, and matter-energy arises in some sense out of mind. Individual minds are not separate (although individual brains may appear to be); they connect at some unconscious level. Ultimately, reality is contacted not through the physical senses but through the deep intuition.

In this frame of reference, the physical world is to the greater mind as a dream image is to the individual mind. It is difficult, although not impossible, to be aware of the dream-nature of one's experience *while dreaming;* yet, once awake, the fact becomes obvious and requires no proof.

Similarly, the organism may have to be subjected to rather drastic treatments (e.g., demanding meditative disciplines or ascetic vision quests) for the person to awaken to the "real Self." But the dream-like quality of ordinary consciousness and the dream-nature of physical reality become from that vantage point self-evident, requiring no proof. In fact, no "proof" could be concocted from the unenlightened, ordinary-consciousness state. But in the awakened state, it is apparent that "we, the collective dreamer" create unconsciously the world we then experience consciously.

In this frame of reference, furthermore, consciousness is not the end-product of billions of years of material evolution: rather, consciousness was there all along. Its existence was not contingent on the development of neuronal cells within the human cranium. In contrast to the usual assumption that consciousness is a non-material attribute arising out of material evolution, this third metaphysic starts from a totally different assumption. *Consciousness is.* Out of universal mind is created the evolution of the physical universe. The development of life forms is "pushed" by natural selection, but it is also "pulled" in certain preferred directions (e.g., increasing awareness, freedom, complexity).

We should not think of this third picture of reality as some abstract theological or philosophical theory to be debated. Rather, it would seem to be a universal insight of which at some level of ourselves we are already aware. As we have noted, it has appeared again and again in the "perennial wisdom" esoteric understandings of the world's spiritual traditions. In those traditions, we are urged not to analyze it or argue about it, but through meditative and other disciplines to *experience* it. (In this regard, we see the potential importance of the fact that a widening group of people throughout the world are exhibiting interest in the "perennial wisdom" traditions, as well as being involved in meditation, yoga, and other "spiritual fitness" disciplines.)

At first thought, the idea that science might be reconstituted on the basis of this third kind of metaphysic may seem as outrageous a proposition as the heliocentric universe did to many in early seventeenth-century Europe. The idea of matter emerging out of consciousness seems quite foreign to the Western mind; at any rate, it would have seemed so a quarter of a century ago. Any such idea as the phenomenal world being a thought in the Universal Mind seemed to belong with the philosophies of the East. However, a growing fraction of the professional, business, and scientific world (as well as just plain people) have been quietly reporting that when they take their total experience into account, it is this latter metaphysic that feels most satisfactory.

The modern world long assumed that there was a fundamental conflict between science and religion. For a time, this conflict appeared as a series of battles over such issues as the age of the earth, the meaning of the fossil records, evolutionary theory, the Freudian re-interpretation of the human psyche, and so forth. Religion always seemed to lose. Then, as the world moved well into the twentieth century, the conflict subsided and people tended to live their religious lives apart from whatever they thought science was telling them about the nature of reality. The price paid for this schizophrenia was that neither science nor religion seemed to be satisfying the person's deep desire for some kind of understanding that would be secure enough to base one's life on.

It now appears that what is happening is a resolution of this conflict in a somewhat unexpected way. There may indeed be a conflict between dogmatic exoteric religion and positivistic science. However, there is *not* an inevitable conflict between the esoteric "perennial wisdom" of the world's spiritual traditions and a science based on the third kind of metaphysical assumptions identified above.

It has been necessary to dwell on this point because it is potentially so important, and one's initial inclination is likely to be not to take it seriously. Improbable as it may still seem to many persons, the world appears to be experiencing a "second Copernican revolution," wherein the reassertion of the importance of inner, subjective experience is challenging the adequacy of positivistically biased science. As people have increasingly looked to their own inner experience as the realm in which matters of value and meaning are resolved, and come to trust their own deep intuition as the ultimate authority, the heretical "secret" has been more and more openly shared: the world of experience is not the "reality" they taught us in science class! There is another way to look at things that retains the value of scientific knowledge, but is more true to the totality of human experience.

And so we find the "new heresy," growing in power. Compared with the "scientific heresy" it seems equally comprehensive and fundamental. Just as "the earth goes around the sun" became the somewhat inadequate summary of the Copernican revolution, so "consciousness as causal reality" could be taken to be that of the "second Copernican revolution." *If* this picture of a shifting metaphysical base proves to fit—that is, if this "third metaphysic" continues to capture the allegiance of a widening group of people until it ultimately prevails—then the world of the twenty-first century may be as different from the present as modern times have been from the Middle Ages. Obviously, this has the most profound implications for any concept of development.

The Development of "Developed" Nations

All countries are "developing countries." The highly industrialized nations such as the United States face a different set of development options and questions from the non-industrialized poorer countries. Because of the interconnectedness of the modern world, we need to explore development paths for the richer industrialized countries before the context for the others can become clear.

Before doing that, however, let us summarize what has gone before. The Western industrial paradigm, which supplanted the medieval paradigm in Western Europe, has been phenomenally successful in its own terms. Its characteristics of materialism and manipulative rationality helped it to dominate the planet and to prevail over competing cultures. Those same characteristics are now the source of serious societal and global problems, problems of a sort that raise doubts as to their solvability within that paradigm.

At the same time that this global crisis is so evident, there appears to be a spontaneous and spreading attraction to the world of inner experience; a rediscovery of the "perennial wisdom" of the world's spiritual traditions; a growing appreciation of the need for balance of masculine and feminine qualities and values; and a realization of the need for a non-exploitative relationship with Planet Earth, its creatures, and its peoples.

This suggests that the value emphases, represented by the "Green" political movements, "deep ecology," the "feminine perspective," and the "inner peace" end of the sprectrum of peace movements, are reinforced by, and indeed probably partly rooted in, a spreading shift in basic assumptions. Thus not only are the new value emphases and perspectives likely to have staying power, but they are seen as part of a whole-system change that will include major institutional changes.

THE EMERGING VALUES AND PERSPECTIVES

These values and perspectives, as distilled from statements by the various Green-related movements, can be summarized as follows:

- *Wholeness:* Resolution of the world's dilemmas will come only from a whole-system view. People do not behave like "economic man," and the economic system cannot be adequately considered apart from the greater society.

- *Ecological awareness:* The holistic view includes awareness of the finiteness and multiple-connectedness of the planetary ecosystem, and the inextricable interdependence of all human communities and dependence on the planetary life-support system.

- *Peace and common security:* Present "national security" policies diminish both security and well-being. The psychological climate of insecurity stemming from the nuclear arms race affects all, especially childen. Resources going to the world arms races, nuclear and "conventional," are in effect stolen from the world's poor. Arms spending reduces the capability of the state to provide programs that would increase the well-being of its citizens. Thus achievement of sustainable global peace and nuclear disarmament is imperative.

- *Decentralization; human scale:* Bigness and concentration of power contribute to the feelings of alienation and depersonalization in modern society. The desire for high quality of life will require decentralization of much social and political activity, rebuilding of community, an appropriate technology (i.e., human scale, ecologically compatible, "kind" to human beings and to the planet).

- *Postpatriarchal perspectives:* Sensitivity is needed to the destructive aspects of patriarchal society and masculine competitive, aggressive, exploitative values. There must be a counterbalancing of these values with feminine nurturing, cherishing, conserving, cooperative values, and general appreciation of the feminine perspective.

- *Transmaterialist beliefs:* The new emphasis includes self-realization, transcendent meaning, and inner growth leading to wisdom and compassion.

- *Social responsibility:* It is imperative that appropriate measures be taken to ensure that the poor and working classes will not get hurt by programs to restructure the economy and consumer society along lines that are more ecologically sound.

- *Solidarity with the Third World:* The future of the Third World is of intimate concern to the industrialized countries. As economic growth is not an adequate goal for the developed countries, so economic growth alone is not an appropriate goal for the developing world. An emerging redefinition of growth and development includes emphasis on human development and well-being, social and cultural goals, and self-reliance.

- *Steady-state population and economy:* Finiteness of the globe dictates both that world population should approach steady-state conditions and that the interaction between the total world economic activity and the earth-system should approach some kind of equilibrium. The latter will require new concepts of work and of the healthy economy, since the creation of jobs through boundless economic growth and consumption is not in the end a viable strategy.

- *Cultural pluralism:* The richness of cultural diversity is a planetary resource just as the richness of diversity of plant and animal life. The tendency of the world industrial economy to stamp out competing cultures must be corrected.

- *Non-violent change:* Necessary and fundamental societal change must come about through a spreading awakening. The political manifestations of this must involve non-violent change if the change process is to be compatible with the ends desired.

- *Empowerment of people:* For the other conditions to be met, the emphasis must be not on goals but on process, on people becoming empowered to take responsibility for their own lives and for changing society as necessary. The process is an evolutionary one and the goals are emergent.

SOCIETY'S NEW "CENTRAL PROJECT"

We asked earlier, what comes after a production-focused society? What is the central purpose of an advanced society when it no longer makes sense to continue with the principal goal of economic production? The answer becomes apparent from the emerging value emphases and beliefs about the nature of human being. It is to advance human growth and development to the fullest extent.

The best example from the distant past of a society that actually accomplished this is the Athenian model of *paideia*. The Athenians assumed that the primary function of society is to promote learning in the broadest possible definition. Every institution of society was directed to that end. *Paideia* was the Greek term for this larger concept of education and for the social matrix that was its manifestation. *Paideia* was education looked upon as a lifelong transformation of the human personality, in which every aspect of life plays a part. It did not limit itself to the conscious learning processes, or to inducting the young into the social heritage of the community. *Paideia* meant the task of making life itself an art form, with the person himself being the work of art. In theory, at least, the achievement of the human whole—and of the wholly human—took precedence over every specialized activity or narrower purpose. The cornerstone of this social curriculum was, according to its foremost scholar Werner Jaeger, "the search for the

Divine Center."

The motivations implicit in the emerging belief-and-values structure fit very well with this Greek concept of a "learning society." They clearly do not fit with mindless consumption, material acquisition, and endless economic growth.

In the "learning society," the occupational focus of most people is learning and developing in the broadest sense. This focus includes a wide diversity of such activities as formal education, research, exploration, self-discovery, various specialized roles, and participation in the community of concerned citizens to choose a better future. These activities contribute to human betterment and fulfillment. They are humane, non-polluting, and non-stultifying. They can absorb unlimited numbers of persons not required for other sorts of work.

"Learning society" implies reversal of a number of aspects of the long-term industrialization trend. It almost certainly involves something like the "intermediate technology" or "appropriate technology" concepts of E. F. Schumacher and others. These terms refer to technology that is resource conserving, environmentally benign, frugal in the use of energy, relatively labor intensive, and understandable and usable at the individual or community level. Such technology tends to complement a strong ecological ethic; strong identification with nature, fellow human beings, and future generations; a lifestyle characterized by voluntary frugality ("doing more with less"); appreciation of the simple life and simple virtues; and the kind of work that fosters these attitudes.

The Redefinition of Work

Thus there is involved a redefinition of work. Our present conceptions about work were formed in an era when the primary societal function of work was the production of necessary or desired goods and services, and in which one could foresee no end to the social desirability of increasing the economic productivity of the individual laborer through technological advance. Yet today, as we have seen, these assumptions lead to a fundamental dilemma. On the one hand, if labor productivity in a country does not continually increase, the industry in that country tends to become non-competitive in the international market. On the other hand, if productivity does increase, the economic product must increase (by definition) to maintain the same number of jobs. As various resource, environmental, political, and social constraints tend to limit economic growth, chronic unemployment becomes an instrinsic characteristic of the future.

Underemployment, the failure to utilize the individual's full potentiality, is also characteristic of the extrapolated future. Many of the jobs in industrial society are boring and stultifying. Rising educational levels mean that there will not be job opportunities to match the expectations that traditionally have been associated with acquiring academic degrees.

If it were really true that human beings basically seek to escape from work, then industrial society might be considered a great success, since it has made possible the elimination of so much work that humans once had to do. But both from observation of worker behavior and from the findings of psychological research, there is ample evidence that *people seek meaningful activity and relationships.* Humans thrive not on mindless pleasure, but on challenge. Therefore, although full employment is no longer needed from a production standpoint, *full participation is essential from a social standpoint.*

The social-roles function of work is enhanced when work is done in the environment of the home, community, and small corporation. Thus we would expect the "learning society" to be more decentralized. Many production and service activities would be removed from the mainline economy; a significant amount of production would be in the household and community. (The household economy is already far from negligible. Were its exchanges counted in such economic indicators as the GNP, it would be about one-third the size of the official economy.)

One of the traditional functions of work has been to facilitate equitable distribution of income and wealth. However, the logic of linking income with labor contribution to economic production becomes less convincing as the degree of automation of production increases. We are seeing a decrease in the relative importance of income, as compared with opportunity for meaningful activity and relationships. Furthermore, the informal economy is increasingly being favored, and income distribution is far less of an issue in a society where much of the exchange takes place outside the formal economy, such as through communal work, barter, trade, and gifts—

and where much of this exchange is non-monetized.

Thus the puzzle of how to achieve fair distribution of overall societal income, when only a fraction of the population have jobs in the mainstream economy, may be less difficult to solve than might appear at first thought. One aspect of the change is a partial divorcing of income distribution from jobs in the mainstream economy. Among the alternative ways of achieving income distribution, appearing on the whole to be good for people, are through communal exchange as well as such grants as scholarships, research fellowhips, and assorted forms of patronage. These latter may come from both the private sector and the public sector, perhaps preferably so. Some amount of government transfer payments would undoubtedly be necessary to take care of the most needy cases.

Again, I feel impelled to say that we are not attempting here to theorize about some idealized society, but rather to report some of the observed changes that appear, when considered together, to amount to a fundamental shift in the direction of social evolution.

The New Business of Business

If there is anything at all to the proposition that a fundamental transformation is already under way, we should see signs in the business community. For one thing, business is all-pervasive in modern society, and reflects any major change in any portion of it. Moreover, business is extremely sensitive to changes in its environment, and tends to respond to them promptly. The modern business corporation is probably the most adaptive institution humankind has ever devised.

There are indeed indications of a new concept of management in business, and a new concept of the corporation. They show up most clearly in the sorts of executive development seminars that proliferated in the past decade. A central theme of these courses and workshops is the untapped power of creating and holding a vision of a desired individual or collective goal. Another basic premise is that all persons can find, in their deep inner experience, a sense of purpose of wanting to contribute to the whole. The emerging concept of management involves creating an organization in which a pre-eminent objective is to accomplish something together which is in alignment with every member's sense of purpose. Profit is relegated to the role of a control signal, not an end goal. Management is less a matter of using power to direct resources toward achievement of a goal set by top management, and more a matter of empowering people in the organization to use their own creativity, both in setting and achieving goals. The central function of the corporation is less a matter of rewarding those who have invested money in the firm, and more a matter of actualizing the potentialities of those who are investing their *lives*. Corporate excellence is not efficient management toward maximizing short-term return, but the ability to attract and hold the most creative people.

There are many questions yet to be answered regarding the future of the large corporation and the world business system as a whole, but these new concepts in executive development are surely one of the indicators deserving attention.

The Displacement of Economic Rationality

Economic rationality has assumed a place in modern industrial society that is unwarranted. There is no *a priori* reason to assume that economic logic will lead to socially desirable decisions. For example, it is economically rational to discount the future at some rate related to prevailing interest rates; but in a social sense that is equivalent to building into the decision-guiding structure the propostion that the well-being of future generations do not count. Economic arguments would seem to indicate that providing a good education for everyone or insuring citizen protection on city streets amount to drains on the economy, whereas a new arms contract or a gambling spree at Las Vegas adds to the GNP!

The economy is the dominant institution in modern society; the performance of the economy is judged on the rate of consumption of goods and services. These goods and services tend to use up scarce resources, materials, energy, fresh water, topsoil, livable space, endangered species, wilderness. We are inclined to forget how recent was the value shift by which we in the industrialized societies became no longer ashamed to be called "consumers." Two generations ago frugality was still a virtue and hedonistic consumption was a vice. Then in only a few years (perhaps as an unconscious response to the fear of return to the Great Depression after World War II), consumption became a virtue and frugality was understood to be bad for the economy. If the mass-consumption societies were to become frugal again, their economies would collapse. But the entropic handwriting on the wall is clear: frugal we must become.

We have remarked above on the paradox of work. Modern society has rightly considered employment (i.e., constructive and satisfying social roles) to be essential to the well-being of all its citizens. Yet, capitalist societies have also considered employment to be a mere by-product of economic production, the amount being a function of various economic variables. (Some socialist societies, on the other hand, attempt to so manipulate the economy in order to create full employment opportunity that they often pay a high price in featherbedding, inefficient makework, low morale, and social consequences such as alcoholism.)

This peculiarity of the pre-eminence of economic rationality is a characteristic of our bureaucratic age. Decisions of the highest import are defended, if not decided, on the basis of economic analyses; furthermore, this is on the whole considered to be rational behavior. To a visitor from another civilization viewing us for the first time, this elevation of economic institutions and economic rationality to such a pinnacle position would appear to be the utmost craziness. Throughout history, that pinnacle position in the durable societies has been reserved for the repositories of such wisdom as are deemed worthy of guiding the great decisions—usually institutions of religion or of the highest knowledge.

It is difficult for us to look at this fundamental issue without prejudice, so steeped are we in the cultural concept that economic rationality "naturally" dominates. For generations, it has been an unspoken sign of progress to have an ever-increasing fraction of human activities of all sorts accounted for in the mainstream economy; to have economic logic displace philsophical discourse or even political expediency as the prevailing rationality for guiding momentous decisions; to incorporate the most profound human considerations into an economic cost-benefit analysis as mere "externalities."

There are now indications that this fetish relationship with economic rationality is approaching an end point. The value emphases of the emerging culture are not well reflected in the sorts of economic and financial control signals that have received major attention in the past. A social rationality of some sort will tend to carry more weight than economic rationality as these changes proceed further.

The Prospects for Alternative Development

In other sections of this essay, there have been various attempts to describe the *promise* of some form of alternative development, the *reality* of attempts to create such a development in the face of a dominant world system antagonistic to it, and the *prospects* for future development along these lines. The burden of my observations here has been that (1) the *reality* is that prospects for all forms of alternative development are rather dim *unless* there is a fundamental change of mind that sweeps the world (particularly the developed world), and (2) the *prospect* of such a change happening is more promising than one might think.

THE CALL FOR "ANOTHER DEVELOPMENT"

The concept of development that dominated for the quarter-century following the end of World War II was strongly influenced by the success of the Marshall Plan and the International Bank for Reconstruction and Development in reconstructing war-torn Europe. A similar approach was proposed for the Third World. The main factors to be supplied were injections of capital, technologies, and technical expertise.

The chief factor left out of these calculations was that of cultural difference. Some societies, particularly around the Pacific Rim—notably Taiwan, South Korea, Hong Kong, and Singapore—found a match between their cultural traits and the characteristics of the growing world industrialized economy, such that they not only were able to compete, with the Western nations but in some respects excel. But many other cultures emphasized other values and found the price of adapting to the alien Western industrial culture too high. Of course, a number of other factors entered into the situation—geography, climate, natural resources, demography, among others. But the net result was that although a few of the developing countries were able to enter into the global economic game and compete, the bulk of the Third World drifted into a relationship of economic exploitation. They were not only progressively and relatively poorer but so badly mired in debt that, despite the appearance of development aid, poor countries seemed to end up subsidizing the rich through low-wage labor and excessive interest payments.

This economic schism grew, dividing the world into extremes of affluence and deprivation. A few countries with a minority fraction of the world population are characterized by over-abundance, over-production, and over-consumption. Those containing the vast majority of the population are characterized by concentrations of poverty, scarcity, unemployment, and deprivation. Moreover, resources from the poorer countries tend to be steadily drained out to fuel the world economy. Because of the weakness of their position, the Third World countries have been able to do very little to rectify this fundamental inequity. (The temporary successes of OPEC were, of course, a notable exception.)

There is in the world situation a fundamental paradox, with a number of dimensions. We live in an age that has witnessed the end of empires and seen the dawn of independence for scores of nations, and yet it has turned out to be an age of increasing domination of the world by a few great economic powers. A century of unprecendented material progress has also been one of sprawling misery and widespread deprivation. Despite world agricultural production now surpassing population growth, the availability of adequate food is denied hundreds of millions of people. On balance, there is a net flow of nutritional resources from the poorer and more populous regions of the world to the richer and less populous. Policies of "aid" and technology transfer have, in effect, turned out to be a net transfer of surpluses from the poorer to the richer countries. All of these aspects of the fundamental paradox suggest that something is basically wrong with the way modern man has gone about constructing his world.

In reaction to these conditions, the "Group of 77" Third World nations, in the 1974 Special Session of the General Assembly of the United Nations, made a forceful demand for a "New International

Economic Order." This was in essence a response to the perceived situation, wherein the control of world trade and finance by the advanced industrialized nations left much of the Third World impoverished. It was a call for a restructuring of the global system to reduce these perceived inequities. The demand failed to produce significant results, partly because the powerful nations were unwilling to make the concessions of economic power that were implied by the NIEO, but also because the required restructuring goes much deeper than can be reached by changes in policy or, in fact, that governments can bring about.

There followed a stir of activity around the concept of "alternative development," of which this project is a part. Broadly speaking, "alternative development" is defined as development which builds on indigenous cultural roots, places human and community development above economic development per se, and which fosters and employs local and national self-reliance. Above all, it is development which comes out of the local culture and rejects domination by the alien Western industrial culture. The latter is characterized by its use of knowledge as an instrument of domination—domination over the unpredicatble forces of nature, over social forces and institutions, and ultimately over relations between societies and between cultures and races.

The paradox we spoke of a bit earlier is the reflection of a fundamental axiom regarding power, which can be seen to operate throughout history. That is, that the more power—social, economic, political, or military—one has, the better position one is in to obtain even more power. This tends to be true whether one is thinking about one individual, one organization, or one nation. Every enduring society, whether ancient feudal, or modern capitalist, involves some tacitly agreed-upon mechanism for limiting that natural tendency for power to accumulate. But there is no such mechanism at the *global* level, and that poses a fundamental limitation on the abilities of countries to pursue diverse paths of alternative development.

We have spoken earlier of the global development dilemma. Concepts of "alternative development" are extremely useful in that they point to the direction of fundamental change that will be required to resolve that dilemma. However, they describe viable paths for individual countries *only insofar as the global context changes to foster those paths*. The force that could bring about such a change in a global context, if it continues to grow, can be thought of as a change in perception. We noted earlier the elevation to the global level of what was prior to World War II mainly a domestic issue. That issue was the legitimate right of all (planetary) citizens to satisfaction of certain universally felt needs. We observed there that this idea of restructuring international society around a newly recognized fundamental right is "as profound in its ultimate implications as was the concept of democratic government, two centuries ago." The political power of *re-perceiving* a previously unclaimed right is typically underestimated.

Sociologist Ralph Turner has observed that many profound changes in history have come about through people shifting from the perception of certain conditions as unavoidable circumstances or misfortunes to *their re-perception as injustices, hence leading to a new sense of rights*. Therefore, in the European Reformation, re-perceiving religious authoritarianism as unjust led to the concept of a right to religious freedom. The democratic revolutions involved re-perception of authoritarian governments as unjust, and hence the right of democratic participation. The socialist movements had to do with re-perceiving economic slavery, poverty, and extreme disparities of wealth as basically unjust, and therefore to a concept of a right to economic security.

The "development revolution" that is now spreading around the world can be thought of in a similar way. Persons in the industrially advanced countries had in the past been willing to accept air and water pollution, industrial blight, environmental degradation from logging and mining, the weakening of traditional and communal structures, the dying out of crafts and small family farms, sporadic unemployment, alienation and depersonalization, and so forth as part of the "price of progress." These are now being re-perceived as ills that must be righted. Similarly, in the developing countries, people had to some extent been accepting of poverty, famine, disease, and unhealthy living conditions as misfortunes, or even as their own fault. The more common attitude now is that such conditions are injustices, fostered or caused by deliberate or systemic exploitation, and therefore conditions that must be corrected. While this re-perception provides the motive power necessary for fundamental change, in the main there is little understanding as yet of how basic the change would have to be in order for alternative development paths to, in fact, be feasible.

THE REDEFINITION OF DEVELOPMENT

We have examined some indications of a worldwide "awakening" under way, a fundamental change in perception. This "awakening" involves re-perceiving the present world situation and its origins. It involves re-perceiving the basic rights of people and societies around the globe. At its most fundamental level, it involves re-perceiving the culturally accepted picture of reality and the authority structure behind that. As (or if) these changes proceed, there will be a departure from the equation of development with "modernization" and economic development. Development will be defined differently for different cultures and different societies. Human and cultural development will be central factors in these definitions, with economic development demoted to the status of means rather than end.

Up to now it has been extremely difficult for a society or a nation to pursue a development path different from the path dictated by the mainstream world economic system. Several factors will make diverse development paths more feasible in the future.

One of these factors is the increasingly evident conclusion that the past ways of development do not, in the end, lead to a viable future for the world. The highly industrialized countries are going to have to find some development path for themselves that, without necessarily sacrificing quality of life, does not make such voracious demands upon the resource base and effect such gross insults to the ecological and life-support systems of the planet. As a result, the developing countries will find the advanced industrialized countries a less attractive model, and will be freed to search for their own uniquely suitable form of development.

A second important factor is the growing sense of a crisis in meaning in the developed world. As individual riches are not always found to produce a happy life, so the allurements of affluent industrial society and its trappings fail to provide the kind of shared meanings that make a society cohesive and inspire mutual loyalty.

Then, too, there is the growing sense in traditional societies, as noted above, that "modernization" does not necessarily bring about the development that is best for them in human terms. This concern is reflected within the industrialized countries by a growing appreciation of the value to the world of diverse ecology of cultures. Thus there is an emerging vision of transformed society; although the entire vision is not yet clear, certain characteristics can be discerned. The vision is distinct from either Marxism or Liberalism, although it shares some of the same human goals. It is transnational, with different emphases coming from different cultural backgrounds. Because it is emergent, there is no clear articulation to be found in any single country or any particular political movement (although the various Green movements probably come closest).

THE PROMISE OF TRANSFORMED DEVELOPMENT

To give this vision some definition, let us summarize it with five defining characteristics:

- Man in harmony with nature;
- Man in harmony with man;
- Individual self-realization;
- Honoring cultural diversity; and
- Globalization of global issues.

We will discuss these briefly, both as characteristics of individual societies and as characteristics of the global system that would foster alternative development.

Man in Harmony with Nature

We mean the word "man" in the sense of man/woman or human beings, although if truth be told the disharmony is in good measure due to the activities of the male of the species. This harmony contrasts sharply with the exploitative attitude toward nature that has been a hallmark of industrial society. So-called primitive societies typically have had more cooperative, less exploitative relationships with nature. In some cases, for example, among many Native American tribes, there was a clear tradition of caring for Earth. Thus there is much precedent for the ecological ethic that now seems dictated by increasingly serious environmental problems.

One indication of a shift toward a different relationship with the planet can be found in the "Gaia hypothesis" seriously advanced by a few scientists. The central concept is that Earth can well be thought of as a living organism, with self-regulating capabilities regarding temperature, chemical composition of atmosphere and oceans, climate, etc. The relationship of humans to the overall Earth organism is somewhat like the relationship of the various micro-organisms in our bodies to their human hosts some of their activities are positive with regard to, and some inimical to, the state of well-being of the whole. In this view, it is especially obvious that the future well-being of the human family (or any part of it) is intimately linked to that of the planet.

The shift toward becoming more in harmony with nature is only partly due to the threat of what will happen to us if we do not change. It is more directly rooted in the reassertion of spirit, of the transcendental, which as noted previously is an aspect of the contemporary waves of change.

Man in Harmony with Man

The emerging vision emphasizes community in the small view, and global cooperation in the large. Institutions are to be person-centered and non-discriminatory with regard to sex, race, and culture.

On the world scale, there is to be a "great leveling" of rich and poor societies, not in wealth alone but in equity and equality of opportunity. The Western concept of economic development toward a "consumer society" is to be eschewed in favor of "liberatory development," emphasizing liberation of spirit and energy, self-reliance, preservation of cultural diversity and identity, and reassertion of group history. There is to be a casting off of the mental yoke of fatalism, self-denigration, and submission to external authority, and increasing emphasis on human productiveness, autonomy, and global cooperation. For these conditions to be possible in the individual societies, there has to be a reshaping of the international order in a manner compatible with the legitimate goals of developed and developing countries. We have already indicated how the motive force for that reshaping is growing.

Individual Self-Realization

The new order is to be one that fosters movement from self-subordination—to superiors in a hierarchy, to institutions, to "advanced" or powerful nations—toward self-realization. Especially in the workplace and in the development of Third World countries is this emphasis on self-actualization of central importance.

The basic idea involved here is summarized in psychologist Abraham Maslow's concept of "deficiency needs" and "self-actualization" or "being" needs. It appears that persons, after their "deficiency" needs—food, shelter, warmth, sex, belongingness, esteem—are reasonably well satisfied, are then motivated by "being" needs. This was well expressed in a counterculture slogan of the late 1960s: "We don't want to have more, we want to *be* more."

Manifestations of this emphasis in the industrialized countries are to be found especially in the various "liberation" movements (of women, minorities, the elderly) and intentional communities. Similar manifestations are found in the worker self-government and "industrial democracy" movements of northern Europe. In the Third World, the emphasis is seen most clearly as an insistence upon casting off all shackles inherent in the acceptance of poverty and exploitation by landlords, rich ruling classes, or imperialists. In both cases, the emphasis is on awakening to the realization that one has been imprisoned by "buying into" a set of beliefs which, once this is realized, one need not accept.

Cultural Decentralization

There is implicit in the new vision a repudiation of the centralist tendencies of both capitalist and socialist management and production, as well as of the continued urbanization tendencies of both industrialized and developing societies. Espoused, instead, is decentralization of population concentration, of community, of agriculture, of management and control, of technology, of economic production, and of mass culture.

The issue of decentralization is particularly apparent in the "appropriate technology" movement, with its emphasis on human-scale technology under human control.

Globalization of Global Issues

Coexisting with the decentralization characteristic, and not in conflict with it, is the global management of those affairs that, by their very nature, are concerns of the entire population of the earth. These include use and care of the oceans and atmosphere, exploitation of non-renewable and some renewable resources, control of weapons of mass destruction, and control over the diffusion of hazardous chemicals.

The Importance of Timeliness

While it is important to see clearly the long-term resolution of development-related problems, it is equally crucial to understand the constraints that will be operating during the transition period. It is not improbable that this period will see some sort of partial breakdown of the world economic system. This could be triggered by any number of factors, but the oppressive debt structure is a likely candidate.

Such signs of fundamental change tend to be threatening to many people, particularly if they lack understanding of its cause. Response to perceived threat is likely to lead to non-constructive actions. There are two common forms of such response. One is an attempt to "turn back the clock" and return to an imagined time when family and community values were strong, consensus was easily come by, and generally things "worked." The other involves an irrational strengthening of faith in the old ways of dealing with problems—through new technology and new centralized management approaches.

Nothing could be more crucial to this time of transition than sharing interpretations of why the transformation is necessary or appears to be happening. There is no conversation more critical today than that around the question: What is viable global development? What is a "world that works for everyone"?

As dialogue leads to a deeper understanding of this major evolutionary change of direction, there can result an easing of anxiety and a lessening of the likelihood of large-scale human misery attendant to the transition. Men of action have often given the advice: "Don't just talk; get out there and do something." Perhaps the best advice for the short term is: "Don't just do something; get out there and talk."

The most important element of the dialogue is to affirm that the goal of true global development is feasible; nothing less is tolerable. The goal of a global commonwealth is one in which each of Earth's citizens has a reasonable chance to create through his or her own efforts a decent life for self and family and in which men and women live in harmony with Earth and its creatures, cooperating to create and maintain a wholesome environment for all. It is also one in which there is an ecology of different cultures, the diversity of which is appreciated and supported; in which war and other flagrant violations of human rights in the name of the state have no legitimacy anywhere; and in which the entire planet lives under the rule of laws that respect the individual and the community. This goal ultimately leads to a deep and shared sense of meaning in life itself throughout all the human family.

NOTES

1. Jonathan Schell, 1982, *The Fate of the Earth*, New York: Avon Books.

2. Roger W. Sperry, 1981, "Changing Priorities," *Annual Review of Neurosciences*, Vol. 4, pp. 1-15.

3. Jacob Needleman, 1975, *A Sense of Cosmos*, New York: Dutton.

Index